SIX MONTHS WITHOUT SUNDAYS

Max Benitz was born in London in 1985. He read Modern History at the University of Edinburgh and South Asian History at the University of Calcutta. After graduating in 2008 he took a local media job in Kabul and then worked at the Royal United Services Institute where he focused on the British Army's role in Afghanistan.

He is best known for his leading role in Peter Weir's *Master and Commander: The Far Side of the World.*

SIX MONTHS WITHOUT SUNDAYS

The Scots Guards in Afghanistan

Max Benitz

BIRLINN

First published in 2011
and this second edition published in 2012 by
Birlinn Limited
West Newington House
10 Newington Road
Edinburgh
EH9 1QS

www.birlinn.co.uk

ISBN: 978 1 84341 056 0

British Library Cataloguing-in-Publication Data
A catalogue record for this book is available from the British Library

MOD Disclaimer: Any individual contributions of a political nature
are those of an individual and are not representative of the Secretary of
State.

Typeset by Iolaire Typesetting, Newtonmore
Printed and bound by Clays Ltd, St Ives plc

For the fallen and the wounded

and

All the men and the women of Combined Force Lashkar Gah,
Operation Herrick 12,
Helmand Province, Afghanistan, 2010

If we turn our eyes towards the monarchies of Asia, we shall behold despotism in the centre and weakness in the extremities, the collection of revenue or the administration of justice enforced by the presence of an army, hostile barbarians established in the heart of the country, hereditary satraps usurping the dominion of the provinces, and subjects inclined to rebellion though incapable of freedom.

Edward Gibbon,
The Decline and Fall of the Roman Empire

I used to get big bunches of Canadians to drill: four or five hundred at a time. Spokesmen stepped forward once and asked me what sense there was in sloping and ordering arms, and fixing and unfixing bayonets. They said they had come across to fight, and not guard Buckingham Palace . . . I told them that when they were better at fighting than the Guards they could perhaps afford to neglect their arms-drill.

Robert Graves (Royal Welch Fusiliers,
First World War),
Goodbye to All That

Contents

List of Illustrations

Mayor Daoud cuts the ribbon declaring Stabilisation Bridge on Route Trident open

Colonel Satir and Major Hugo Clarke conduct a *shura* at Checkpoint Attal

Taj Babi, aged three, is carried by her father to a waiting casualty evacuation helicopter

Colonel Kamullidin talks the Commanding Officer through his men's successful operation

A happy cow and a happy boy after a vet engagement in Basharan

First night back in the Officers' Mess and Lieutenant Tulloch is in high spirits, as Major Martin French looks on

Guardsman Rab McClellan back on the Bucky, St Andrew's Day

Major Kitching leads Left Flank to triumph in the Tug o' War

1st Battalion Scots Guards on parade to collect their Operation Herrick medals, St Andrew's Day

List of Maps

Acknowledgments

If there is one thing the Scots Guards taught me, it is the importance of giving credit, rather than taking. Hence the length of this list.

This book focuses on the young officers, non-commissioned officers and junior ranks of Combined Force Lashkar Gah, especially the Scots Guardsmen. It is you whom I most wish to thank. Without exception you treated me with kindness, humour and patience. Having a civilian whose admin resembles a burns pit thrust on you when you were trying to get on with the much more important business of staying alive meant that you bore the majority of this project's burden. Whether it was squaring me away with a bedspace, scoff or kit, making time to answer stupid questions or watching out for me on patrol, I owe you all a great deal. If this book goes some way to repaying that debt, then I will have done my job.

Having said that, this project would never have happened without the say-so and encouragement of a number of more senior men and women, some of whom took considerable risk in giving me the space and time I needed to get the job done. Lt General Sir John Kiszely KCB MC, Colonel Alistair Mathewson OBE, most especially Colonel Lincoln Jopp MC, who first called my bluff; Brigadier Mark Van Der Lande OBE, Colonel Huw Lloyd-Jones, Lt Colonel James Carr-Smith, Tim David and the Wider Contracts team, Sarah Yuen and Captain Jon Gilbody from the Media Ops world; Majors Martin French, James Leask and Guy Anderson; my friend Captain Malcolm Dalzel-Job (who, by rights, could be the focus of a whole other book), Captain Graham Brady and Regimental Sergeant Major Ali Mackenzie all know how important their contributions were. I thank you all unreservedly. Apologies and thanks to Will MMC, Hamish Barne and Simon Ramsay for putting up with someone who eventually realised he'd be more use outside than in – I hope this book is adequate atonement. Thanks also to Rab for the bum-facing, and to Shrek for calling me a 'ballbag': two uniquely Scots Guards rites of passage.

Thanks to the superb Anna Power and Francesca Barrie at Johnson & Alcock for much valued guidance. True thanks to Hugh Andrew, Neville Moir, Jan Rutherford and all at Birlinn for embracing this project from the outset and sticking with it through a few dicey moments. I owe a considerable debt to Andrew Simmons for turning a stream of dispassionate jargon into a book with, I hope, a soul. Michael Munro did a meticulous job with my copy.

I am grateful to Olivier Grouille, Dr Terence Mac-Namee, all at Military Sciences and beyond at RUSI; Professor John Mackinley for warning me about how hard this would be. Sir John Keegan gave me a start in writing, and since then James Fergusson, Jon Boone, Jerome Starkey, Tom Coghlan, Miles Amoore, Celia Walden, Rob Corbidge, Geordie Grieg, Amy Iggulden, Helen Lewis-Hastely and many others have all helped guide a youngster into print.

Sir Sherard Cowper-Coles and Alex Cartwright are owed much for their wisdom. Personal thanks to Martin Tyrrell for telling me to write and to Peter Weir for showing me what an artist is.

I owe my many great friends a great deal indeed and thank you all for putting up with me. Most of all, thank you to my brilliant siblings without whom I'd be nothing and my parents to whom I promise to dedicate the next book.

For their assistance with the paperback, I would particularly like to thank Air Commodore David Prowse OBE, Lieutenant Colonel Crispin Lockhart MBE and Commander David Gordon at DMC, and Charles Heath-Saunders and Tracy Harrison from Army Headquarters and Wider Markets. Lieutenant Colonel Robert Howieson was most gracious in allowing me to conduct further interviews with members of 1st Battalion Scots Guards, and Captain Graham Brady was very helpful and diligent in facilitating these. As ever, I am indebted to those of all capbadges who agreed to be interviewed, my agent, and everyone at Birlinn.

Glossary

Entries in capital letters are spelt out phonetically in speech – IED, GPMG; those in lower case are pronounced how they are spelt – Mert, Casevac – with a few exceptions where acronyms match existing words – MIST, TRiM. I acknowledge that this is unusual and ask readers to allow flow to beat formality in this work.

1 SG 1st Battalion Scots Guards

4th Mechanised Brigade brigade deployed on Operation Herrick 12 of which *1 SG* is the *armoured infantry* element

.50cal half-inch calibre Heavy Machine Gun round, usually vehicle mounted

5.56mm standard calibre Nato rifle round

60mm Mortar *Company* level mortar that fires high explosive, smoke or red phosphorus rounds

7.62mm calibre for AK-47 variants and British *GPMG*

A-10 tank-busting jet armed with 30mm cannon capable of firing dozens of rounds per second and missiles for strafing runs. More trouble than they're worth

Afghan National Civil Order Police (ANCOP) paramilitary Afghan force bridging the gap between police and army. Usually drawn from outside Helmand

Afs Afghanis, the local currency. Afs 50 = $1 in 2010

Air any support from the air – jets, *Attack Helicopters*, *drones*, as in 'Where's the air?'

ANA Afghan National Army

ANP Afghan National Police. Usually locally recruited

ANSF Afghan National Security Forces. Umbrella term for Afghans in uniform

Apache *Attack Helicopter* extensively used in Helmand. Excellent and far-ranging surveillance capability coupled with 30mm cannon and Hellfire missiles. Terrifyingly able

Arcs the range a weapon can sweep left to right unhindered by physical or visual obstruction. A broad arc would be 180 degrees, a narrow one five degrees, and so on

Area of Operations the patch of a map that a grouping is responsible for

Armoured Infantry *Warrior*-borne unit such as *1 SG*

Attack Helicopters (AH) usually, but not exclusively, heavily armed *Apaches*

Banging ugly

Battalion infantry unit. In the case of 1st Battalion Scots Guards, 550 strong in three rifle *companies*, a support *company* and headquarters company

Battlegroup a *battalion* plus the attached arms (engineers, etc.) that make it semi-self-sufficient. Replaced with *Combined Force* on Herrick 12

Bergen large backpack

Break Contact end a fight, typically through use of overwhelming firepower to kill or supress the enemy and cover a withdrawal

Bund embankment

Casevac Casualty Evacuation. From stretcher to *Mert* to Birmingham.

Cash for Works paying locals to improve their surroundings, thereby influencing them. Schemes include irrigation ditch clearances and culvert repairs

CF LKG Combined Force Lashkar Gah. 700 British soldiers and their 2,000 or so Afghan partners spread across Lashkar Gah District and headquartered in the city

Checkpoint smaller than a *Patrol Base*, and usually a *platoon*-sized base

Chinook heavy lift, twin-rotor helicopter

Chippy incapable of running a chip shop; inept. Not in the civilian sense of harbouring a resentment based on perceived slights or social insecurity

CNP Counter Narcotics Police

Cobra US Marine Corps gunship helicopter

Combined Force a British *battlegroup* plus its Afghan partners, e.g. Combined Force Lashkar Gah

Company sub-unit to the *battalion* or *Combined Force*. Usually consisting of three *platoons* and roughly 140 strong. Holds some assets (small *drones*, mortars) but relies on higher control for most. The intensely local campaign in Helmand is fought at the company level.

Contact interaction with the enemy, typically through small-arms fire or *IED*. Shouted when encountered. Verb or noun, e.g. 'They contacted us with small arms and I shouted "Contact!"'

Counter-IED Counter-Improvised Explosive Device. Any drill, capability, device or specialist used in fight against IEDs. Specialist counter-IED teams may consist of: an IED disposal team, Advanced Search team, dog handler and Weapons Intelligence Specialists as required by the tactical situation

Counter Insurgency military thought has been a Laocoon enveloped by Counter Insurgency since about 2005, with much wailing and gnashing about its nature at Staff Colleges. There are Counter Insurgency Academies, Counter Insurgency Centres and a sprawling network of defence analysts spending an indecent amount of time defining and studying it. Basically, the principles are: 'wisdom is better than weapons of war: but one sinner destroyeth much good' (Ecclesiastes 9:18) and do whatever works best in your *Area of Operations.*

Drone Army vernacular for a Remote Piloted Aircraft System (RPAS). Sometimes armed with Hellfire missile, usually just observing. They range in size from hand-launched Desert Hawk to Predator and Reaper

EOD Operator Explosive Ordnance Disposal Operator. A senior non-commissioned officer, warrant officer, or officer trained to dispose of IEDs

Fire Support Group a mobile heavy-weapons team

Fire team four-to-five-strong half-section commanded by a Lance Corporal. Two to three per *multiple.*

Firing Point identified origin of hostile fire. Examples could be a *murder hole*, a clump of trees or other cover

Foot Guards five regiments – Grenadier, Coldstream, Scots, Irish and Welsh Guards in order of seniority – make up the Foot Guards. They are the senior infantry regiments of the British Army. Together with the Household Cavalry, they are the Household Division and wear a distinctive Blue-Red-Blue shoulder flash.

Forward Line of Enemy Troops the frontline

Gimpy see *GPMG*

GPMG 7.62mm General Purpose Machine Gun. Each *platoon* carries three GPMGs – often referred to as *gimpy* in speech – and besides the gunner, men will carry spare *link* to keep this primary weapon going in a firefight. Also vehicle-mounted. Superb

Grenade Launcher for the British, a tube under the barrel of a rifle that fires 40mm high-explosive and red phosphorus grenades several hundred metres

Grenade Machine Gun fires 40mm high-explosive or red phosphorus rounds 500 metres with accuracy. Surprisingly quiet as it fires, louder if you are the target, one imagines.

Guards see *Foot Guards*

Guardsman *Foot Guards* equivalent of a private soldier. Also, umbrella term for all members of a Guards regiment, as in: 'Once a Guardsman, always a Guardsman.'

Hazara separate ethnic group who are predominantly Shi'ite Muslims living in central Afghanistan. There are pockets of Hazaras throughout Helmand.

Helicopter Landing Site/helipad anything from a fully modern concrete airfield with refuelling pens to a patch of dirt rapidly *Valloned* in the middle of a firefight.

Herrick/Op Herrick codename for ongoing British operations in Afghanistan since 2001. Numbered sequentially, each Herrick lasts six months and is led by a particular brigade. Herrick 4 in 2006 was the first in Helmand. This book focuses on Herrick 12.

Hesco brand name for the ubiquitous four-and-a-half-foot high geotextile sacs supported by a steel mesh and filled with earth. They protect against bullets and blast and have largely replaced the sandbag.

Hexamine/Hexy Hexamethylenetetramine (a solid fuel resembling Kendal mint cake that burns without smoke)

IEC Independent Election Commission of Afghanistan

IED Improvised Explosive Device

Illumination hand-launched or mortar-fired flares for lighting up the battlefield at night

Insurgent catchall term for those hostile to *Isaf* and Afghan National Security Forces at a particular moment. Without conducting interviews with each and every one of them, it would be impossible to deduct their motives for resistance and label them correctly. 'Taliban' has a specific meaning and should not be used as a catchall phrase. While many, perhaps most, of those who fight Isaf and the Afghan Government in Helmand are members of or identify with the Taliban (Afghan and Pakistani), to call them all Taliban would be as incorrect as referring to all members of Napoleon's Grand Army of 1812 as revolutionaries. Amongst those who shoot, bomb and spy there are undoubtedly Pashto nationalists; foreign-born Salafists; the young, intimidated and bored poor; criminals connected to the drugs trade and opportunists settling tribal disputes. I acknowledge that this term can be used to rob an armed political movement of its identity

Isaf International Security Assistance Force. Multinational grouping primarily but not solely consisting of Nato members. Present in Afghanistan under rolling UN Mandate and at invitation of the Afghan Government

Jack, jacking when one soldier, through laziness, drops his performance, leaving others to pick up the slack. A 'jack bastard' can 'jack' on the rest of his platoon by being 'jack'

Javelin or Jav anti-tank missile used extensively in Helmand

JChat Brigade-wide instant messaging system

Joint Afghan and British, as in joint patrolling

Kalay hamlet. Typically a number of different families' compounds gathered around a mosque. A more substantial settlement will just have its name, e.g. Sayedebad.

Kandak Afghan battalion

Light Machine Gun 5.56mm belt-fed section weapon that bridges the gap between rifle and *GPMG*

Light Order stripped-down fighting kit, keeping weight to a minimum to enable mobility

Link ammunition for belt-fed weapon

Local Nationals Afghans

Lurk a patrol, typically at night, that stays in an area watching for enemy activity, which can then be disrupted

Main Charge the bit of the *IED* that goes bang. Typically a 25-litre yellow palm oil container stuffed with home-made explosive.

Main Operating Base the MOB in Lashkar Gah houses Brigade and Combined Force Lashkar Gah Headquarters, alongside the *Provincial Reconstruction Team*, contractors and a cast of hundreds. Known as 'Lash Vegas' to the soldiers outside the razor wire-topped walls.

Mastiff large armoured six-wheeled battle taxi. Crew of three, carries another eight and armed with either a machine gun or *Grenade Machine Gun*

Mert Medical Emergency Response Team. Chinook turned flying hospital

MIST Report Method [of injury]; Injury [sustained]; Signs [and symptoms]; Treatment [given]. A brief report to get an evacuation helicopter launched, giving the doctors an idea of what to expect. Also includes the *Zap Number*, sex and age of casualty. Pronounced 'Mist' rather than spelt out

Monging switching off during a task, usually due to exhaustion – especially on exercise. See *Jack*

Multiple roughly half-*platoon*-sized tactical grouping. *Sections* were found to be too small to independently foot-patrol in Helmand, and as not all of a platoon can get out of camp at once, the multiple bridges the gap. Commanded by Platoon Commander or Sergeant. The tactical building block of the Afghan war, as the *platoon* was in the First World War and the brick was in Northern Ireland

Murder Hole opening hacked into a mud wall, typically inside a compound, and used to fire from

Net radio network. There is a *Battlegroup* net; each *Company* has its own net, each vehicle has its own net and there are various other nets for emergencies or to talk to air support

NGO Non-Governmental Organisation

Op/Ops Operation/s

Op Minimise After a British soldier is killed or seriously wounded, all civilian communications back home are suspended to ensure next of kin find out the news through the appropriate channels

Ops Room Operations Room. Nerve centre of a unit from which operations are planned and monitored. At Battalion Headquarters level, a large room full of signallers, *staff officers*, flat-screen TVs, radios, computers and the Battalion Colours. In a *Vehicle Checkpoint*, a radio and a *hexamine* stove with a kettle perched on it

Patrol Base a large garrison, typically a Company Headquarters

Patrolman Afghan National Police rank equivalent of a British Police Constable

PAX private insurance scheme for soldiers on operations to top up MoD compensation allowances

Pedro American Blackhawk helicopter converted for casualty evacuation

Platoon 30-strong group of soldiers commanded by a junior officer and made up of three *sections* or two *multiple*s further broken into *fire teams* and a small headquarters element. Three platoons form a *company*

Positively Identify (PID) ascertain without doubt from where you are being shot at. Without a PID, British soldiers cannot usually engage under their *Rules of Engagement*

Pressure Plate method of initiating IED through the pressure of the victim or vehicle's weight completing a circuit and detonating the *main charge*

Provincial Reconstruction Team (PRT) civilian-led and owned group consisting mainly of Department for International Development and Foreign and Commonwealth Office officials. The lead for governance and development in Helmand

Q Bloke Company Quartermaster Sergeant

Quick Reaction Force group ready to move at a moment's notice to assist in an unforeseen eventuality. A fairly relaxed job until it isn't

R&R Rest and Recuperation. Each British soldier gets a fortnight away from Afghanistan during their six-month tour

RDG Royal Dragoon Guards

Replen replenishment of supplies: usually ammunition and rations

RPG Rocket-Propelled Grenade. Standard Afghan forces and insurgent direct fire weapon with a range of approximately 900 metres. An airburst round provides an indirect fire capability. Plentiful and loud

SA80 5.56mm standard rifle of British Army. Much

upgraded for Herrick, it carries a 4x sight and holds a 30-round magazine

Sangar watchtower

Sapper engineer

Scran food

Section three to a *platoon*, commanded by a Lance Sergeant. Largely replaced by the *multiple*

Shalwar kameez long, night-shirt-length garment worn over loose pyjama-style trousers. Much the most sensible order of dress in Helmand

Shura meeting, frequently between *Isaf* commanders and local elders in a neighbourhood. Can be hours long and fuelled with tea, watermelon and pistachio nuts. A collective decision-making forum.

Smoker all ranks night out, usually by *platoon*

Solar Shower black bag filled with water and left in sun to heat up

Squared Away or Squared ship-shape, sorted

Stabilisation/Stabilisation representative men from the Military Stabilisation Support Team work alongside the rest of the *Battlegroup* to deliver steadying effects to the district. This ranges from cash-funded building projects to more subtle events such as Koran-reading competitions and medical engagements.

Staff Officer those who command paper rather than men and ensure the administrative side of soldiering doesn't break down on operations

Stag/stagging on sentry duty

Tac Tactical Headquarters, normally *Company* or *Battlegroup* Tac. While the bulk of personnel and kit remain at a permanent headquarters, Tac, either on foot or in vehicles, can head out to command the situation on the ground.

Tashakor thank you

Trident British Army-planned route that links up the Patrol Base line between Nad Ali and Gereshk. Designed to be *IED*-resistant and ostensibly built for the Freedom of Movement of Afghans.

TRiM/TRiMed/TRiMing Trauma Risk Management. System of on-the-spot mental health counselling conducted by junior commanders trained to provide a judgment-free environment for traumatised soldiers to discuss recent experiences. Pronounced 'Trim' rather than spelt out

United States Marine Corps by June 2010, there were approximately 20,000 US Marines in Helmand and the British Task Force Helmand came under the command of a Marine Major General heading up Regional Command South West, and Marine attachments and equipment, especially helicopters, were a frequent sight in a British patch

Vallon ubiquitous metal detector used to find *IED*s. Has become a verb meaning to check a route for *IED*s: 'Have you Valloned that track yet?'

Vehicle Checkpoint (VCP) smaller version of a *checkpoint* sometimes with as few as four British soldiers plus their more numerous Afghan partners. Situated on a main road, the garrison of the Vehicle Checkpoint search cars and passengers for anything suspicious.

Warrior Armoured Fighting Vehicle armed with 30mm cannon and chain gun. Carries a section of infantry into battle, drives them to fixed enemy position, where they dismount and assault. Crewed by commander, gunner and driver.

Zap Number rapid identification system for soldiers consisting of the first two letters of last name followed by final four digits of soldier's service number, e.g. MA4219. Marked on items of clothing along with blood group and allergies to assist doctors in Bastion with treatment and identification for the next of kin process.

Zero headquarters on a specific radio net (Blackjack Zero being Combined Force Headquarters, Blackjack One Zero being B Company Headquarters, etc.)

Rank Structure of 1st Battalion Scots Guards, less Attached Personnel

- Lieutenant Colonel – the Commanding Officer
- Major – Second in Command; Company Commanders; Quartermaster; some senior Staff Officers
- Captain – most Staff Officers; most Late Entry Officers; Company Second in Command; senior Platoon Commanders
- Lieutenant – Platoon Commander with at least a year served
- Second Lieutenant – Platoon Commander fresh from training
- Warrant Officer 1 – Regimental Sergeant Major
- Warrant Officer 2 – Regimental Quartermaster Sergeant; Drill Sergeant; Company Sergeant Major
- Colour Sergeant – Platoon Sergeant Major; Company Quartermaster Sergeant; individual appointments such as Signals Warrant Officer and Pioneer Colour Sergeant
- Sergeant
- Lance Sergeant – equivalent to Corporal
- Lance Corporal
- Guardsman – equivalent to Private

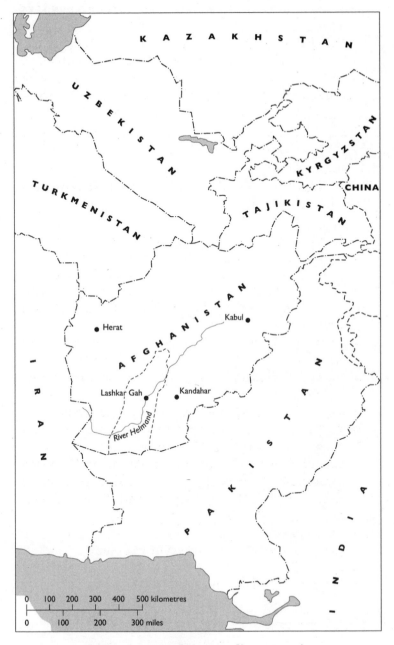

Afghanistan and surrounding countries

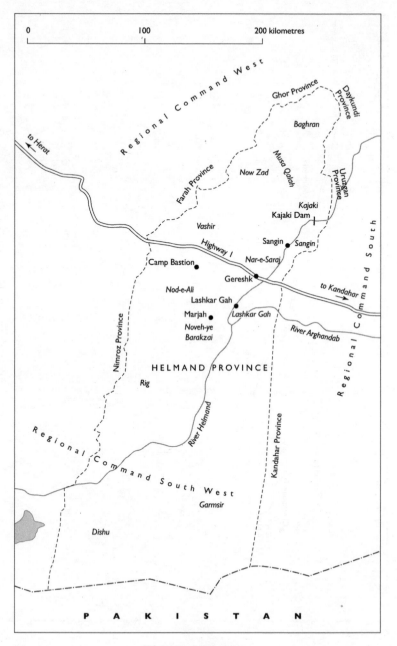

Helmand Province

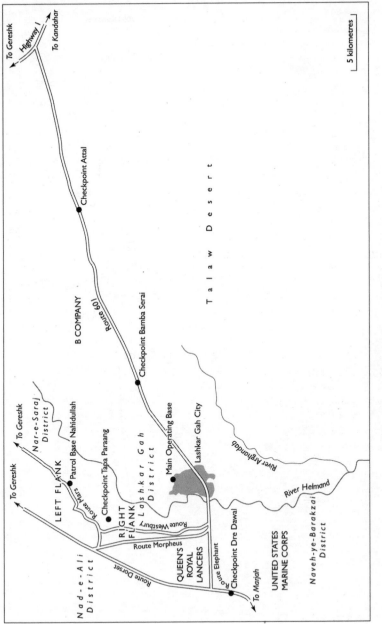

Overview of Combined Force Lashkar Gah

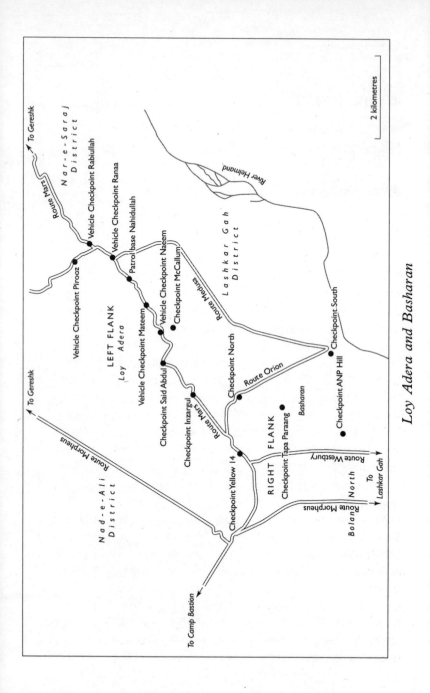

Loy Adera and Basharan

INTRODUCTION

'Getting it'

June–December 2009

The ideas surrounding this book were brought into sharp relief by a walk through Trafalgar Square in November 2009. News had come through that morning of an incident in Helmand that appeared to sum up the war in Afghanistan. Five unarmed British soldiers had been shot dead by an Afghan policeman they had been risking their lives to train. There is a mantra in today's campaign that runs: 'Where's the Afghan face in this?' The answer this time was: 'On a motorcycle, heading for an insurgent stronghold.' The afternoon headlines screamed and news websites ran stories of how the incident brought into question the entire British strategy in Afghanistan.

Looking up, there was a Spitfire. Looking down, there was a crowd. They filled the square to honour a war hero – Air Chief Marshal Sir Keith Park. His statue was being unveiled amidst a flyby. His generation's war, still a fetish in our society, was one of national survival. Leaves and not bombs fell around the drizzly square in 2009 but in 1940 the British people, who just two years previously had been fervently against the idea of a war with Germany, endured random and violent death. Seventy years later, the deaths of five professional soldiers threatened to upend a military strategy and revise Britain's primary foreign policy commitment. Appetites had changed.

By November 2009, a YouGov/Channel 4 News poll found that 57 per cent of the population thought victory in Afghanistan no longer possible and 35 per cent advocated immediate withdrawal. Government and military resignations over the war had begun to trickle in and prevarication was rife in Washington. The mood inside the British Army was also getting nasty. A low grumbling was emerging into the public domain.

In June 2009, Patrick Little, a recently retired infantry officer, wrote a searing criticism of the Army's inability to assimilate lessons. 'All is not well in the British Army and has not been for some time,' he warned. Hubris, a lazy instinct to blame the government for failings, the toleration of 'toxic commanders' and the absence of meaningful internal debate were all deemed by Little to have hindered the Army's performance in the field. Only a 'long and painful journey' of self-criticism would rectify these problems, he argued. Little was not alone. In a frank exchange of views at a conference I attended in October 2009, a slew of mid-tier officers and external experts laid into the generation that commanded. The oft-repeated line was: 'They just don't get it.' Unfavourable comparisons were made with the American military. Facing the possibility of defeat in Iraq in 2005, they had opened themselves up to a process of far-ranging internal chastisement. Colonels called out Generals and Field Manuals were ripped up and re-written. After becoming US Secretary of Defense in 2006, Robert Gates, the British officers noted approvingly, fired a few four-stars.

As an outsider with no military experience these structural arguments at first seemed bewildering – what is 'it' and how is it acquired? Slowly, though, the debates on 'institutional rectitude' and 'constructive dissent' seemed to boil down to a generational shift in military thought.

The young Lieutenant Colonels and below who had won medals directing mini-campaigns in Basra and Sangin were standing up to their elders and telling them that South Armagh was not where doctrine ended.

At the time, Britain was also planning an overdue look at her place in the world through a *Strategic Defence and Security Review*. It was set against the backdrop of the financial crisis. As I sat in conference rooms listening to 'stakeholders' discuss Britain's future, an underlying assumption emerged: Britain's inexorable decline and the need to do some cutting. The people in control were setting the rules of a game that my generation was going to have to play. In an increasingly unstable world, tools were being taken away from us. We were going to be caught between the Scylla of the long-term debt thrown up by our parents' financial recklessness and the Charybdis of defence cuts. The demographically bloated generation that we were going to have to defend and sustain was giving us an empty bottle of whisky and an unloaded revolver and telling us to get on with it.

After the unveiling of the statue of Park, I caught a bus home in time for the evening news. All channels led with the latest from Helmand. Phrases like 'turning point' were invoked. More than one anchor raised an editorial single eyebrow. The uncle of one murdered soldier performed stoically for the cameras: 'It was his job and he loved doing it . . . it's what he wanted to do. That [going to Afghanistan] was part of his job and he knew that.' In order to connect more fully with the audience, people who had never met the man were then interviewed in the street. Words like 'awful' and 'appalling' cropped up. One network then switched to its second story: a student in Sheffield who had decided to drunkenly urinate on a war memorial.

This juxtaposition summed up two threads in British

life today: admiration coupled with misunderstanding for a man who considered the possibility of a violent death 'part of his job', then a story about 'Broken Britain's' youth. The civilian–military gulf and then the self-disgust.

I believe that there are several reasons for these trends. First, there is a growing gap between civilian and military life, meaning that we are unable to understand war. This is partly because we are inured to risk. Simply put, there are more passenger safety notices on a London bus than on a Chinook helicopter in Helmand. Second, the perception of a general breakdown in society means we are unable to accept the desire of our forces to risk their lives on our behalf. Lack of understanding translates into lack of support. This will fatally undermine our military's ability to conclude long-term campaigns successfully.

And through this, my generation was the one doing much of the fighting and plenty of the dying in Helmand. The popular image of Britain's youth is probably more aligned with the Sheffield war-memorial pisser than with soldiers who are killed on action before reaching their twenties. To summarise conventional opinion: we are feckless, feral, binge-drinking, ASBO-courting, hooded knife-wielding hooligans. We are united by attention spans that can be measured in the time it takes to change channels and we spend our time twiddling our thumbs on PlayStations.

And yet, thousands of Britain's young are going to Helmand and some of them are not coming back alive. They accept the risks and do their job. How can this be? These young men and women emerge from a society that believes itself to be broken. It blames much of this decline on the generation it sends to an unpopular war to do a job it can no longer understand. A political class that gamely starts wars but cannot articulate war aims directs a riven military. And yet they go and fight and sometimes die. Who are these soldiers and what is the Army achieving in Afghanistan?

★

A few days later, I was in a post office with a letter in my hand. I had decided to try to go and answer some questions that Spitfire over Trafalgar Square had brought to mind. Most of all, I wanted to 'get it'. I also wanted to see if I was up to war – stupid, naive boy. The letter was addressed to the Commanding Officer, 1st Battalion Scots Guards. My father's regiment, the Scots Guards were preparing to go to Helmand in 2010 for their first tour of Afghanistan as a battalion. The house I grew up in was plastered with prints of pipers and Guardsmen and my father wears a Household Division watchstrap – this, fifty years after leaving the regiment he spent five years with. I'd always wanted to have something to do with the Scots Guards but am barred by temperament and constitution from the British Army. Instead, I would go to Helmand with them as a witness to what they did in today's war – a subtle but important distinction from the journalists who must always keep their distance and find that headline. It was, perhaps, a rather complicated and potentially lethal way of telling my father I respected him. In the post office, I paused a while before dropping the letter. Part of me never expected to hear back. Part of me wondered where it all might lead.

Aside from these arguably questionable personal motivations for going to war alongside the Scots Guards, there were strong reasons why they, and the wider campaign, deserved study at that time and in the way I intended to do it. Given the unpopularity of the war it seemed clear, even in 2009, that the summer of 2010 would be the zenith, or near enough, of military involvement in Afghanistan. While the annual announcement that X will be the most vital year yet in Afghanistan has become as predictable as 'Auld Lang Syne', there was a potent case for 2010. General McChrystal's Commander's Initial Assessment, calling for more troops, had been backed up by Nato's acceptance of the strategic concept for Phase Four of the campaign – the transition to Afghan control. After a lengthy pause for thought, President Obama pledged an additional 34,000 troops on 1 December 2009; the rest of Nato said they would send another 7,000 to complement this surge. The coming year, especially the sadly named 'fighting season' that summer, would be the campaign's moment of maximum effort and perhaps maximum risk. If 2010 went wrong, the war went wrong. The British part of this near-final chance to succeed would be in Helmand Province.

The British Army had broken into this rural backwater in 2006 and the campaign had followed an irregular beat of fatalities, gallantry awards, offensives and policy announcements. The nature of the campaign had taken a lot of criticism. From the regrettable pre-deployment misquote of the then Defence Secretary about 'not a bullet fired' to the 24-hour period in July 2009 when eight British soldiers had died, the British in Helmand had been fighting a tenacious insurgency on the ground and public opinion at home. They had to get it right in 2010. Strategic imperatives dictated from the capital cities, such as the utter minimisation of civilian casualties and the delivery of a popularly legitimate local security sector would be addressed in dusty outposts by young British soldiers. Enduring success would only come if their officers could construct a coherent campaign alongside other British Government departments and, of course, the Afghan Government: no one was arguing that foreign

military force could do it alone or provide the eventual
solutions for Helmand and Afghanistan. Alongside a few
pockets in the east of Afghanistan, Helmand is perhaps the
hardest task assigned to any Isaf force. While some argue
that one could lose Helmand and still win in Afghanistan,
if Isaf could begin to crack Helmand in 2010 then this
would be a strong indicator of the campaign's direction.

I was determined to get to Helmand that summer. I had
spent a few months in Kabul immediately after graduating
from university in 2008 and then worked at the Royal
United Services Institute in Whitehall in 2009. These
experiences gave me some grasp of the strategic stresses
felt by the ministers, diplomats and soldiers at the top.
Now I wanted to get down to the tactical level: to see if
they 'got it'. The battalion is where the campaign is fought
daily and where decisions made at the top have the most
impact. I felt I would be much more comfortable here,
surrounded by men of my generation, doing what the
young do in times of war. The Guardsmen, sergeants and
junior officers were, to a 25-year-old, much more note-
worthy than the brigadiers and generals – fine officers
though I'm sure they all are. There has been plenty
written about Ministry of Defence cock-ups, helicopter
numbers, strategic errors and political missteps, and all
those whys and wherefores. Most reporting of the war has
been couched in these wider terms – as is correct in a
functioning democracy. However, there was a risk, I felt,
that the basic realities of the war (what happens to 18-
year-olds when they go to Helmand) could be lost. I
wanted to write a book about soldiers in 2010 before this
important piece of history was lost. As a civilian, I wanted
to discover what was happening in Helmand and hoped
this narrative would help other civilians develop their
picture of that demanding place; to help bridge that gap
between us and those in uniform. For military readers, my

intent would be to provide an example of what a Battle-group did at this stage of the campaign. Mostly, I hoped to provide a lasting testament to and for the men and women of the Battlegroup. A few weeks after I posted that letter, the Commanding Officer got in touch. I found a publisher and the Ministry of Defence approved the project.

The next eighteen months were, essentially, a kidnap. A tribe initiated and trained me, took me to war and brought me home. I watched them fight and kill, love and hate, laugh and cry; I was witness, anthropologist and, occasionally, friend. I spent more time with a single unit – in and out of Helmand – than any other British author, journalist or artist has done during this war. As a result, this book is 'all for the boys' and they speak for them-selves. There are 550 of them and not all can be mentioned between these covers. My sample is random but repre-sentative and what follows is portrait as well as photo-graph – not every aspect of this group's experiences could be captured in absolute detail. In what follows, I strike out for the larger picture only where it is important to do so or where some context helps explain an event. Another decision was not to examine the soldiers' families. They had enough to deal with and I did not wish to intrude on anxiety and grief. I suspect many of them felt the year more keenly than those who went to Helmand. Their sacrifice and support is the bedrock always mentioned by soldiers and it is right that it is acknowledged here.

During the kidnap, I was only ever given two direct orders. The first was from the Commanding Officer, who simply told me: 'You're not allowed to get killed.' The second was Company Sergeant Major Stretch Halliday, who said, 'Max, remember the plan. Dinnae write a shite book.' I endeavoured to obey them both.

CHAPTER ONE

Three hundred and sixty-eight years

1642–2010

In the Operations Room, in a tent in Lashkar Gah in 2010, two crossed silk flags looked out and silently judged men rushing from phone to computer to radio as they managed the day's battle. These were the colours. On certain anniversaries, a Guardsman would adorn them with a laurel wreath and history's whisper would remind you that men had weaved the silk with blood.

The Scots Guards were raised, as any Scots Guardsman will tell you today, in 1642 – 990 years after the proselytising Arab invasion of the lands we now know as Afghanistan and 65 years before the Act of Union made the Scottish and English Crowns one.

Charles I, King in name of England, Scotland, France and Ireland, was playing golf outside Edinburgh when he heard that the last of these kingdoms had risen in rebellion. Under letters patent issued to the Marquis of Argyll on 28 March 1642, 'one Regiment of our Scottish Subjects consisting of the number of Fifteen hundred men' was raised to fight in Ireland. Charles wanted to lead the expedition, so styled the men 'a Guard for his own Person'. The English Parliament was reluctant to see

Charles acquire a standing force. They refused consent and banned him from going to Ireland. Argyll's men still sailed and fought a bloody campaign. Meanwhile, the fractures between King Charles and Westminster turned to Civil War. The English Parliament then refused to pay the Scots for their service in Ireland. The Regiment sailed back across the Irish Sea, not for the last time, in 1645.

Religious and political factions turned to fighting in Scotland and anarchy in England. The Regiment found themselves fighting for the Scottish General Assembly and then Charles II after Westminster had cut off their founder's head. The men of Argyll's Regiment were appointed 'his Majestie's footte regiment of his Lyffe Guardes' in 1650. They fought and lost to Cromwell and Monck's men at Dunbar. They scattered at the interregnum.

In 1660, Charles II returned from the continent and re-formed his Foot Guards. For the next century, the Regiment that became known as the Scots Guards in the 1680s negotiated the religious skirmishes that continued to dog Scotland, came out for the Protestant William of Orange (who rewarded them by founding a Second Battalion in 1689), guarded the Monarch in London, besieged Namur and were with George II at Dettingen. Names that are found in today's Regiment began to appear on lists of officers. They took no part in the '45, save screening the north of England, and were ordered 'not to laugh' at the Militias raised in panic at the Young Pretender.

With Jacobites crushed, the British Army was employed on the continent and in the colonies. Some 3rd Guards, as the Scots were now referred to, having lost precedence to the Grenadier and Coldstream Guards, always remained at Court. Here they could establish such Standing Orders as those of 1783, which banned double-breasted waist-coats from the Officers' Mess and ordered other ranks to be 'well dressed and in Black Gaiters' when visiting other regiments. In four months in 1793, the 13 or so Guards officers eating daily at the table at St James's Palace managed to get through the vast sum of £5,500 of food and drink.

The wars begun by the French Revolution saw the 3rd Guards engaged heavily across Europe and then in Egypt in 1801. The 1st Battalion fought at Talavera, Fuentes D'Onor and Salamanca, and then headed home on Napoleon's abdication of 1814. The 2nd Battalion went to the Low Countries to show intent as the Congress of Vienna convened. Napoleon escaped Elba before Metternich, Talleyrand *et al*, could establish a settlement that would keep the Scots Guards from the continent for 99 years.

The 2nd Battalion woke up soaking on 18 June 1815 in and around a Belgian farm named Hougoumont. Along with the Coldstream Guards they would hold this position that long day at a cost of at least 239 killed. Sergeants Fraser, McGregor and Aston, with Private Lister, helped shut the famous farm gate.

In 1831 they became Scots Fusilier Guards and were given bearskins. In 1854 they sailed for the Crimea to join an army that was underequipped and poorly led, thanks to decisions made in Horse Guards. Their Colour Party stormed the redoubt at the Alma, won the first four Victoria Crosses ever awarded and were immortalised in Lady Butler's painting. It hangs in the Officers' Mess today. They fought at Inkerman, then froze and died of want that winter. Once home, they appointed their first Pipe Major. They were not involved in the Afghan Wars. In 1877 Queen Victoria finally returned the Regiment to its old styling as Scots Guards.

Two companies of Scots Guardsmen in the Guards Camel Regiment rode to rescue Gordon on camels; 1st and 2nd Battalions fought the Boers. A 3rd Battalion was raised and disbanded. In 1910, some 215 years after the event, a Select Committee awarded the Regiment a battle honour for the Siege of Namur. The next year, a young Home Secretary named Winston Churchill called them out from the Tower of London; they fired on anarchists at the Siege of Sidney Street in the East End.

In 1914 they crossed the Channel. Four years later they returned, 2,841 men short. Little names from France and Belgium – Ypres, Loos, Somme – made their way onto the colours. The Privates of the Brigade of Guards were renamed Guardsmen by George V.

Between the wars life was becalmed and focused on the ceremonial. 2nd Battalion went east of Suez for the first time in 1927 for a garrison tour in China. They brought a Dragon Boat back to startle the rest of the Guards Boat Club with. The Officers' Mess became a staging post for the Scottish aristocracy in London. Men like Lord Lovat, who would go on to wade ashore in Normandy with his piper and commandos, served a few years.

War with Germany resumed in 1939. The 5th (Ski) Battalion was formed with a vague idea of supporting the Finns against the Russians. The unit never deployed, to the chagrin of Lieutenant David Stirling, who went off to join the Commandos, then formed the Special Air Service (SAS). Between them the 1st and 2nd Battalions fought through Norway, North Africa, Italy and Western Europe on foot; the re-formed 3rd Battalion were put in tanks and landed in Normandy.

A remarkably varied generation of Scots Guardsmen served in that war; amongst them a future Archbishop of Canterbury, Deputy Prime Minister, Marshal of the Diplomatic Corps, chief ballet critic of the *Sunday Times* and David Lean's special effects guru – Oscar nominated Guardsman Eddie Fowlie, who died in 2011.

The 2nd Battalion were sent to the Malayan Emergency

in 1948. The Guardsmen went after the Communist insurgents with ferocity in the jungle. In Britain, the varied interests of the Officers' and Sergeants' Messes were shown when Major Petre won the 1948 Grand National and Company Sergeant Major Rioch beat off all challengers for his title of Imperial Services Champion at Bayonet Fighting. The event was discontinued in 1956 by which time he was 44.

Years of skiing and exercise in Germany were broken up with tours of Cyprus, Malaya and Borneo, Kenya, Belize, Oman, Hong Kong and Northern Ireland, as the British Government decided where to hold or disengage.

Occasional shocks arose. The 2nd Battalion headed to the Falkland Islands in 1982 amidst cries from much of the Army that a battalion who had been on the forecourt at Buckingham Palace for two years were the wrong men to send. They stormed Mount Tumbledown at the point of the bayonet, losing eight men to well-dug-in Argentine Marines.

In 1991, 1st Battalion helped the liberation of Kuwait, while 2nd Battalion lost out in the MoD's 'Options for Change'. The battalions merged in 1993. The rest of the 1990s passed in the Balkans and more tours of Belfast and East Tyrone.

The events of 9/11 meant two tours of Iraq for the Scots Guards and then the warning order to deploy to Helmand in the spring of 2010.

If the above account appears long, then that is because the history is long. It is also important. It still informs what the Regiment does in an age of unmanned drones and Improvised Explosive Devices (IEDs). It is a recruiter, a unique selling point and a reference. Guardsmen slap the Ever Open Eye sticker of the Guards Armoured Division on anything that's nailed down, non-commissioned officers tattoo the capbadge on their shoulders and officers wear their divisional blue-red-blue ties. Old boys wearing blazers with buttons in threes (3rd Guards) come to funerals of serving soldiers they never met. This shows the young that they are part of something much larger than today. No one bores on about the history now but it is there, a silent hand on the shoulder. It is no better or worse than any other regiment's history, but it is the Scots Guards'.

★

The Book of Judges describes how one tribe caught out imposters: 'Say now Shibboleth: and he said Sibboleth: for he could not frame to pronounce it right.' 1st Battalion Scots Guards (1 SG) has a network of shibboleths seemingly impenetrable to the outsider. They have no CO, Adj, RSM, CSMs, Sarjs, Screws (full or half) or Privates. They do have the Commanding Officer, the Adjutant, the Regimental Sergeant Major, Company Sergeant Majors, Colour Sergeants, Sergeants, Lance Sergeants, Lance Corporals and Guardsmen. In speech, the 'Lance' in front of Sergeant or Corporal is not mentioned. This gives the men a verbal promotion to go with the extra chevron they wear in gift from the Monarch. Full Sergeants are marked from Lance Sergeants through a shiny capstar and a red sash on parade. As neither is much worn in Helmand, telling the difference is impossible unless you know every man in the Battalion, which about three people do. Making head or tail of where brevity is welcomed, as in changing Company Quartermaster Sergeant to Q Bloke, and where it is not, as in shortening Regimental Quartermaster Sergeant to RQMS, is another verbal minefield. Some of this had filtered through to me in unknowing osmosis from my father but I still made howlers. When I called Company Sergeant Major Johnstone 'Sergeant

Major' one day, he turned on me and said with genuine disappointment: 'Come on, Max. How long have you been here? You should know by now that there's only one Sergeant Major – the Regimental Sergeant Major. Honestly.'

Battalion insults also follow a strict gradient of rank. There are belters, ballbags, bangers, mutants and, finally, the electric. Belters are generally a bit too by the book and just give off the wrong impression. They generally sit above you in the rank structure. Officers make up a healthy percentage of the Battalion's belters. Ballbags (scrotums) are people who screw up on occasion and are told so to their face, as in: 'Eh, Ballbag – get the fuck over here!' If someone is doing something wrong, then he's a ballbag. It's a transitional term rather than a label for life. Everybody has been a ballbag in the past and has the capacity to be a ballbag again. One of the moments when I knew I was on the right track with Battalion was when a Guardsman on Salisbury Plain called me a ballbag – a genuine baptism. Try as I might, the publishers of this book wouldn't go for *Eh, Ballbag!* as a title, much to the disappointment of the Guardsmen. Bangers come next and are just out-and-out wankers. Mutants are the youngsters (officers and men) who unwittingly mess up situations and who might take a while to learn from their mistakes. There is still hope for a mutant. At the bottom are those classified as electric. These are the men who no one believes made it through training. Having a few electric Guardsmen around can be a bonus in certain situations. Anyone new is a crow. Not really an insult, just a way of telling an officer or a Guardsman that he's new, as in: 'Eh, crowbags, how many operational tours have yooz done?'

★

Like many rivalries in the Army, the inter-company one in the Scots Guards is probably as ancient as anything between siblings. Competition is used to encourage professionalism, as letting the platoon, the company or the regiment down in front of their nearest rivals (who constantly pick over each other's performances) is a cardinal sin.

In Battalion, Right Flank is a breed apart. They are named after their position on the parade square and on the old pitched battlefields. As the senior company, 'The Flank' takes the pick of the taller Guardsmen and has a reputation for groupthink and hardheadedness. Known to the rest of Battalion as 'the Borg' after the ruthless race of *Star Trek* villains who claim that 'resistance is futile'. This feeling of separateness was reinforced in 2007 when they were detached from Battalion and sent to Helmand for Operation Herrick 6/7, while the majority of Battalion went to Basra for Operation Telic 11. Right Flank pioneered the use of Warrior Armoured Fighting Vehicles in Afghanistan and the insurgents named them 'Desert Devils'. This experience meant that they were the natural choice to act as Armoured Infantry Company on Herrick 11/12. As there is only one Warrior-borne company in Helmand, the rest of 1 SG got out of their wagons and trained as Light Role infantry. Right Flank would leave months before Battalion and the expectation was that they'd not be seen for the duration of the tour.

Alongside the Reconnaissance Platoon, B Company provide heavy weapon support with a platoon each of mortars and anti-tank missiles. The Company attracts more seasoned soldiers – 'the old sweats' – who have earned the right not to be micro-managed as many are in rifle platoons. The weapons platoons would conventionally be split into small detachments amongst the rifle companies. For Afghanistan, some would split to a Fire

Support Group role while others were down to act as Police Mentoring teams.

As the central rifle company in the line, C Company traditionally took the smaller Guardsmen, known as 'rabbits'. The uncertainty of what Battalion would do in Helmand led to the Company being split to the Flanks.

Headquarter Company keeps the show on the road. A 250-strong group of men and women across 16 departments, they range from clerks to cooks. Many are in 1 SG on attachment from other parts of the Army. For instance, as an Armoured Infantry battalion, 1 SG retains a platoon of men from the Royal Electrical and Mechanical Engineers. Scots Guardsmen to their very skilled fingertips are the Pipes & Drums. These soldier-musicians have the enviable task of slaking the seemingly unending thirst the rest of the world has for bagpipe music. In recent years, they've toured Ghana, Bermuda and North America. All that is put away come tour time. The men are split around Battalion to earn their keep as riflemen, drivers and intelligence analysts. Most found room for their pipes when they flew to Afghanistan.

Left Flank was the junior rifle company. With the demise of C Company and Right Flank's detachment from Battalion for the tour, they would be the largest sub-unit. Whether a result of a few characters in key appointments or of a long-standing ethos, the Company had a welcoming but professional attitude.

★

After their first farewell to Mother on the steps of their prep school, the majority of Scots Guards officers learn about the gradual privileges accrued by rank and seniority. Ten pence a week in the tuck shop becomes 50p by the age of 13 – a whole pound, perhaps, if a monitor. At public school sugar rationing ceases. Alcohol and tobacco are the new illicit substances. Entrance to the Sixth Form permits the occasional beer. Heads of House may visit local pubs. The shock of university – girls, cooking, laundry – can be vast. Some never recover. Many make straight for Sandhurst and then the Officers' Mess – the finest boarding house devised and one in which you are paid to live. Unlike school, there is an honesty bar and always someone to have a beer and a fag with. Unlike most universities, there is a team of friendly staff that mothers, cooks and serves decent food. There's even a charming lady who cleans bedrooms and places a four-leafed clover on the pillows of young men heading for war. And that's the catch.

It's jacket and tie at supper each night, except for the Piquet Officer, who wanders round camp afterwards in Mess Dress – forage cap, cane, and worsted red-and-blue jacket – checking the armouries are locked. The number of officers with double- and even triple-barrelled names means following conversations in the Mess can be impossible for outsiders:

'DH, have you seen MMC?'

'MMC? I think he's with DJ. Where are you off to?'

'To see KHC. Have you heard LG's been posted to Australia?'

The fact they mostly went to the sort of schools that fascinate the press informs their behaviour in the Mess – they have the relaxed ease and immaculate manners that system can breed. More important is that most hold degrees from Russell Group universities. Many have deep family connections to Scotland but all the Sandhurst entry officers have English public school accents. All, though, have the wit to realise that being aggressively posh just isn't clever or cool today. Many are the sons and grandsons of Scots Guards officers. Some are the sons and grandsons of Scots Guards generals. A few may go on to be generals. Whatever their background, it stops on the walk to work in the morning. Accents and attitudes aren't hidden but soldiers won't abide a snob, especially an incompetent one. A bad relationship with 'the boys' kills a career in Battalion stone dead.

Lieutenant Jimmy Murly-Gotto was like the player in the card game 'Hearts' who 'shoots the moon' and picks up every card going. He'd followed the Eton, Oxford, Guards trajectory beloved of 20th-century high-flyers. This was combined with attractively vulpine features and skilled athleticism. I have met many who hold just one of these assets and are stained with arrogance. Murly-Gotto, 25 and from Dorset, was not. He would lead 1 Platoon to Afghanistan.

Padre and Captain Colin MacLeod of the Royal Army Chaplains' Department was a son of the Manse and from the Isle of Lewis. Now 41, he'd joined the ranks of the 4th Royal Tank Regiment aged 17 and served six years. 'It couldn't have been more different from what I see the boys doing now,' he said, recalling halcyon days with the UN in Cyprus. He went on to university, then sensed his calling to the ministry. Ordained into the Free Church of Scotland, he re-joined the Army, this time as an officer and man of God in 2005. He was the first Padre from his denomination since the Second World War. He ministered to the Argyll and Sutherland Highlanders in Afghanistan in 2008 and was then posted to the Scots Guards. Hailing from an island where the Sabbath is still sincerely observed, he would head back to Afghanistan for another tour where the days of the week would blend into one. Another six months without Sundays. Like the Late Entry Officers who had commissioned after decades in the ranks, the Padre was a bridge between officers and men. Major Jock Dunn was the senior Scots Guardsman, with 30 years' service from Guardsman to Regimental Quarter-master. Coming into the Mess for a bowl of soup at lunch, he would nod at the colours and growl at a young officer, 'Tell me, Hamish, what Battle Honour is it today?'

★

Many of the 170 members of the Sergeants' Mess reminded me of Sartre's famous Parisian Waiter: their performance is so spot-on that it makes the observer aware that is just that. Away from the disciplinarian in the field and the legend in the Mess, there is usually a family man who, frankly, misses his wife and kids like hell during the long separations his career demands. That they can't show this on operations and always have to look to their men first makes the strain placed on them almost unbearable. They are the absolute heart of Battalion.

Their chief was Regimental Sergeant Major Ali Mackenzie. Another Lewis man, and young for 37, he had a Scots Guards uncle who went through Malaya and then taught him at school. 'I'd always wanted to be a soldier. Everything was about playing with your toy soldiers – there was nothing else,' he told me in a soft Western Isles accent harshened by 22 years on parade grounds. The Sergeant Major had followed the best route to the top: Junior Leaders at the Guards Depot aged 15, East Tyrone aged 18 and then to Armagh with the Close Observation Platoon. He went through the Infantry Battle School with a distinction and was a Platoon Sergeant on operations at 26. Top appointments at Sandhurst and in Battalion followed and then the main role. Vitally, he'd hardly missed an operational tour during his career so had the experience to take 550 Guardsmen to war. He knew the potential costs. An Afghan Policeman murdered his great friend, Regimental Sergeant Major

Darren Chant of the Grenadier Guards, in 2009. They had gone through Pirbright, Brecon and Sandhurst together. Competitive but not by nature a shouter, Mackenzie had two real loves: family and catching salmon in an estuary back home.

The other route up was the one taken by Company Sergeant Major Tam McEwan. When they were both crows, he was the Commanding Officer's gunner in Iraq in 1991. Red-haired, Glaswegian and capable of fitting more words into a minute than any other Scots Guardsman, he hadn't paused for breath since. 'It took me a bit to get promoted to Lance Corporal for various reasons – I was namely normally in the jail – got promoted to Lance Corporal in about 1997.' He then set about catching up with and then overtaking many in his peer group through Northern Ireland, Germany and Iraq. He would be Operations Warrant Officer on tour.

Company Sergeant Major Neil Lawrie had joined the Army to 'escape the drugs and the dramas in Glenrothes', his hometown in Fife. Now he would take a rifle company through Afghanistan's poppy harvest and fighting season. His job would be equivalent to the chief operating officer of a multi million-pound organisation employing hundreds. It is almost inconceivable that he could have found a similar role in the civilian world after leaving school at 16.

Stories from a grandfather about the war in Italy had drawn Sergeant Tony Gibson to the Army. Like about 40 per cent of the Scots Guards, he was from the north of England. He'd gone into a recruiting office aged 16 and said he wanted to be in the infantry. A dozen years later, he was 11 Platoon's Sergeant. Sergeant Craig McAlpine was the son of a Scots Guardsman who'd served 22 years. 'Since I was a boy, I wanted to join the Army,' he said. He travelled round the world with his father until, aged 16, he was 'frogmarched' into the same Army Careers Office at which his father had joined.

★

Guardsman Rab McClellan looked out at the room of faces staring up at him. He'd done well on the selection weekend for British Army recruits. One of the final tests was this two-minute 'Ice Breaker' talk on himself or a subject he knew well. He cleared his throat. 'Buckfast Tonic Wine, or Bucky to you and me, is a fortified wine first made by the Benedictine Monks of Buckfast Abbey in Devon in the 1870s. It is 15 per cent alcohol by volume. To open it, twist the metal cap on the glass bottle 11 clicks to the right and then enjoy . . .' A few years later, Rab and his brother Davie were preparing to fly to Afghanistan as Guardsmen in 1 Platoon, Right Flank.

Guardsman Matthew Mears from Preston joined at 25. He'd done spells as a bar manager in Magaluf – 'not all it's cracked up to be' – and in the Royal Navy since leaving school. Bored with sitting in Plymouth and Portsmouth, and knowing the pub trade was still 'dying out', he'd moved across to the infantry to 'do something a bit more physical'. Like many, a thirst for a challenge, combined with hard economic realities, had led to the Infantry Training Centre in Catterick. Life there was 'hard at times but pretty much what I expected'. After getting, 'bored out of my skull' working as a security guard, Alex Maclachlan had looked at different regiments to join. Although born in the Midlands, he wanted to reconnect with his Scottish roots. 'The Scots Guards had all the history – all the other Scottish Regiments had melded together. You know if you do something, like stagging on Buckingham Palace, people have been doing that for 300 years. You're proud of your history.' His brother had tried to get him to join him in the Parachute Regiment, 'but they're all a bit dodgy in that side of life', the Guardsman concluded. Guardsmen Mears and Maclachlan would both leave wives behind when they deployed to Afghanistan with 12 Platoon, Left Flank.

Family tradition played just as much a part with Junior Ranks as elsewhere in Battalion. Guardsman Lee Sample had followed his father into the Irish Guards. He'd left school with nine passes at GCSE (many more than most who end up in the infantry) and knew what he was was getting into. His father had left the Irish Guards as a Colour Sergeant. Sample sought an attachment to the Scots Guards 'as a way of making my own little name'. As he went around his parent unit getting his papers in order for the move to 1 SG, the older men had warned him, 'You don't want to go to the Scots Guards. You think *we're* Victorian in our attitudes – you'll get a shock up there.' Sample had enjoyed the first months of the attachment and slotted into the Reconnaissance Platoon. Guardsman Amornsin Wannuwat had followed a slightly different tradition. Many of his uncles were in the Royal Thai Army. Wannuwat's immediate family had brought him to Britain aged ten. After tiring of work in a factory, he decided to continue the martial tradition in his new homeland. The Scots Guards were the first regiment with space on a training course, so he'd slipped into their ranks. Once he understood some of the choicer accents in his group of recruits, he'd enjoyed the 28-week course that turns civilians into soldiers. His entire family turned up to his Passing Out Parade.

Very much Scots Guardsmen, though very much *not* Scottish, were the overseas soldiers who made up around 7–8 per cent of the Battalion. Their representative in the Officers' Mess was Lieutenant Dan Krause-Harder-Calthorpe from Germany. Born in a country constitutionally disabled from aggression, he had made his way to

Sandhurst after national service in the Bundeswehr and a tour of Iraq as a Private with the British Parachute Regiment. A proud and natural soldier, his experience of Airborne Operations would serve 2 Platoon, Right Flank, well in Helmand.

Lance Sergeant Waldo Serfontein, 31, was a senior South African in 1 SG. Like all those from the Commonwealth, he was welcomed into the British Army. 'The British Army is definitely one of the most professional out there. It's one of the most active, so that was a no-brainer. Scots Guards – I read up about the Regiment, liked the sound of it and here I am today,' he told me. He'd gone through Helmand with Right Flank before. On Herrick 12, he would help mentor a company of Afghan National Army (ANA) soldiers. Guardsman Naibuka Suguturaga, 25, was one of the rugby team or so of Fijians in Battalion and had joined aged 19. He came from an island of fewer than 1,000 farmers and hadn't been back since joining. 'I'm not a qualified person – like in education – and I've got a brother-in-law who joined. He said, "Wouldn't you like to come over and join the British Army?" He sponsored me,' Suguturaga said. The first time he left Fiji was to fly to training in Britain in midwinter.

*

Soldiers are drilled in training to respond to certain situations without thinking – a matrix of mental associations that will trigger actions that should keep them alive in a war zone. This is then combined with a group ethos of social pressures acquired in their unit. This further conditions the soldier to act in certain types of scenarios, as not every situation can be anticipated in training. By the time he reaches the front line the soldier has had a powerful set of behaviours grafted onto him. It is fortunate that in the British Army core standards ('As a soldier your behaviour must always be lawful, appropriate and totally professional') are also drilled into soldiers. This is meant to endow them with the ethical framework to cope with certain situations where moral ambiguity is prevalent and bad decisions will end lives. One of the most noticeable traits that this training breeds was immaculate manners towards an outsider like me. Nothing seemed too much trouble, no question too ridiculous (though many of mine were). This from men whose primary job it is to close with and kill the enemy.

From Catterick, newly minted Scots Guardsmen head down to London for a spell of ceremonial duties around the Royal Palaces. They have a crash course in the dignified side of the British constitution: Trooping the Colour, State Opening of Parliament and, some years, providing a 'Pony Platoon' for stalking parties at Balmoral. Time away from bearskins is spent picking up driving qualifications and maintaining the soldiering skills they'll require when in Battalion. Most move back to Catterick after roughly six months in London.

'It's different and better in Battalion,' Guardsman Wannuwat told me. Challenging exercises, live firing on an array of new weapons and specific training for operational tours keeps men busy. First stop for all is a rifle platoon. In the Scots Guards, these work along similar lines to a large Victorian family – at least in barracks. The Platoon Commander is father – firmly in charge, fairly remote and there to provide guidance. He is usually only consulted about issues that might affect the whole family. The Platoon Sergeant is mother and runs the housekeeping. They ensure everyone has everything they need to get through the day and manage the minor issues with their own brand of discipline. The junior non-commissioned officers are trusted elder siblings to the Guardsmen, for whom everything is provided but who are also kept end-lessly busy.

A huge bonus for the junior ranks was the Single Living Accommodation Modernisation (SLAM) rooms they had in Catterick. Multi million-pound blocks housed men in private rooms. 'In Windsor,' said Guardsman Sample, 'my bed was held together with bungees and I didn't have locked doors. I thought I'd been put in the wrong place when I was shown to my SLAM room here. It's like a hotel.' Some thought SLAM isolated men into a routine of Xbox and television over shared time in communal areas. However, the privacy and near luxury it gave may have been a reason that not one Scots Guardsman signed off to leave the Army in 2008–09.

*

Though thinking about the tour had begun almost as soon as 1 SG had returned from Iraq and Afghanistan in 2008, the build-up only really began with the arrival of the new Commanding Officer, Lieutenant Colonel Lincoln Jopp MC. 'What's he like, Tam? Can you see us all right with him?' a few senior sergeants had asked Company Sergeant Major McEwan when the Commanding Officer arrived in Catterick in December 2008. 'Lincoln Jopp will give you nothing,' McEwan replied. It was to the Company Ser-geant Major's credit that he told the story to the Com-manding Officer and to Jopp's credit that he told it against himself. He had commanded Scots Guards platoons and companies on operations and won his Military Cross in Sierra Leone. A fan of *The West Wing,* he took a copy of Andrew Rawnsley's latest dissection of New Labour on tour with him and was a natural politician. He was equally happy quoting General Petraeus and Lord Buddha. He drove his men hard. Once in command of the necessary information about a situation, he was straight with his men and expected them to be straight with him. He was always the Commanding Officer, never Colonel Lincoln, as a less rigid man might have been.

Initial training had its moments of farce, as when equipment shortages had Guardsmen using broomsticks as dummy metal detectors. There was also a succession of rumours about what their role would be in Helmand. This reflected the fluidity of political will for the Afghan campaign. Would Britain stick or twist in Helmand? Would they move lock, stock and barrel to Kandahar? What effect would the general election have on the campaign? What, above all, were the Americans planning? Would General McChrystal's leaked calls for troop increases be pipped by Vice President Biden's desire to focus on counter-terrorism? President Obama, who had used tough talk on Afghanistan to show how right he had been on Iraq, plumped for a surge. This secured British involvement in Afghanistan for 2010. However, the new question arose of which regions and roles in Helmand the US Marine Corps would grab. This line of strategic uncertainty led directly to Guardsmen prepping for war and caused a succession of about-turns in the tentative Orders of Battle Brigade and Battalion formulated.

The Battalion ambition was to be a ground-holding Battlegroup in Helmand. In early 2009 the focus was preparing for exercise in Canada in their Warriors. A good performance there might mean a plum role in theatre. A soaking gunnery camp in Wales preceded the long flight to Alberta. Some effort had been made by the exercise controllers to simulate Helmand realities. A dummy Afghan bazaar and village was in place, complete with a 'suicide bomber in a bucket' splattered across the main square in one part of the exercise. This built up to a live firing exercise across the prairie. This was great for Right Flank, who would be in Warrior for Helmand, but the rest of Battalion must have questioned the benefit of storming trenches from vehicles they'd not see in theatre. After the traditional three-way brawl between the Taser-armed Alberta Police, the Duke of Lancaster's Regiment and the Scots Guards, the men flew home.

The Brigade Commander was delighted with 1 SG and appointed them Regional Battlegroup South. This meant they would be a helicopter-borne reserve expected to fly into trouble spots across southern Afghanistan to shut down insurgent activity and reinforce ground-holding units. This was a great result – better even than traditional ground-holding. Then bad news came. The job was nicked off the British Army and given to the Americans, now planning to 'surge' into the south. It was announced that Britain would not resource another Battlegroup role – an unexpected draw-down. For a while, it looked like 1 SG, apart from Right Flank, wouldn't deploy. The Battalion's carcass was picked over for parts: Major Dunn appointed Camp Bastion Quartermaster, Drill Sergeant Grierson sent to Kabul's training establishments.

Realising that uncertainty was the only certainty, Battalion trained generically. The array of different vehicles and weapon systems meant men had to be sent on an alarming number of external courses. Over 4,500 man training days were spent on driving courses alone. All this got in the way of collective platoon and company training. Right up to the final exercises, men were missing from their sub-units. This meant that the opening night in Helmand was also the first dress rehearsal for some teams.

Desperate for a role, 1 SG leapt at the Police Mentoring Headquarters job offered before Christmas 2009. This then mutated into the Afghan National Security Forces (ANSF) Development Headquarters. The changes meant new sets of qualifications were required. The plan called for teams to split from 1 SG and go to the corners of Helmand. This would deprive headquarters of the chance to oversee a real Battlegroup in action and they would merely deploy in a support rather than command position. The Commanding Officer began talking about how the stars would realign in Helmand and a ground-holding role would be found for 1 SG. No one believed him. Real kit arrived and low-level training on actual Vallon metal detectors could begin within the companies as the final months ticked away. Before Christmas, the round of Battalion functions kept spirits high. The night before the Officers' Mess vs. Sergeants' Mess rugby, five new second lieutenants arrived in Catterick fresh from training. They were given a brutal welcome on the pitch the next day, then met the men they'd be leading to war.

Amidst the training, there was tragedy. Lieutenant Peter Rous died on selection for the Parachute Regiment in November 2009. He had dreamed of leading the Guards Parachute Platoon in 3 PARA. A few weeks later, Guardsman Andrew Gibson was murdered outside a nightclub in Darlington. He had joined the Army at 16 as a Junior Soldier and then spent one year with F Company in London before joining 1st Battalion in Catterick. He was the son of a Scots Guardsman who had fought in the Falklands in 1982 with 2nd Battalion. Gibson was the second Scots Guardsman murdered by civilians in less than six months. In October 2009 Guardsman Paul McGee was stabbed outside his front door in Lochwinnoch after his taxi driver and his mother were attacked. He died outside his home; he had been attending a charity night. He'd won a Queen's Commendation for Bravery in Iraq in 2007 trying to save the life of a fellow Guardsman. The Regiment had lost three men and hadn't even got to Afghanistan.

In the New Year, Right Flank disappeared to their role in Helmand. For the rest of Battalion, the uncertainty of who would deploy where, when and in what role increased strain on families barely glimpsed. Only at the start of the Mission Rehearsal Exercise, on 7 February, was word received that a ground-holding Battlegroup role had indeed been found. It would be centred on Lashkar Gah, Helmand's capital. All of 1st Battalion Scots Guards would deploy to Afghanistan in April 2010. I would join them in May.

Playing FTSE with Insurgents

Guardsman McHugh watched the Sky News tickertape roll constantly on an August morning in Helmand. 'British and Afghan forces succeed in taking Taliban stronghold of Saye-debad, Southern Afghanistan,' it read.

'Aye, have they fuck. We killed all the Taliban there in February,' he said.

'Who's gone in?' asked Guardsman Stafford.

'It's the Lancs,' McHugh replied.

'The Lancs? Chippy as fuck.'

'Aye. And they gone in with seven companies.'

'We did Sayedebad with one.'

'All they'll find there is deid Taliban, lots of brass and a bloke who answers to Mr Miyagi and loves boil-in-the-bags', said Sergeant Kirkwood, who'd wandered over from the Operations (Ops) Room in the checkpoint 1 Platoon, Right Flank had been manning for the final part of their tour. They'd be home in a week.

'What's this patrol then, Kirky?'

'Just a wee walk up Route Orion. Staffy, what's happened to your 'tash?'

'Shaved it off.'

'Taliban won't like that. Taliban don't like change.'

'I've changed my trousers and all,' said Billy Stuart, an enormous Lance Corporal.

'Oh dear,' said Kirkwood. He stared at the screen. 'At least the FTSE's up.'

The eight of us walked out of the checkpoint with two Afghan National Policemen. One, a bearded bear of a man, was improbably dressed in a Guards Training Company

T-shirt and carried a Kalashnikov with a folding butt dwarfed by his frame. The other looked like a 50-year-old junkie. Which was probably what he was.

It had been hot for longer than anyone could remember. 500 metres up Route Orion, the road the checkpoint was designed to watch over, we swung east into the Green Zone. Over our right shoulders was Muktar Fort, looking over the Helmand River, and beyond that Lashkar Gah. In order to minimise the risk of IEDs we walked through springy grass and then ploughed fields, taking a route a drunk might pick. The figure in the white robe watching us stood out against the mud compound walls. He watched for several minutes and then disappeared into a nest of compounds to the north.

Ten minutes later we were walking through chest-high corn when Lance Corporal Stuart turned and said to everyone in particular, 'Good spot for an ambush.' As we left the corn, we came into open ground flanked on three sides by compounds. Inevitably, we got shot at.

If you showed an Eskimo a rattlesnake he would not need to be told that the fangs pack haemotoxic venom capable of rotting your organs. He'd just know to get away, thanks to that file nature gives us marked 'avoid'. Getting shot at is similar. So rich and unnatural are the cadences of bullets aimed to harm you that you just know to make yourself low and small as soon as those first rounds skip around. 'Fuck' becomes your favourite word until it ends.

'Get that fucking Gimpy going!'
'Fucking hell!'
'Will you fuck off?'
'I'm having a stoppage every fucking round.'
'Fucking nice – fucking get some.'
'Keep your fucking eyes down there.'
'I'm fucking running low on ammo.'
'Where the fuck are they?'
'Fuck me, lads!'

'*Smash that fucking green door right now.*'

'*I've been fucking smashing it all day.*'

The initial rounds came from the north, then other firing points opened up from the west. High-velocity single rounds were mixed in with bursts of automatic. Sergeant Kirkwood was up front with the policemen who were darting about waving bursts of automatic around the compounds and generally giving the Guardsmen some room. After a while Kirkwood got bored with getting shot at and took the platoon light missile off Guardsman Peters. He fired it into a compound to end the contact from the north, then re-joined the rest of the patrol bunched up against a wall on the edge of the cornfield. Everyone's starting to have a wee chuckle. Another burst – medium machine gun and high-velocity single shots – this time from the rear.

'*Where the fuck's that?*'

'*What the fuck?*'

'*Right, we need to fucking move.*'

'*Who the fuck is firing over there?*'

'*Whoa – fuck me!*' *as an RPG sails in from another firing point.*

And it's kit on and run through the corn, firing as they go, trying to see where the people who want to kill us are. Halfway through the field there's a grassy track that couldn't be more than three metres across but seems a mile wide under fire. Quick pause, assess, and then on and over it and back into the sweet-smelling corn. The field ends and we're in open ground next to another route. A Warrior has rushed up the road and the sight of its powerful cannon is enough to end the contact, finally. The guys peel down the route taking on water, marching out quicker than they marched in. There are two white flags on the route, insurgent markers showing the population that they control this area, even though it is only a kilometre from the nearest Isaf checkpoint. Lance Corporal Stuart goes up to a flag and pulls it down. The police take the other. 'It's all good. It's all good,' Stuart says. It has been the longest and shortest, best and worst 18 minutes of my life.

Back in the checkpoint it's time for a group photo with the trophies, endless cigarettes, bottles of water and peeling-off kit. Taking off my kneepads, there's a white mineral crust as thick as a line of teacher's chalk: a tidemark of sweat and a reminder of a morning's work.

'Oh, the FTSE's still up,' says Sergeant Kirkwood, looking at the screen.

'And the Lancs are still in Sayedebad.'

'That was quite a cheeky wee contact.'

'Nothing like Sayedebad, though.'

'Oh no. Nothing like Sayedebad.'

'Tell me about Sayedebad,' I say.

CHAPTER TWO

'Are there tigers in Afghanistan?'

Christmas Eve 2009 to 10 February 2010

Initially, Right Flank weren't meant to go on Operation Moshtarak and if they were, they'd have gone in Warriors and not to Sayedebad, which hadn't been considered in the early stages of the plan.

Moshtarak, Dari for 'together', was an operational plan that emerged from Isaf's Regional Command South in Kandahar in the late autumn of 2009. Operation Panchai Palang in August of that year had brought Isaf into insurgent-held areas but left ungoverned space across central Helmand. Moshtarak would close some of these spaces down. The focus of the operation was getting the US Marine Corps into the town of Marjah, south of Lashkar Gah. North of the capital, in the British area of operations, a similar ungoverned space known as the Char-e-Anjir Triangle, or CAT, would be dealt with.

In November 2009, orders confirming Moshtarak were issued. The Grenadier Guards Battlegroup was asked to plan their part of the operation, slated for February 2010. The Battlegroup had deployed in October and was partly based along a line of patrol bases north of Kawshhal Kalay (village). Kawshhal was a known insurgent hot spot and beyond it lay an area of ungoverned space that had the potential to turn into an insurgent stronghold once the Marines had squeezed the insurgents from Marjah.

Along with their role in clearing the CAT to their east with the 1st Battalion Coldstream Guards, the Grenadiers put together a plan to clear Kawshhal Kalay in the days before Operation Moshtarak began. However, the intent was not to roll into the village and destroy it for the sake of eliminating the opposition. Instead, the Grenadiers wanted to move into the village slowly and, hopefully, without too much force, building relations with the locals and then a permanent patrol base for their Afghan partners. This would be much easier if the focus of insurgent activity was elsewhere.

Operations are designed around enemy activity and available resources. A resource that was not in Helmand at the time was Right Flank, sent away on pre-tour and Christmas leave with the promise of a solid month off and a leisurely report to barracks in mid-January. Moshtarak had been constantly delayed due to the strategic importance of allowing enough properly trained Afghan National Army soldiers to be ready on the start line. By 2009, Isaf's exit strategy had begun to rest on the creation of a decent Developing World-standard security sector in Afghanistan. No one was trying to mint Scotland Yard or Aldershot in Afghanistan but the evolution of a competent force that could defend the Afghan Government from threats internal and external would hasten the West's exit. Most importantly, in my opinion, it would mean they wouldn't have to come back to Central Asia. Hence Moshtarak (rather than the sub-Clive Cussler operational code names of the past) and waiting for competent Afghan soldiers to make the operation truly 'together'.

It therefore seemed Right Flank was safe in letting go over Christmas. Much of their training had been in formidable Warrior Armoured Fighting Vehicles. Armed with a 30mm cannon and chain gun, the Warrior is designed to charge enemy positions, disgorge a section of infantry and provide covering fire as they close with and kill the enemy. The expectation for 2010 was that they would build on previous experience and bounce around the desert, outflanking the IED threat and closing down insurgent ability to manoeuvre. The Guardsmen had prepared themselves to be taxied round Helmand in 30-ton behemoths that would provide shelter from both enemy and conditions while carrying their kit. As the only Armoured Infantry Company available to the British, it seemed a safe bet that they'd be in their wagons all tour.

For the Grenadiers' charismatic Commanding Officer, Lieutenant Colonel Roly Walker, the question remained of how to draw the insurgents away from the push into Kawshhal Kalay. This would allow his men to conduct the population-focused counter-insurgency operation that the war in 2010 demanded. The doctrine touted in Afghanistan by this stage of the campaign was that the enemy should no longer be the main objective in operations. Instead, it would be winning the support of the people of villages such as Kawshhal Kalay that would dictate victory or defeat for Isaf and their Afghan partners in Helmand. Once gained, this support could then feed into the narrative of success Isaf hoped to pitch to Afghan and international audiences. However, the enemy always have a vote and they were known to be numerous where Walker was sending his Battlegroup. His solution was to insert a rifle company into the insurgents' local headquarters in order to focus their efforts on protecting their rear, thereby disrupting their reaction to events elsewhere. Initially, thinking lay with putting Right Flank into the area in Warriors but the terrain was assessed as unsuitable for the tracked vehicles. Discussion then focused on a helicopter assault using another company more used to light infantry soldiering and therefore more suitable for the operation. Eventually, it was decided to bring Right Flank to Helmand a month early and assign them a role once they arrived.

★

Like every member of Right Flank, Lance Corporal Mick Little, a 23-year-old from Govan in Glasgow, remembers the precise moment Operation Moshtarak ruined Christmas. He had returned home for leave and was frantically picking up final odds and ends in his local Asda on Christmas Eve. The phone rang, and he was told to report back to Catterick a fortnight early. At first, he thought it was a typical squaddie wind-up, so phoned the Guardroom back. They told him the call was genuine. He phoned his fiancée, who was naturally upset, and then made his way to the checkout, only to be ID-ed by the checkout girl for the alcohol he'd bought. 'That pushed the boat out for me. I had to walk away because I was a bit annoyed,' he said.

In the rush, Right Flank was still undermanned. F Company was asked to draft the final few. As an unmarried Guardsman, Tyrone Peters, a 24-year-old fresh from training and originally from Grenada, was informed he'd be going to Afghanistan very soon and was sent to Catterick to join his new company. On arrival, and knowing only the other Guardsmen from F Company, he was marched into his new Platoon Commander's office.

'Right, well, I'm Lieutenant Murly-Gotto and this is Sergeant Kirkwood, the Platoon Sergeant. I'm sure you've got a lot of concerns about getting sent to Afghan on such short notice. I know I would, but look, you'll get most of your training just by watching the other guys in the Platoon – listening to what they're saying. Just keep your ears and eyes open as much as possible. Welcome to 1 Platoon,' said the young officer.

Sergeant Colin Kirkwood, an Ayrshire man, put Guardsman Peters under the wing of more experienced members of the platoon and had his kit issued within a few hours. Peters had been in a Warrior once in training and had never set foot in a helicopter.

The Company rushed through the last administrative hurdles to deployment: vaccinations, hearing and dental checks. The possibility of failing one of these tests after so much training worried many. Guardsman David McHugh, 20, had been in the Scots Guards for three years since deciding to, 'do something interesting' with his life. He was 'just dying to go'.

'It sounds daft,' he said, 'but I was pure paranoid about stupid things like your audio and that. Paranoid I wouldn't be able to go to Afghan. I just wanted to go to Afghan; I wanted to have my own experiences. Everybody else had done theirs, like Iraq or Northern Ireland and that, and I hadn't done nothing, so I just wanted to put my mind at rest.'

A few of the company failed and were left behind. The rush cut goodbyes short but some, like Lance Corporal Greg Harris, a north Londoner in The Royal Army Medical Corps attached to the Company, were grateful: 'The longer you have to say goodbye, the worse it gets a lot of the time.' On the afternoon of 11 January the company, some nursing final hangovers, others yet to sober up, laid out their Number 2 Dress uniforms and medals on their beds in case the worst happened, changed into fresh desert combats and assembled on a snow-draped parade square ready for the coach journey to RAF Brize Norton in Oxfordshire.

★

After a long journey, delayed for some by a frozen runway in England, the Company arrived at Camp Bastion. Some were distinctly underwhelmed by the sprawling mass of tents and sand that comprises the hub of Isaf operations in south-west Afghanistan. As with all other units arriving, Right Flank was put through an in-theatre training package. Theirs was tailored to their Warrior role. This chimed with everything they had been told to date. As 2 Platoon's Lance Sergeant John Norwood from Glasgow put it: 'Loads of our training before we deployed was all Armoured Infantry based and basically that was our understanding of what our role was going to be – constant Warrior.' Commanders, drivers and gunners got used to the wagons they expected to call home for the next six months and got them almost to combat readiness. Then rumours began to fly about camp.

'Right Flank were linked with every job,' according to Sergeant Kirkwood. The Guardsmen participated in the age-old custom of making things up to confuse one another. Rumour control was such that Lance Corporal Thomas 'Peaches' McGonagle was able to convince more gullible members of the Company that he'd been sent away on a submarine commander course for a special operation up the Helmand River. One rumour that failed to gain traction was that some sort of secret operation was planned and that Right Flank would be dropped by helicopter. As Guardsman McHugh put it: 'The strongest option, the one that was pushed at Guardsman level, was going to Pimon [a large Patrol Base on the west of the Green Zone] with Warrior – we got a long brief on that. The second option was also in Warrior. Third option was the heli-op and everyone just said: "We're going to Pimon, then." It [the helicopter assault] sounded stupid, no one believed it at all, it just sounded daft. Then it was on.'

It turned out that Right Flank would act as the spearhead for Operation Moshtarak. As more details of the operation began to develop and the initial shock wore off, men became more excited at the prospect. Any reservations that soldiers used to being taxied right up to the point of assault, having their kit carried for them, would struggle in a new environment were dismissed.

Training for the operation was laughably simple. The troops went to the flight line in Bastion, where a Chinook was parked. They got on. Then got off. Then went back to their tents. For 2 Platoon's Lieutenant Krause-Harder-Calthorpe (KHC for short), this was adequate, as airborne 'wasn't rocket science. It is basic soldiering. The main effort is to have a quick exit, get into a formation that is controlled and easily manageable, and provide immediate all-round security.' The Company Commander, Major Iain Lindsay-German MBE, also drilled the prospect of landing under fire into commanders' heads during the familiarisation day and during the increasingly complex Orders Groups held prior to departure. Other elements started to come together. The operation dictated that Right Flank should bring everything and everyone they needed in the field with them. As Moshtarak had been sufficiently delayed to prepare the Afghan National Army for full participation, Right Flank took with them an 18-strong platoon split between their three platoons along with four Afghan interpreters. A 13-man counter-IED team was also assigned to Right Flank to clear an IED belt if it developed and exploit any unexpected finds in Sayedebad. They were joined by two Royal Engineers to help with demolitions and other tasks and an RAF Flight Lieutenant to coordinate helicopter moves. To help link up communications with neighbouring units that were not British, a two-man US Marine Air Naval Gunfire Liaison Company team also joined the operation. Finally, it was decided that Right Flank would need more fire support on the ground than their weapons provided. The Grenadiers offered two two-man Javelin teams to fill this gap. They were commanded by Lance Sergeant Thomas Loder, a 31-year-old from Lincolnshire who plays prop for his battalion and who, he said when we talked in an office overlooking St James's Park that summer, seems to be in the wrong place at the wrong time' whenever he goes on tour.

Javelin is an American-designed and British-modified anti-tank missile that has come to be used extensively in Afghanistan in an anti-personnel role as, essentially, a 16-kg sniping round. Its thermal sight gives it a surveillance capability and it is highly accurate up to 2,500 metres. Key to its popularity is that it is a Battlegroup asset and as such does not need Brigade clearance to fire. If the operator has done his job correctly, the round cannot miss and will follow the target even if it tries to run. Insurgents know it as 'the missile that follows you'. Due to the nature of the weapon, it should also kill the target without destroying any structure he might be using as cover, making it a relatively low collateral damage weapon. After Apache helicopter pilots, Javelin operators must have the most confirmed kills of anyone in Afghanistan.

Lance Sergeant Loder arrived in Bastion, assembled his teams and went to visit Right Flank's Headquarters. Aware that they were fresh into theatre, he wanted to check that they were happy with the capability he was bringing and the terms on which it could be used. Loder was also apprehensive about working with another regiment on operations, especially one new to theatre. He dismissed these concerns after chatting with a few members of Right Flank. All Guardsmen train together in Catterick and the *esprit de corps* of the Foot Guards meant that Loder, though having to adapt to a few new accents and customs, quickly felt at home. After looking at some live surveillance footage of Sayedebad shot from drones to try and pick up on the pattern of life and the relief of the area he'd soon be dropped into, Loder left to brief his teams, who would be split between 1 and 2 Platoons.

With these additional assets and limited space on the Chinooks, there was not room for all of Right Flank. It came as a blow for 20 of the company when they were left behind to bring the Warriors up to scratch and sustain the operation from Bastion.

Sayedebad had seen no Isaf forces for two years. It was a predominantly Shi'ite Hazara community, a rarity in Helmand. Alongside these farmers there was known to be a core of insurgents using the village as a command and supply hub due to its proximity to the Isaf Patrol Base line to the north. The village itself was built around a cross-roads. Running north–south was a collection of mud shacks with metal shutters knitted together by a warren of alleyways that made up the bazaar. Away from the road were smaller clusters of thick-walled mud compounds. The intelligence assessment remembered at Guardsman level was that the men they would immediately face had low morale and perhaps five rounds of ammunition each. By paying the area an unexpected visit, it was hoped that Right Flank would draw more insurgents into a fight, allowing British troops to the north to ease into their objectives without recourse to heavy firepower. US Marines would push south along the western bank of the Nahr-e-Bughra Canal at the same time.

With these orders and resources, and against this in-telligence picture, Right Flank went about putting to-gether their detailed plan. It was decided to split the Company into its three platoons and give each a com-pound to occupy for the first part of the operation. To the north, 1 Platoon, commanded by Lieutenant Jimmy

Murly-Gotto, would land almost on top of the bazaar. To the south-east and in the centre, 3 Platoon, under Second Lieutenant Henry Greeves, would bed down with Company Headquarters. They would thus be within sight of the rest of the Company for ease of command. South of them, and completing a roughly dog-leg formation, 2 Platoon under Lieutenant KHC would land furthest from the village. After getting into their compounds and establishing rudimentary defences, exploratory patrols would push out and set up Vehicle Checkpoints on the roads to isolate it. Further patrols would orbit the village to gain a greater understanding of the area and its people. If the area was permissive, the village could then be searched in detail using the counter-IED team. The platoons would then move about the area, occupying different compounds each night to keep the insurgents guessing. After the Grenadiers were happy that Right Flank had achieved what was needed, they would leave by helicopter. Resupply and life-support would be by air only and the company had to land with enough rations and water for 48 hours and kit for eight days' combat. This meant that each man would have a 'disgusting' amount of kit on his back. A Guardsman could typically carry his rifle with six magazines ready and ammunition for a further ten magazines in a bandolier, 1,000 rounds for a General Purpose Machine Gun (GPMG), 300 rounds for a Light Machine Gun, a shovel, lightweight stretcher, team medic kit, six litres of water, rations plus any personal kit. This was all rammed round the body of his heavy counter-IED kit. The platoons also had mortar rounds and Javelin missiles split between them. Guardsmen generally come in two models: the five-foot-five street fighter and the six foot-three bull-necked. For those in the wee category, they were carrying at least their body weight. Initial packing was cancelled when the daypacks kept snapping at the shoulder straps and larger packs were ordered. These still didn't allow sufficient space for sleeping bags. The idea of clipping the sleeping bags to the outside of the sacks was immediately dismissed as looking unsmart, 'chippy' and not becoming of the Scots Guards. The notion of one between two was also dismissed by many. Most decided to go with a thin rubber jungle sleeping bag combined with a bit of warm kit stashed somewhere, the general feeling being: 'Aye, nae dramas, we're in Afghanistan, it isnae goin' to be that cold,' according to Lance Sergeant Norwood. In an effort to keep weight down, some went without any sleeping bag and even discarded their toothbrushes. Smokers still found room for enough cigarettes, though Guardsman McHugh carried only one pack: 'I was planning on giving up in Sayedebad,' he said.

By the time I began interviewing Right Flank about Sayedebad in May, they had formed a very clear narrative of the build-up to and execution of the operation. They welcomed the chance to tell their story. They were also happy to tell stories against themselves. For instance, many mentioned the appalling weight they'd carried, how cold it was and where mistakes were made. This was refreshingly honest and allowed me to put together an account of events I hadn't witnessed. In traits I noticed in many Scots Guardsmen, the emphasis was always on giving and not taking credit, a lack of bravado about one's own role and the ability to laugh at yourself. I think the most telling aspect of the story about the weight of kit carried into Sayedebad was that no one in Right Flank thought to weigh their packs in order to establish bragging rights later on.

Like all modern armies, Britain's relies on battery power in the field for night sights, radios and counter-IED kit. It was clearly impossible on top of all the munitions to carry enough batteries for eight days. A generator was required. In order to lighten the load during the insertion and for any Casualty Evacuations (Casevacs), Company Sergeant Major Andrew Johnstone was given a crash-course on a quad bike, during which he crashed twice. Once briefed, the company's medics decided to take themselves to the hospital in Bastion and gain as much hands-on experience as possible before leaving camp.

While Guardsmen worried only about the weight on their shoulders, junior commanders were rapidly facing up to the responsibility of getting their men through an experience none of them had trained for. 'I didn't want to show it to my Guardsmen but I was a bit worried,' admits Lance Corporal Little. At 23, he was young to be stepping up as a section commander and was always thinking of the responsibility he would have to take if his multiple commander, Sergeant Kirkwood, became a casualty. In an effort to allay the fears of his fiancée, Little phoned her before the operation and said he had a cushy job in Bastion and not to worry.

Three days before the operation, Orders were issued to the platoons by their commanders. Lieutenant Murly-Gotto, who had just celebrated his 26th birthday in the Bastion Pizza Hut (a shipping container with holes cut in the side), told 1 Platoon that they would occupy Compound 21, right on top of the bazaar. Near to the bazaar, which previous aerial reconnaissance had shown to be of interest, it was a large compound for the area. Lieutenant Murly-Gotto had some reservations about the compound: did its size indicate that the people there were wealthier than their neighbours and, if so, what was the source of their wealth? Knowing that he could be dropping onto anything – an arms or drugs factory, an insurgent bed-down location – he watched footage from a drone flying over the compound exactly 24 hours before he would be knocking on the compound door. Huddling round the black-and-white screen, looking at the live infrared footage, he noticed a number of bright white spots moving around the compound. 'Probably just dogs,' said Bombardier Chris Kirkup, the Company Forward Air Controller.

The night before Landing Hour, the platoons reassembled for a final chat and then junior commanders took their smaller teams away to gear them up and give them confidence in their commanders' confidence. Lying in bed that night and away from the penetrating gaze of their Guardsmen, young commanders could admit to themselves that, for them too, this was going to be new and potentially challenging.

After a few hours, those that had slept were woken and got kitted up. Men were leaning forward under the weight, trying to walk with their heads up. Anyone who sat down needed two men to lift him. On the Flight Line, Right Flank did two things that are rare in Helmand. First, they came off Card Alpha, the usual Counter Insurgency Rules of Engagement, and were placed under 429 Alpha, a less restrictive set of rules about who can be engaged when. Second, they cocked their weapons before boarding the Chinooks on the assumption that they would be hit as they stepped off, as had happened to a helicopter assault the previous night elsewhere in Helmand. Despite these signs of what was to come, Lance Sergeant Davey Walker managed, as always, to find humour and taunted 2 Platoon by saying that he and 1 Platoon would have to come and rescue them at some stage of the operation.

At 03:00 on 4 February, Right Flank took off. Nerves built on a half-hour flight that felt much longer. Men leant against the frame of the helicopter or against one another – anything to take the weight off their burning shoulders and taxed calves as they flew in near-total darkness to the unknown. Guardsmen Peters didn't enjoy his first flight by helicopter, feeling 'seasick' throughout. This sensation was replaced with another when the Chinook gunners opened up on targets on the ground.

★

As 1 Platoon's Chinook came in to land, Lance Corporal Little was one of the first to jump off, almost immediately putting his foot into a shallow ditch and rolling over on his ankle. Unable to get up with the weight, he lay stranded with his arms and feet flailing in the air, until other men got off and dragged him up. The platoon got into a broad V shape pointing away from the Chinook, which was away in moments. The whirr of 30mm cannon fire from the Apache Attack Helicopters (AH) above them rang out across the muddy ploughed fields around Sayedebad. This was drowned out by the detonation of a helicopter-launched Hellfire missile. It found six armed men moving towards 1 Platoon. Another missile was then launched from a drone. 'It's happening here,' thought Guardsman McHugh. It was 03:30. Adrenalin had seeped into bloodstreams, giving Lance Corporal McGonagle the feeling that 'You can leap over a compound in a single bound'. Despite the high, during the two-minute 'soak period' as the Platoon Commander got his bearings, it was apparent to Sergeant Kirkwood that his men were crumbling under the weight and would not be able to fight with it on their backs. The younger Guardsmen looked to Kirkwood and other experienced members of the platoon, thinking, 'What's happening here?' They were met with a practised look of outward nonchalance. They in turn relaxed in spite of the noise.

Confident that the RAF had dropped them in the correct place, 1 Platoon slowly moved off towards their compound. Reformed into their sections, Lance Corporal

Little took his men forward and checked a perimeter away from the compound with Vallons and identified entrance points. Once this perimeter was clear and a base formed for fire support, Lance Sergeant Walker's section swept a route up to the compound wall. As they got closer, a cacophony of dog barks greeted them – the analysis of the previous night's drone footage had been accurate. Walker drew his pistol and made to shoot the dogs, but Lieutenant Murly-Gotto worried that gunfire would be worse than barking, so they moved on. Two ladders were placed against the wall and scaled by machine gunners who looked into 1 Platoon's new base. With all clear, Murly-Gotto took Gul, his interpreter, and the Afghan commander forward and banged on a large metal door reclaimed from a shipping container; Gul was on his first mission with Isaf, and was understandably nervous. Un-surprisingly, the occupants were already awake and opened the gates. The family elder greeted Gul and seemed relatively relaxed as he was told that Isaf were occupying his compound for an unspecified amount of time and his family had to leave. Lieutenant Murly-Gotto pushed Afs. 50,000 ($1,000) into his hand and agreed that he could stay to look after the livestock. Everyone looked the other way as the women and children left in a hurry. Any concerns that the compound was anything other than a family residence were gratefully dismissed.

As the light began to come up, the rest of the Platoon entered the compound. It was decently kept, with strong high walls, various stables and living rooms. The elder, a small Hazara man, bore a striking likeness to the sage in the *Karate Kid* films and his home was immediately re-named 'Mr Miyagi's Compound'. The men removed their kit and began building up 'sangar' or fortified sentry positions on the corners of the compound. From the roof, and with the light firmly up, civilians were seen streaming from neighbouring compounds. They were dragging their livestock and possessions away in a hurry. Lance Corporal Little was on the north-east corner pushing up single sandbags to provide basic cover to the sentries. They would be on guard for the next eight days. The first rounds came in before Little could even draw up his initial sketch of the area.

'What's that?' he asked the Guardsman he was with.

'We're getting shot at!' he replied as rounds began to bounce off the roof and into the overcast sky. Identifying the compound engaging them 200 metres to the north, Little realised that this was real and that the people he could see were neither that far away nor that friendly. He slipped a high-explosive grenade into the launcher under-slung to his rifle, fired and missed. 'You dropped short, Mick!' the Guardsman with him teased. Engaging the firing point with his machine gun from the cover of a single sandbag, the Guardsman silenced the insurgent fire.

In the yard of the compound Sergeant Kirkwood set about organising the platoon into the traditional troika of guard, patrols and Quick Reaction Force, as Lieutenant Murly-Gotto tried to raise the other platoons via radio around 06:30.

3 Platoon and Tac were in a fairly ropey compound. An initial patrol to clear a helipad was fired on at once. The compound was then hit with sustained accurate fire. While leading another patrol after 13:00, 3 Platoon's Sergeant, Tam O'Donnell, was shot through the left femur and knee. After receiving first aid from Lance Corporal Harris, O'Donnell was bundled out of the compound to a Pedro Casevac helicopter that came in under sustained fire. The American pilot left with a souvenir of his moments with Right Flank: a Kalashnikov round through the arm. Inside the compound, Guardsman Allen writhed on the ground

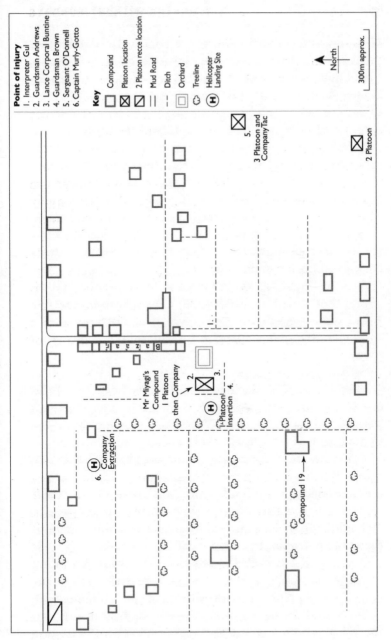

First Sayedebad Mission

Point of injury

1. Interpreter Gul
2. Guardsman Andrews
3. Lance Corporal Buntine
4. Guardsman Brown
5. Sergeant O'Donnell
6. Captain Murly-Gotto

Key

☐ Compound
⊠ Platoon location
◨ 2 Platoon recce location
═ Mud Road
┄ Ditch
▢ Orchard
♠ Treeline
Ⓗ Helicopter Landing Site

300m approx.

North

3 Platoon and Company Tac
2 Platoon

Mr Miyagi's Compound
1 Platoon
then Company

1 Platoon
insertion

Company
Extraction

Compound 19

screaming, 'I've been shot in the cock!' Harris whipped the man's trousers off but there was no wound visible. A round had passed close enough to the skin for the Guardsman to feel its heat. 'I'm framing those trousers,' Allen said. The round had come through a fist-sized murder hole the Guardsmen had cut to defend themselves.

2 Platoon had enjoyed a similar morning. An exploratory patrol led by Lieutenant KHC came under sustained fire when they pushed up to what was later identified as an insurgent dressing station. KHC called in Attack Helicopter support and extracted back to his bullet-pocked compound. From the walls, the rest of the platoon could see rounds splashing at the feet of the patrol as they peeled back through the sodden fields.

Back in Miyagi's Compound, Lieutenant Murly-Gotto approached new boy Guardsman Peters, who had recovered from his first helicopter flight that morning.

'Peters, I've got a surprise for you: you're point man today.'

'Alright, sir. Let's go.'

Murly-Gotto had decided to take Lance Sergeant Walker's section out to get a sense of the ground and have an initial probe of the bazaar. Walker was very much the go-to man in the Platoon. An experienced Lance Sergeant at 36, his relentless sense of humour couldn't mask a cool professionalism. Exiting via the metal doors at the south of the compound, they headed into a narrow alleyway and turned right towards a large field bordered by compounds 200 metres to the south. They were contacted throughout the short patrol and headed back.

Sergeant Kirkwood decided to try his luck patrolling towards the bazaar to the north and perhaps put in the vehicle checkpoints, as per the original plan. If contacted, he'd try to draw insurgents out from the bazaar and into the open. From the metal doors, they turned left and headed into a field north of Miyagi's Compound. Lance Corporal Little was at the back of the patrol with Guardsman McHugh. They were engaged as soon as they turned their backs to the bazaar, fewer than 100 metres to their east. Getting down and trying desperately to identify the firing points, Lance Corporal Little noticed the rounds landing between McHugh and him. 'This is for fucking real here. We're getting proper shot at,' he shouted over the fire. Unable to identify the firing point and unwilling to shoot at houses that could be occupied by civilians, Sergeant Kirkwood had his men check fire. In training they'd all heard of murder holes. They had reckoned that in Warriors they wouldn't apply to Right Flank. It was apparent they would. Eventually, Little identified a firing point and launched a grenade straight into it, ending the contact and allowing the multiple to pull back to the relative safety of Miyagi's Compound.

In the central compound, Major Lindsay-German was having a think. His location was unworkable. Increasingly accurate fire from five or six places at all points of the compass was coming in so frequently that his signaller, Lance Sergeant Ryan Sinclair, had given up bothering the Grenadier Guards' Ops Room with Shot Reports. 'Don't worry, sir. They're bound to run out of ammo soon – they've only had five rounds a man!' said Sinclair, remembering the intelligence brief. Lindsay-German had also lost one of the company's key men and an old friend from South Armagh days. As getting Sergeant O'Donnell out had resulted in the wounding of a pilot, a further Casevac flight might not be forthcoming. Finally, there was a report that a group of insurgents were moving into the area with anti-personnel mines to encircle him. He was in danger of becoming permanently fixed. A few years earlier, a commander in his position would have lit the area up with artillery, but the risk of civilian casualties restrained his options. After a conference with his Second in Command, Captain Chan Monro, and the Company Sergeant Major, he decided they couldn't stay put. While he was achieving his mission by drawing the insurgents into a fight, the risk to his men was unsustainable and a new plan was needed. After a company radio conference, it was clear that Miyagi's Compound had the best protection, sat on slightly elevated ground, was large enough for all of Right Flank and had the best emergency helipad. At 20:00 it was decided to get everyone up there.

In the soon-to-be-abandoned compounds, men re-packed their kit. The Company Sergeant Major, an intimidating perfectionist, came into the Headquarters. 'I hate to be the bearer of more bad news, sirs, but the quad's bust,' he said. There was a stunned silence for a few minutes as everyone digested how they were meant to carry a generator and other heavy kit without the quad. No one could quite believe that their luck had got worse. Eventually, some bottom-of-the-barrel laughter broke out.

After dark, the men of Tac, 2 and 3 Platoons made their way up to 1 Platoon. They looked, to Captain Monro's eyes, like 'some ridiculous scene from the retreat from Moscow'. Those who avoided falling into the six-foot-deep irrigation ditches and kept upright were slowed by thick mud that clung to boots. Each step was a struggle. Halfway through the march an enormous explosion tore through the night. Even those who had been briefed that the engineers were going to 'deny' the quad and generator with a pair of mines were shocked by the noise. Many assumed an IED had been struck or an ambush initiated. With any pretence of a quiet getaway gone, the stream of Glaswegian curses as yet another Guardsman rolled over into the mud reached quite a pitch. Miraculously, the insurgents had gone home for the night and didn't engage this slow-moving train of targets. There was palpable relief when all elements of Right Flank got into Miyagi's Compound around midnight. This turned to disbelief when it was realised that a signaller had left a sandbag full of radio batteries back in 3 Platoon's compound and that they would have to go back out and get it before first light. At around 03:00 everyone was finally in. For the men on the ground it had not felt like a very successful first 24 hours in Sayedebad.

★

With the company complete in one location, what 1 Platoon had been doing the previous day trebled in scale as the three-way rotation of patrols, guard and reserve was now on a company scale. With the Javelin teams reunited, Lance Sergeant Loder could now provide almost 360-degree coverage. He started identifying likely firing points that his second team could engage from the north-east corner of the compound. The plan to bounce around the area and satellite Sayedebad was clearly bust. Instead fighting patrols were sent out to push up against the insurgents and engage them.

The first fire of the day came late, at around 08:30 from a line of compounds 750 metres to the south-west. From his Javelin sentry position, Lance Sergeant Loder picked up the smoke of insurgent weapons at the corner of a compound through his binoculars. Switching to the thermal sight on his weapon, he could pick up two men, one lying in a ditch preparing a medium machine gun while the other fired his Kalashnikov at Miyagi's Compound. Bracketing his sight onto the targets, he could pick out their hottest features – faces, chests, weapon barrels – and called out, describing his target to the Company Commander, who checked the compound on his map and gave Loder the go-ahead. As the missile initiated, the sight's screen changed to the picture seen from the on-board camera. He closed the brackets on the sight further, selected a direct rather than a top attack and held the initiation trigger. Crosshairs flashed up on the chest of one of the insurgents and locked on. This is where the missile will hit, even if the man runs. After pulling the fire trigger, there is a slight pause followed by a small blast, as the missile jumps six or so metres from Miyagi's wall. The rocket motor starts and the missile takes approximately six seconds to cover the distance. There is no more firing from the position. Everyone cheers.

Keen to follow up on this success and not keep static, 1 Platoon was sent on patrol. Lieutenant Murly-Gotto took Lance Sergeant Walker and his men out to the west, as Sergeant Steven Smith, a very welcome additional full sergeant, took his multiple into the bazaar. To the east, Sergeant Kirkwood's men were soon engaged and called in the whole platoon for support. The fire was sporadic and inaccurate, but men were still instinctively getting down on their bellies each time a shot came over. The break in momentum worried Sergeant Kirkwood. Once men were down with their heavy packs, they'd take motivating to get back up. Kirkwood decided to order his men to ignore the firing and advance through the contact, relying on the shoddy marksmanship of the insurgents to prevent casualties. He could see many of his men were shocked to be walking through enemy fire. Murly-Gotto came up on Kirkwood's right flank, keeping Smith's men in the rear. He couldn't quite believe that he was executing a textbook Infantry Battle School platoon advance to contact 36 hours after leaving base.

The multiples paused in ditches. Intelligence reported that the insurgents were going to fire a large calibre weapon at two soldiers standing beside a wall. Lieutenant Murly-Gotto told the Platoon to remain alert. Lance

Corporal Little looked at Guardsman McHugh. They looked at the wall next to them. Sergeant Kirkwood also noticed the coincidence and told them to start moving away when they saw a puff of smoke. One hundred metres to their west, an insurgent had broken cover and fired his Rocket Propelled Grenade (RPG) directly at the pair. It landed close enough to knock both off their feet. Mud, shocked from the earth by the explosion, rained down on Little, bringing him to his senses. He checked for his arms and legs. Everything was where it should be, apart from his hearing. The rest of the patrol, some convinced that they'd just taken casualties, returned fire. The machine gunner had a stoppage, so Sergeant Kirkwood stood up, trained his sights on the insurgent and shot him through the neck. More fire was coming from a compound next to the dead insurgent. Whipping the light missile strapped to his back round and onto his shoulder, Sergeant Kirkwood struggled to remember the quick chat he'd had on the Bastion ranges. He recalled something about aiming a tad high. The missile flew directly into the doorway of the compound and a man ran out on fire. Kirkwood and Little followed up with grenade launchers, setting the compound on fire. By this point, Apache was providing cover but their arrival had subdued insurgent firing. Back in Miyagi's Compound, Tac asked the helicopter to back off a bit to encourage the insurgents to renew their fight with 1 Platoon. This worked and once the insurgents had shown their firing points, the Apache closed in again and fired a Hellfire Missile into the troublesome compound. 1 Platoon decided to head home. Sergeant Kirkwood's men were in first, followed by Lieutenant Murly-Gotto's multiple. As Sergeant Smith's men closed in and crossed the road 100 metres from the compound doors, Gul, the interpreter on his first Isaf mission, was shot in the back. Shouts of 'Man down!' were heard in the

compound and Sergeant Kirkwood's multiple headed
back out under fire to get the interpreter in. The Pedros
were summoned from Bastion and came in to take the
wounded man out of Sayedebad. Knowing it was a callous
thought, Lieutenant Murly-Gotto was thankful that it
wasn't a Scots Guardsman who had been shot.

After a few hours' rest, 1 Platoon were sent out after
dark. There were fears the insurgents could use the night
to dig in an IED belt around Right Flank and then fix
them in Miyagi's Compound. Countering this each night
were patrols sent to 'lurk' in the darkness. As with every
night of the operation, it was extremely cold as the
Guardsmen lay down in wet ditches and waited for the
water to freeze around them. Lance Corporal McGonagle's temperature dropped below 35° Centigrade and he
had to take off his boots and socks and use his desert scarf
to warm up his feet. Some muscle memory from training
kicked in amongst the Guardsmen and they could be seen
getting up and marking time – as on a drill-square – in an
effort to keep their feet from freezing solid. Later that
night the sangar spotted a pair of men digging in an IED. 1
Platoon was guided onto the pair and engaged them. By
the time McGonagle told me this story in August I could
hardly believe Afghanistan could be that cold, so extreme
are the summer temperatures Right Flank had to deal with
later in their long tour.

That night, Major Lindsay-German was able to report a
much better state of affairs than 24 hours previously in the
nightly radio conference he held with Lieutenant Colonel
Roly Walker. Despite losing Gul, the effect they were
having on the insurgents was marked. Already, they
believed they had killed 26 of them. Key to this success
was using the options given to Right Flank by Apaches
and Javelin. When combined with the ability of highly
disciplined Guardsmen to advance through enemy fire,

Isaf simply had more possibilities available to them than the insurgents. As far as the Grenadiers were concerned, Right Flank was doing its job very effectively. Their purpose wasn't to put themselves in danger for the sake of hitting Sayedebad. Instead, they were to disrupt the enemy south of the line of Isaf bases that they were seeking to extend into Kawshhal Kalay. If Right Flank could do that simply by having a presence and allowing the insurgents to attack them, then they were achieving their mission and making the Battlegroup aspect of the wider operation much easier. That Right Flank was also being proactive was a bonus.

★

1 Platoon's night in the cold paid off early the next morning. When fire came in on the compound, the men, unseen by the insurgents, identified the Firing Point, which was out of view of the rest of the company, and guided the Javelin team onto it. For the remainder of the morning, harassing sniper fire continued to hit the compound. At one point, a bright Guardsman put a glove on a stick to tempt fire. The ploy worked and once again Lance Sergeant Loder's Javelin locked onto a target with success. Loder had to be very careful not to compromise his positions. Clearly the insurgents knew that this fearsome weapon emerged from two specific corners of the compound. Once locked on, the camouflage surrounding the missile had to be moved prior to firing. In an increasingly fraught game of cat and mouse, Loder's teams had to keep the heads of any potential insurgent snipers down with small arms and grenade launchers, while their teammates locked on and fired the missiles.

A consistent irritation was Compound 19, roughly 300 metres south of Miyagi's Compound. This was one of the only double-storey compounds in the area, and the fact that rounds were hitting the southern roof of Miyagi's Compound led to the assumption that much fire was coming out of 19. As it was impossible to assert that there were no civilians in the compound, flattening it was clearly out of the question. During contacts from 19, the only option was to cut it in half with small arms fire and hope that rounds would hit insurgents in their murder holes. On that third morning, a patrol was sent out to try to get into 19 and investigate it. The rate of fire was such that the patrol was forced back. As they returned, they found a number of suspected IEDs, increasing fears that the insurgents were trying to put in a belt of devices. As the platoon pulled back from their suspected find, an Afghan National Army sniper hit and killed an insurgent, providing a boost to the Afghan platoon's morale. They had been viewed suspiciously at first, especially their Platoon Commander, who flatly refused to go on patrol but was happy to send his men out. At their first meeting in Bastion, the Afghans had assured Right Flank that this sort of operation was 'very easy for us'. Any doubts about this boast were dispelled in contact. During patrols with 3 Platoon, the Afghans 'would just get up and run every-where. They'll get up and fight everything,' according to Lance Corporal Harris. Under contact, the Afghans were happy to stand up and walk towards firing points, letting go with their American-supplied M-16 rifles. Although command and control could be an issue, the prevailing wisdom became that if the troops wanted to run ahead, they'd be allowed to. Guardsmen were also grateful to have the Afghans go first into compounds to talk with locals and secure them – perhaps the most dangerous part of compound clearance.

After the earlier IED find, another fear was realised on the third day when the compound came under mortar and airburst RPG attack. Given the size of the compound and the paucity of cover, it seemed inevitable that casualties would be taken. Luckily for Right Flank, the fire was inaccurate and not repeated. Despite the various threats, Mr Miyagi's family then decided to visit. After they knocked on the door, Second Lieutenant Greeves, resplendent in the waxed Barbour jacket he had brought on operations, opened the metal doors to the family. 'Mrs Miyagi, I presume?' he said, receiving only an odd look from the woman. He was too young to remember the *Karate Kid* craze in the 1980s and had assumed 1 Platoon was addressing the compound owner by his actual name. After the family had left, Captain Monro wondered: 'Is the end for this bloke once the Taliban come back?' There was no way of knowing.

The fire on the compound was taking an irregular pattern by now. Insurgents would transit between compounds without weapons to hand. They'd then begin their attacks from the apex of an L-shape of compounds, before moving unseen along ditches from place to place. When engaging Right Flank's foot patrols, the insurgents, with their much lighter loads, had an edge in manoeuvrability. Darting along irrigation ditches, out of the sangar's watch, they could outflank and fire on patrols. Patrol commanders then had a choice. They could advance and have the insurgents in a straight gunfight but risk walking into an IED ambush, or remain static and rely on Isaf's technological superiority to get results before the courage of the Guardsman on the ground broke. 'Because you're staying on the ground, it encourages them to keep shooting at you and because they're shooting at you, the guys with the Javelin can get a fix and destroy them. So we're kind of using ourselves as bait,' explained 2 Platoon's Lance Corporal Kieran Bradbury to me later. To counter their vulnerability, especially from the air, insurgents would use civilians as cover, many members of Right Flank maintain. When fired at from a compound, patrols would request air support. On arrival, the pilots would state that the compound courtyards were full of women and children, making any strike impossible. In addition, the insurgents were unable to see round the next corner with thermal sights and eyes in the sky – unlike Isaf. They got round this handicap by engaging patrols from compounds and then getting women to repeatedly go out and pump water wells to report on Isaf's reaction and interdict return fire. 'So, they have no regard for the safety of these people or they have full confidence in our rules of engagement. It was a bit of a reality check to see what they are prepared to do, to be quite honest,' Captain Monro remembered when we sat smoking and talking in a calm checkpoint months later.

Word had come back from Bastion that Sergeant O'Donnell and Gul would both survive their serious injuries and were out of initial surgery. A little later, orders came that Right Flank would stay an additional 24 hours in Sayedebad to continue absorbing insurgents for the benefit of the wider operation. It was undoubtedly an exciting entrance to Afghanistan – the sort of gunfight that many join the army to get into but relatively few actually see. Going on stag, the perennial bane of a Guardsman's life, became exciting and, during the day when it wasn't cold and there was plenty to shoot at, something to look forward to. Men would come off the roofs with stories of close calls looking 'wired, as though they'd just been out partying – nervously excited about the whole thing. It was an odd situation to be in,' remembers Lieutenant Murly-Gotto. Life in the compounds was far from glamorous, though – 'Crap, nae niceties,' said Lance Corporal Little. For those unlucky enough to be sleeping outside, the compound recalled 'Passchendaele – once it rained,' said Lance Corporal Bradbury. There was always a niggling task for the junior men to do. Whether replacing the bullet-emptied sandbags along the sangar positions each morning, bringing in resupplies of rations, water and ammunition and, on that night, a new quad and generator from the helipad, or simply cleaning weapons, men kept busy.

That night Lance Sergeant Al Reid took his 3 Platoon multiple on a lurk to the west of Miyagi's Compound. By now, Right Flank had adopted the basic infantry tactics of the insurgents and was sticking to the irrigation ditches as much as possible. The risk in this was that the insurgents would notice the new pattern and exploit it through placing trip wires in the ditches. Reid's men were therefore split into two fire teams, with each watching a ditch for the course of the bitterly cold night. After a few hours of staring through their night vision, Reid came over the net:

'Are there tigers in Afghanistan? Something's just come past my position with fucking big teeth and it wasn't a dog.'

'Watch your arcs, Reidy, it's a dog,' replied Lance Corporal Andrew Bennett from the next fire team. Five minutes later Bennett picked up a heat signature through his night sight. It appeared to be melting into the water 40 metres ahead of him up the ditch, and coming closer. The lurk had paid off and an insurgent was trying to emplace an IED, Bennett thought, quietly telling his fire team to get ready for a contact. Refocusing his sight, he could see the figure was closing in. It was a leopard crawling along the ditch. His machine gunner fired five bursts in its direction, incredibly missing with every round. Inside the compound, men woke up and began getting ready to stand to. Bennett reported what had happened to Second Lieutenant Greeves.

'Sir, that wasn't a contact. A big cat just got within 40 metres of our position and wasn't stopping.'

'Right.'

The cat had disappeared when shot at, but over the course of the night kept probing the lurk for a weakness, stalking the Guardsmen.

'Sir, I understand our number one priority out here is to engage the enemy, but that's the third time that cat has attacked my position,' an exasperated Bennett reported towards dawn. 'Are they going to throw anything else at us this tour?' he thought. 'It's already ridiculous.'

★

By the fourth day, and in light of Gul's injury on day two, Guardsmen decided that perhaps the most hazardous parts of any patrol were getting in and out of the compound. Here they were most channelled and had to go out into what became known as 'Sniper Alley' before fanning out. Before heading out, the strain was clearly visible on men's faces as they stamped like horses before a race. 'Everyone was lined up and ready to go and everyone was looking at the ground thinking: "It might happen to me, I have to be switched on here; none of this monging it like you did on training or exercises" ', Lance Corporal Gary Archer recalls. The frenzied stamping would reach a pitch as the doors opened and final cigarettes were tossed to the ground. Some patrols chose to double out to clear Sniper Alley as quickly as possible. Other commanders preferred to walk out, trying to keep their men calm and perhaps show any observers that taking fire didn't overly worry them.

Inside, the compound was beginning to show the effects of 140 unexpected visitors. Mud stairs leading to the rooftops had begun to collapse under the weight of heavily armed men dashing up and down. The roofs under the sangars had also begun to sag with the weight – making it impossible to further fortify them. Guardsman McHugh thought the sangar positions themselves already looked 'like they'd been there about nine year. Where the Javelin was, there were burn marks and brass everywhere.' The engineers, confined inside the four walls, decided to make themselves comfortable and had dug a small seating area. Another pit had been dug to burn rubbish; one unenviable Corporal from Tac had the responsibility of making sure that the aluminium foil shit-bags the men used burned correctly. No complaints could be made about the living conditions, as everything was shared equally; Guardsman Stafford was even handing out the 200 cigarettes he'd somehow managed to stuff into his pack, much to the delight of Guardsman McHugh, who had realised that he couldn't have chosen a worse week to try to quit smoking.

On the fourth morning, eight local elders turned up at the compound door wanting to talk. Working on the assumption that at least some of them would be insurgents wanting to have a look at the compound's interior, they were shepherded into a small room right next to the metal doors without having a chance to glance round the defences. Major Lindsay-German kept them waiting a few minutes as he searched for a comb and wetted his hair in order to give as good an impression as circumstances allowed. The elders tried to tell Right Flank that it would be best if they moved into a 'better' compound, a schoolhouse east of Sayedebad. Knowing that this was the compound 2 Platoon had been engaged from on the first morning and having reassessed it as an insurgent headquarters no doubt laced with IEDs, Major Lindsay-German told them he'd consider the suggestion and thanked them for coming.

The next priority was to confirm the IED finds from the

previous day. Multiples went out to provide as secure a cordon as possible so the counter-IED team could work in something approaching safety. As non-infanteers, the specialists could not reasonably be expected to head into the type of contacts Right Flank had been experiencing outside the compound walls. With the cordon in place and under the compound sentries' cover, the counter-IED team pushed out and after a careful search found nothing and collapsed back into the compound. I was consistently impressed with the counter-IED teams I encountered later in the tour. There was a brilliant mutual incomprehension between them and the infantry. Roughly, one side said, 'I don't know how you go out bomb hunting,' and the other replied, 'Well, you're the nutters who get shot at.' It takes all sorts, I suppose.

Buoyed by the news that his company weren't sitting in a minefield, Major Lindsay-German tasked 2 Platoon to take over a compound one kilometre north-west of Miyagi's Compound. This would outflank the L-shape of buildings to his west, where the insurgents were typically engaging him. Before 2 Platoon could take over the compound, 1 Platoon was ordered to reconnoitre it that afternoon. As they prepared to leave, multiple firing points to the south engaged the sangars. The order was given to double out into Sniper Alley. Turning left out of the gate, Lieutenant Murly-Gotto took his multiple, followed by Sergeant Kirkwood's multiple, into the large field to their north and away from the fire on the sangars and the alleyway. Under 100 metres from the doors, they were hit with accurate fire. Lieutenant Murly-Gotto managed to get his men to a bund line (embankment) to the north, while Sergeant Kirkwood's men were pinned down in a shin-deep ditch. The Afghan soldiers with them began to eat oranges. Sergeant Smith's multiple was the last out and would clearly face fire from north and south. Guardsman Andrews doubled out and was shot in the shoulder, falling to the ground saying that he felt like he'd been punched. It was a mercifully short Casevac into the compound, where he began joking about his insurance payout while waiting for a taxi to Bastion. The platoon was still pinned down outside, crouched in ditches during a sharp, cold downpour. They had to move into another set of ditches to provide ground security for the Pedro that once again came in under heavy fire. Sergeant Kirkwood was 'really angry when wee Andrews was shot. You bond as a platoon for months. They feel like your kids.'

Soaked through and a man light, Lieutenant Murly-Gotto decided to continue the reconnaissance patrol. With the fire showing no sign of letting up, Kirkwood and the other non-commissioned officers took the lead in standing up and moving forward as calmly as they could, their Guardsmen following. Pushing through a hedgerow, they surprised and killed three insurgents in open ground. Moving further west, Lance Corporal Little reached the target compound and approached the Hazara owners, who seemed friendly and willing to tell of insurgent dispositions to the south. Little made notes on the approach routes and subtly took some photos to show 2 Platoon later. Turning for home, the Platoon was engaged again. One insurgent on a rooftop drew the attention of Sergeant Kirkwood, who fired a missile that detonated on the roof. Other insurgents fired back at Sergeant Kirkwood, shooting his radio antennae from his back. By now it was getting dark, tracer was visible from the sangars as they guided 1 Platoon to safety and mortar-fired smoke rounds could be seen sailing against the dusk before they burst and covered the withdrawal. Lightning began hitting the area. One bolt blasted Compound 19, the troublesome Firing Point Right Flank had been unable to destroy due to concerns about civilian casualties. 'That's from Thor!' screamed Sergeant Kirkwood.

A little later the Platoon made it back inside Miyagi's Compound. 'We're going to have to get you a new watch, sir,' Lance Sergeant Walker told Lieutenant Murly-Gotto.

'Why's that?'

'You said we'd only be an hour.'

Everyone was happy to hear that Guardsman Andrews sounded all right. Lying down in their soaked clothes once the adrenalin of the six-hour contact had subsided, reactions differed. A youngster such as Guardsman McHugh could be thinking how much he wanted the buzz again. 'I know it sounds daft,' he admitted to me later. Guardsman Stafford hurriedly repeated his mantra: 'This place is nuts, just fucking nuts.' Lance Corporal Little, having briefed Lindsay-German and 2 Platoon on the new compound, kept thinking 'what if' as he replayed the numerous close calls they'd all had. 'You're over-tired, so you can't sleep and all the thoughts are running through the head: "Fuck me, I could have been blown up today . . . That was quite close when I got shot,"' he said. 'But obviously you're not showing that to your Guardsmen because you're a section commander and they look up to you, and you look up to your platoon sergeant, and that's how it worked.' Sergeant Kirkwood had his own thoughts, wondering how much longer his men could keep up this sort of pressure.

At 01:00, 2 Platoon headed out to the new compound and were settled in by 04:00. The owner and his elderly mother were terrified of these men coming in in the middle of the night. The man told Lieutenant KHC, 'in no uncertain terms', that he was going to be killed as soon as I left. He begged me not to go into his compound. But clearly I had my orders.' The owner calmed down and began to loosen up. He said which compounds were used as headquarters, and confirmed that the schoolhouse was indeed riddled with IEDs, suggesting that the men from the *shura* were tempting Major Lindsay-German into a trap.

★

The fifth day was quieter. Even though 2 Platoon weren't engaged, it seemed likely the insurgents knew something was there so the western flank was kept suppressed. Major Lindsay-German decided to go into the bazaar next to Miyagi's Compound the following day. Early intelligence had suggested it was of interest and the locals' consistent requests to go in and recover 'our things of value' pricked suspicions. The counter-IED team was warned off for a dawn operation.

With 2 Platoon continuing to lock off the western flank, the bazaar search went in on the sixth day without resistance. 3 Platoon isolated the bazaar and the counter-IED team closed in to begin to search the buildings. Inside, they found 28 intact IEDs, ready to go into the ground, along with various pressure plates and batteries. They even found a packet of combs, which was good news for Lindsay-German, who'd lost his after the *shura* and was beginning to feel rather unkempt. As they cleared other buildings it became apparent that the bazaar's stock in trade was essentially weaponry, as mortar ammunition and grenades were added to the haul. This was clearly a devastating blow for the local insurgents but gave Right Flank a boost. Even months later, for medic Lance Corporal Harris, 'It made the whole job feel worthwhile. They were quite big devices and the engineers said they were ready to go into the ground. Maybe if we hadn't found them then the following day they would have been in the ground. They couldn't get into the bazaar to get the IEDs because we had eyes on. It might explain why they hit us as soon as we landed. They could have been thinking "Fuck, we're going to lose these." A lot of expertise has gone into them. They're high value and it must have pissed them off massively.' While Sayedebad was a known logistics hub and the sort of distance from the front line that the insurgents typically place their IED factories, actually finding one remains an exceptional stroke of luck.

Major Lindsay-German pushed the news up to the Grenadiers. They were as surprised as Right Flank by the scale of the find. Despite being initially amused by the unfamiliar tones of young Scottish signallers talking on the Battlegroup radio net, the Grenadiers had been impressed by Right Flank's reticence during the week. As a new Company in theatre facing particularly fierce opposition, Right Flank could have been expected to talk the situation up and get over-excited. They had not fallen into this trap and seemed rather calm about the spot they were in. News of the find rapidly spread up the command chain, attracting the Media Operations machine that managed to splash the news across the tabloids. The derring-do news coverage slightly sank Lance Corporal Little's white lie to his fiancée that he was in perfect safety back in Camp Bastion. Lieutenant Colonel Walker considered visiting by helicopter but couldn't as Right Flank remained constantly in contact.

With the bazaar half cleared, 3 Platoon and the counter-IED team returned to Miyagi's Compound after blowing up their haul. Insurgent commanders used the explosion to claim to their fighters that they'd successfully struck Right Flank with a massive mortar barrage rather than lost a key asset. This was consistent with a pattern of psychological tricks used to influence their foot soldiers and confuse Isaf. Knowing full well that their enemy's intelligence gathering was active, they would constantly spread rumours about 'bringing the big thing', presumed to be a large weapon system that never materialised apart from one token and inaccurate mortar attack. A real-time piece of battlefield intelligence, such as when Lance Corporal Little and Guardsman McHugh realised they were about to be hit by something next to a wall, was rare. More frequently, insurgents would say they were going to pop up from an identifiable landmark and then hit the patrol from two other firing points. One night an insurgent left on stag complained that he was cold. His commander's response was, 'If the Infidels can do it, then so can you.' Most of the intelligence gathered was simply self-evident statements. Given such an easy target to parody, Lance Sergeant Walker spent the tail-end of the week stating confidently, 'intelligence suggests we're getting shot at', while in contact.

While the bazaar clearance had gone relatively smoothly, that afternoon more heavy fire came from the south aimed at the sangars. Lance Sergeant Loder, tired of taking yet more incoming from Compound 19, finally reckoned he had a firing solution for the trouble spot and shouted down to the Company Commander, asking for permission.

'They're firing at us.'

'How much?'

'Enough for me to ask.'

'Hold on, I'll come up.'

Major Lindsay-German climbed up the ladder to the lip of the wall.

'Right, sir. I'll stick my head up on the left and start firing at 19. If you then get up and have a look so you're happy where it is on the map. Happy?'

'Yes.'

Loder popped up and began firing. As Lindsay-German poked his head up, a round, aimed at Loder, hit the sandbag right in front of Lindsay German's face, ricocheting over.

'Fucking hell!'

The firing then stopped, possibly due to the machine gunner firing at the compound. The Javelin stayed in its tube.

Later that afternoon, Lance Sergeant Loder spotted a two-man sniper team in a semi-derelict building 800 metres to the east. As the snipers lay down, they placed wet blankets in front of their barrels to prevent any dust kicking up and giving their position away. Major Lindsay-German immediately gave permission to fire and the missile hit before they got a round off. Further back from the targets he'd just destroyed, perhaps 1,100 metres from his sentry position, Loder could see a group of five slightly older men in black *shalwar kameez*. They were paying close attention to how the battle was going from a rooftop – a typical procedure of an insurgent command group. 'I really, really wanted to engage them. I knew who they were, they knew that I knew who they were,' said Loder later. After watching the sniper team get wiped out, the men got off the roof, picking up their weapons as they went. There wasn't time to engage them and they were never seen again.

Five days earlier, Hellfire missiles, Apache strafing runs and Javelins would get cameras out of pockets and produce big cheers. By now, young Guardsmen were hardly batting an eyelid. Guardsman Stafford told me he 'just got used to it. You'd just chat shit and smoke fags and then go, "Oh, a Javelin just went off."' The buzz of contacts was fading and the level that they'd been oper-ating at was beginning to tell. Stag duty still had to be pulled, though sightings of 3 Platoon's leopard, now known as the Beast of Sayedebad, kept sentries alert. For Stafford, like everyone else, the cold was 'fucking brutal'. In the sangars, the young Guardsmen of 1 Platoon were often kept company by Lieutenant Murly-Gotto. As a Platoon Commander he was excused guard duty so didn't have to put himself at this additional risk, though his men, such as Guardsman McHugh, knew that 'he was an aggressive officer. Loved to go looking for it. Pure loved it.' After dark the final replen came in during a downpour. Right Flank was due out the next night after finishing the bazaar clearance so only needed an extra few crates of rations and water. The RAF had other ideas and the Chinook pilot managed to drop crates of water from too high, exploding the packing cases and spreading the bottles over hundreds of square metres. 1 Platoon was out for hours, picking up each bottle. If the insurgents could get a reasonable fix on where the helicopters dropped their supplies at night, they could feasibly put in IEDs (if they had any left) or an ambush. Tired of carrying ten bottles at a time, Lance Corporal Little dragged his bivouac bag out with him and filled it with bottles, eventually coming back into the compound looking like a very angry, very small and very Glaswegian Father Christmas. The quad and generator also left that evening. Amongst the standard rations, the Company Quartermaster Sergeant in Bastion had stacked Lambert and Butler fags and 'fun bags' of Rice Krispie Squares and other goodies for the Guardsmen. There was another special package with a note attached: 'For the Officers. I'm sure you must be finding it very hard, so I thought I'd send this small jar of Gentleman's Relish. I'm afraid I couldn't find any roast swan in Camp Bastion.' I always loved this low-level jousting between officers and men. Coming from completely different ends of Britain's social spectrum, humour was the best way to jump the hurdle.

Guardsmen had immaculate Old Etonian accents ready to mock their young officers, who could come back with a line about getting "pure ragin" after a bottle of Bucky. On occasion the class divide seemed so enormous that one group viewed the other like a separate species; I'll never forget one Guardsman asking an officer recently returned from R&R, 'Sir, what *are* posh birds like in bed?' The banter never seemed disrespectful (in either direction) and spoke, for me, of the affection all ranks mostly held for each other.

By that night's radio conference, Battlegroup could tell Right Flank that the wider picture was going well. The ploy of putting them into Sayedebad and sucking the insurgents into a gunfight appeared to be working. The initial clearance into Kawshhal Kalay had gone well. Appearing in numbers along an unexpected route, D Company, 1 Royal Welsh and their Afghan partners had got into the village without a shot fired. Sadly though, an IED had killed three Afghan soldiers. Two other bombs were found. The insurgents had melted into the community and the atmosphere in the village seemed poisonous. While their potential reinforcements were tied up trying to displace Right Flank, there was little the Kawshhal insurgents could do other than wait.

*

By dawn on the seventh day, 2 Platoon were back in Miyagi's Compound in readiness for that evening's return to Bastion. With the Company complete, 1 and 2 Platoon were sent out to provide security for the clearance of the second half of the arms bazaar. The search found more bomb components and military hardware. Multiples on the ground were engaged intermittently after being reported to the insurgents by the women Right Flank believed they used as scouts. The cordon and clearance took up most of the day. Once the platoons were back in, the process of packing up camp began. The water bottles so lovingly harvested the previous evening were emptied out and burnt along with everything else of any perceptible value to the insurgents. Lance Sergeant Walker went to work singing another of his ditties, this time to the tune of Tina Turner's 'We Don't Need Another Hero':

> We don't need another replen
> Because we're sick of rations and water.
> We just want a Margarita
> Or a dirty chicken fajita.

Miyagi, who had been kept reasonably happy with firewood, rations and especially chocolate, must have been glad to see Right Flank prepare to leave. Unfortunately the engineers' seating area he'd been eyeing rather covetously was turned into an additional burns pit to cope with all the rubbish and then filled in. Observing the company gathered for warmth around the pits, laughing and swapping stories, Sergeant Kirkwood turned to Lance Corporal McGonagle: 'Funny how weasels are acting like it's the end of a fucking exercise.'

A few hours later, Right Flank were ordered to stay in Sayedebad for an extra 24 hours. Having burned everything, it appeared that they would, in fact, need another replen.

*

On the morning of 11 February, which they were assured would finally be their final day in Sayedebad, Right Flank shook themselves from sleeping bags and sentry positions. Jimmy Murly-Gotto spent his first day as a captain – his promotion had come through that day. His Platoon had been pinged with a lurk the night before and went straight onto guard. After a week in the cold, some of the Guardsmen had finally succumbed to minor frostbite on their toes. 2 and 3 Platoon were sent out on a final patrol to the north to draw in any insurgents thinking of heading towards the American Taskforce over the canal to the west. The patrol went quietly until they were engaged from two firing points as they turned for home. With two platoons on the ground, this was a good opportunity to push through and exploit a contact. 3 Platoon went left flanking while 2 Platoon moved to the right to get a better position on the compound engaging them. Overmatched, the insurgent fire died down. The Guardsmen headed for home. By the orchard that bordered Sniper Alley fewer than 50 metres from the doors, Lance Corporal Stephen Buntine was shot in the leg in the first burst of a sustained and accurate attack. Immediately, the sangars provided covering fire and were in turn engaged as the casualty was dragged into the compound. Lieutenant KHC, running the firefight on the ground, saw Guardsman Martyn Brown fall next to him and assumed he had tripped but then saw blood coming from his boot and shouted for another Casevac party. The insurgent fire intensified as more men poured out of Miyagi's Compound to bring Brown back in. Inside the compound, Guardsman McHugh was ripping through neatly packed day-sacks, longing to find more link for the gunners on the roof, who were running low. Men straining to identify the firing points felt the contents of sandbags jump against their shoulders as bullets struck. In the courtyard Lance Corporal Harris and the other medics fought the blood and prepared the casualties for the Pedro teams that were coming in fast. Rushed to the helicopter under fire, the casualties were away just 23 minutes after getting shot. Over the course of the week, Right Flank had 40 confirmed and many more suspected kills. They had also disrupted a major logistics hub. Despite this, the insurgents around Sayedebad still appeared numerous and well armed as that final patrol showed.

With the flight confirmed for 20:30, Major Lindsay-German called the men together. He had noticed men slacking off in the compound that day and cries of 'Endex'. He reminded them that the most important part of the mission lay ahead – getting out. The insurgents would surely know that their opponents would leave at some stage and could be waiting to spring an ambush as the men boarded the helicopters. With the weight, the men would be vulnerable and their ability to fight back hampered. 'No fucking about tonight please, gentlemen,' the Major said.

There was less to burn than the previous evening and by 18:00 everyone was ready to leave. 1 Platoon headed out first, followed by the Company Commander and his signaller, then 2 Platoon, the bulk of Tac and finally 3 Platoon. Miyagi was left in a sudden silence when the door closed quietly behind the Company Sergeant Major, who counted each man out and was the last to leave. The helicopters would land a 500-metre march to the north-west. There was less ammunition to carry, though the casualties' kit and a week in the field made the march out as gruelling as the march in.

Guardsman Peters and Du Toit, who after their first week with 1 Platoon could hardly be described as new boys any more, had been picked to go forward with Captain Murly-Gotto and Vallon the landing sight for IEDs. The rest of the Platoon waited about 50 metres back. They cleared the bottom half of the landing sight without incident and worked their way to one another along the northern edge of the box. Captain Murly-Gotto cracked infrared markers at the corners to show the safe area to the pilots. He was just preparing the final marker when he saw a green laser pass his chest and then come back on to him. The first burst caught him through the legs and punched him, and every man out that night, to the floor. The fire was accurate and disciplined.

In training, marshals walk behind exercising troops, occasionally designating them casualties. They are told to fall over and start screaming and writhing so others will know to help them. Captain Murly-Gotto did exactly this as the second burst passed over his head. He then realised that playing dead would be a good idea.

'Check fire! Check fire! It's friendly fire! Peters, Peters! Help.'

Here we go.

'Can't reach Battlegroup, I can't reach Battlegroup!'

We're going to take massive fucking casualties here.

'It's fucking friendlies over the canal.'

I give up.

'Do not fucking fire! Get in the fucking ditches!'

Another burst, is it going to be us?

'Put up Illumination!'

Is it going to be me?

'Hello Kryptonite Zero Alpha, this is Kryptonite One Zero Alpha. Check fire, check fire, it's friendly. We've got a casualty: it's me. I'm sorting myself out.'

The Grenadiers were conducting the evening Battle-group Conference when Captain Monro managed to get through with a report and Casevac request. The Grena-diers called their Liaison Officer at the US Headquarters, who rushed to tell the American Commander what was going on.

Captain Murly-Gotto was shot by a .50 Calibre Nato round from a vehicle-mounted weapon. The bullet left the barrel at approximately 2,910 feet per second or, to put it another way, it could have covered London to Edinburgh in a little under ten minutes, were gravity and the other forces that get in the way of Newton's First Law suspended. Such is the force of this thumb-sized round that it may not have even hit him, just passed close enough to remove his right calf muscle, cleanly cauterising a wound too large for the dressing Peters tried to apply once he'd managed to crawl to his officer. Two flares go up to tell the firing forces that they're hitting friendlies and Captain Murly-Gotto feels very vulnerable and very lit up in a field in Helmand.

Lance Sergeant Walker hears a low moaning from 50 metres away. 'Somebody has to help him,' he says. He leaps up, hoping but not knowing, that the flares have stopped the firing, and runs for his Platoon Commander. Lance Sergeant Macfarlane follows Walker. When they get there, Walker turns on his torch.

'Have you given him morphine?' asks Lance Sergeant Macfarlane.

'No.'

'How no? Give us it.'

Still in shock, one of the young Guardsmen produces a can of spray-paint used to mark the IED safe-lane.

'And what the fuck am I meant to do with that?'

Lance Sergeant Walker assesses a shivering Captain Murly-Gotto, who knows he's going into shock, and asks for more morphine.

'You're all right, sir, you've still got your cock and you can buy yourself a new watch with the insurance payout – yours never did work, did it? Kryptonite Zero: stand by for MIST report but basically his right leg's really fucked . . .'

Captain Murly-Gotto has stopped speaking but hears all this through the radio plugged into his ear.

The two US Marine fire-controllers with Right Flank finally get comms with the forces over the canal. The Pedro comes and Captain Murly-Gotto leaves war forever. Lance Sergeant Walker finishes Valloning the landing sight and the Chinooks come in and take the men. Relief floods through the helicopters as they take off.

When they land, the Guardsmen are sent straight to the shower blocks. 'Any other unit would have been "Go and ring home right now." But it's the Guards, so it's "Go and get a shave and get clean combats on and then you're allowed to phone home,"' thinks Lance Corporal Harris. The showers are cold but still delightful. Horrible little beards are removed; some brush their teeth for the first time in a week. There's a lot of anger about Captain Murly-Gotto. Major Lindsay-German calls his Company together and tells them the story straight. The two US Marines who had been a part of Right Flank for the week are visibly relieved when they hear it wasn't an American unit that fired – until that moment they had blamed themselves and were in tears.

*

The unit that fired on Right Flank were a Canadian mentoring team. There are a number of reasons why they shouldn't have opened fire. First, all week the no-fire line along the canal that acted as a border between the two taskforces had been rigidly adhered to. Permission to fire across a no-fire line, even if Mullah Omar has been spotted taking a nap under a tree, is always sought from higher control. Second, through their night-vision goggles the Canadians would have seen 140 heavily armed men moving in formation. Their profiles would have been unmistakably those of men wearing bulky body armour, helmets with infrared beacons attached and carrying backpacks. None of this is consistent with insurgent practice. Third, Captain Murly-Gotto had cracked three infrared markers and was in the process of cracking the fourth when he was shot, again inconsistent with insurgent practice. That the firing started is almost as unforgivable as the failure of the call sign responsible to ever offer Captain Murly-Gotto and Right Flank an apology. There was still plenty of anger about the loss of a good officer in such an avoidable way when I interviewed the men who'd known him months later.

'He was close to the guys, in a way,' said Guardsman Peters. That's about as high a compliment as officers get from Guardsmen.

Homecoming

Inside the blacked-out helicopter flying for Bastion, the Ketamine begins. Captain Murly-Gotto is strapped to a stretcher but thinks he can move. He knows he has to move: the medics are jumping out of the helicopter, the pilot has abandoned the controls and bailed out. If only he can crawl to the cockpit, Murly-Gotto can stop the bird crashing.

At Helicopter Landing Site Nightingale, a crowd is waiting as the Pedro comes into land. The officer is stoned as they wheel him into the Intensive Care Unit. Murly-Gotto had taken his platoon round the hospital a fortnight earlier to reassure them about how good the care would be if they made it to hospital alive. He didn't expect to return himself. As the medical system swallows him, he sees two familiar capstars as the rear echelon Right Flank Warrant Officers smile. 'Fucking hell, sir, you're a bit early!' says one. In the operating theatre, it feels like hundreds of hands are all over him as they cut his clothes away to check for more wounds and hook him up to machines and drips. It is a very bad trip. The anaesthetic kicks in. The team works through the night to save the leg.

He wakes up surrounded by his men and is still high. He thinks he's the funniest man alive and the Guardsmen laugh gamely at his jokes. Lieutenant KHC volunteers to phone his friend's parents: 'Don't worry, your son is just as handsome as he always was. He's had some damage done to his leg. You're going to see him soon.' There is confusion with his girlfriend's name. His brother officers know her as Tilly; the name on the form is Nathalie. Who is Nathalie? Does Murly-Gotto lead a double life? They decide not to call. Over the next year, Tilly will be the rock Murly-Gotto's rehabilitation is built on. Within a few hours, he is knocked out again and on a C-17 Globemaster. Over the thrum of the four huge jets, he hears a calm Welsh voice in his ear, reassuring him all the way to Birmingham, 'You're nearly home, James.'

He is put on an ambulance and driven to Selly Oak hospital. He is in surgery for nine hours. His parents and girlfriend are waiting for him when he wakes up. 'Thank God I've still got my balls,' he tells them, 'I'll only be here a few weeks and then I'll get back out to Afghanistan.' He is drugged for days; time is hard to recall as he lists with morphine. One day he looks under his sheet. His right leg looks like a piece of shrinkwrapped meat, discoloured with iodine. He is intrigued rather than disgusted by this new reality. It occurs to him what has happened as he sobers up. Surgeons begin to discuss options. Prosthetics are remarkable these days . . . He elects to keep his leg and fight the wound. There is more surgery. Muscles are taken from his back and fused with his calf; bones are grafted into his shin. The surgery works and he wakes up with a cylindrical metal frame encased in plaster around his leg. He doesn't know that this frame will be his companion for a year. That night he dreams he dives into a swimming pool injured and comes out the other side fixed instantly. The reality in the morning is a realisation that the active phase of his Army career is over and a different type of work is beginning that will stay with him for the remainder of his life. He never regrets having joined. He will remain on the Army List until the rehabilitation phase is over, so hospital becomes just as much a part of his career as Sandhurst or platoon command.

He stays in a ward in Selly Oak for six weeks. In the bed next to him is a triple amputee. After some persuading, he gets up with the rest of Right Flank's wounded and they get each other through this stage in their recovery. The morphine makes him sick and itchy, so he weans himself off. He hates being stuck in bed, his independence shattered, the indignity of the bedpan. The Übermensch created in training has been arrested very suddenly. By increments he forces himself better: 'Today I will sit up in bed . . . Today I am going to get into that chair over there . . . Today I will have a shower.' Visitors are endless but he misses Ross Kemp. He starts some tentative physio.

He makes his way to Headley Court Military Hospital in Surrey for rehabilitation. After an initial month there he has three weeks on, three weeks off for as long as it takes – there is no set date to work towards when the frame will come off and he will walk normally. Mentally, he must also put himself back together. There are dark days when the frustration of not being able to perform simple tasks sours his mood for hours. His subconscious never gives in, and after the initial swimming fantasy, never acknowledges the metal frame: many nights he dreams he is running. Headley Court astounds him. The facilities are superb and evolving – a shamed government and Help for Heroes have seen to that. The staff want to be there and tread the line of understanding without mawkish sympathy well. He gets stronger. The atmosphere is half military and half civilian. Guardsmen call him 'sir', the physios 'James'. As 1 SG's seriously wounded come through Headley Court over the spring and summer, he finds a new role – the senior Scots Guardsman in the system and a man to approach with problems or concerns. They are bound, even if they never met in Battalion days.

The welfare side is strong. The Scots Guards Welfare Officer, Captain John McCallum, is nailed to a phone when he's not driving between Catterick, Birmingham, RAF Lyneham and Surrey coordinating the flow of wounded and dead Scots Guardsmen coming home. With support from his family and girlfriend, Murly-Gotto begins to rebuild his life. He buys a ground floor flat in Dulwich and is transferred to the London District Recovery Unit, who visit him *fortnightly to ensure he is progressing. Payouts kick in. Like all of Right Flank, he has private PAX Insurance and collects. The Armed Forces Compensation Scheme also scales his injury and gives him his entitlement. He finds himself in the Welfare State as Mobility Benefit and a Blue Badge are granted. The system largely works in 2010. It is a completely new experience for the young officer to see an area of the Armed Forces so well resourced and seamlessly managed.*

On Christmas Day, Tilly accepts Murly-Gotto's marriage proposal. In February 2011, a year on from Sayedebad, the frame comes off. Murly-Gotto keeps it as a toy for the two Siamese kittens he bought his fiancée and the four of them settle into London life together. The prognosis remains that he will never run again and there is still the chance he may lose the leg above the knee. 'I want to prove them wrong,' he says. 'There are all sorts of stories about people given prognosis and then going on and beating the odds . . . I still feel like when people tell me that I can't do something, I want to challenge it.'

CHAPTER THREE

'Troops, keep your heads down'

11 February–20 February 2010

'Right, that's it, then. Warrior time,' thought Sergeant Kirkwood as he headed back to his tent after the flight from Sayedebad. After an unconventional start to their tour as the Armoured Infantry Company and with the vehicles firmly ready to go, it made sense to think that Brigade would now put Right Flank to the use they had trained for. With Captain Murly-Gotto bound for hospital, Kirkwood, who like every man in the army was trained in the role one senior to his own, would act as Platoon Commander until a replacement could be flown out. One of his first duties was to tell his men to pack 'grab-bags' filled with their personal kit and stow them by their iron beds in Bastion. Each time a casualty had been taken in Sayedebad, the Rear Party had torn through their kit searching for mobile phones and wallets to send back to the UK with the wounded man. Across the Company, five beds were now empty. Wondering why he'd been asked to get the bags ready, Sergeant Kirkwood thought another operation might be on, especially as the Company remained the Brigade reserve for Operation Moshtarak.

The Royal Welsh at Kawshhal Kalay had succeeded. Checkpoints were up, Nad-e-Ali's District Governor, Habibullah Khan, had visited and held a *shura* with the local people. Operation Moshtarak was due to get properly under way in the next few days. The Americans would flood into Marjah with the aim of establishing another zone of government-controlled land to the south of where the British had been operating. However, a feeling remained that the balance hadn't quite tipped in Kawshhal Kalay. Since Right Flank had left Sayedebad, the atmosphere had soured, with an increase in harassment of locals by insurgents. The risk was that early successes could be undermined if more insurgents re-infiltrated Kawshhal Kalay at this delicate early stage. Brigade made the decision to fly Right Flank back to Sayedebad.

Lance Sergeant Loder wandered over to the Right Flank Headquarters to clear up some admin before heading back to the Grenadiers. He saw Major Lindsay-German hunched over a set of maps for the new operation.

'I just came to say goodbye and thank you, sir. I'm kicking about camp for another few days if you need me, though,' Loder said.

He walked out, firmly believing that his time with the Scots Guards was over. Twelve hours later, he was at Right Flank's planning conference for the next operation.

'Oh fuck!'

Lance Corporal Harris's reaction to the news was matched by many in Right Flank. Some wondered if this was going to be the tempo for the entire tour – dangerous week-long operations behind enemy lines with a few days off between each. Others just hoped they'd have to carry less kit than the first Sayedebad – or Sayedebad Part One, as it had now became known. The next operation – Sayedebad Part Two – took on the air of a blockbuster sequel in men's minds.

The plan rapidly emerged, as Right Flank turned around from the first operation. They would land around one and a half kilometres north of the last operation. This meant proximity to Isaf lines. This was good for fire support but the intelligence picture spoke of a heightened chance of dropping into an IED belt. Major Lindsay-German had to balance this risk with achieving his mission. His men would land at night, attempt to enter one of two compounds and then push out patrols in the local area. If the insurgents decided to take on Right Flank, then this was all to the good, as it would draw them away from the Grenadiers to the north and the Household Cavalry Regiment, who were clearing a route towards the US Marines in Marjah to the south. A Sky News team would also come along, as would a platoon of Afghans.

Between packing and weapon cleaning, men tried to relax. 1 Platoon decided to watch *The Hurt Locker* for a spot of IED training. The film ended and they got into their beds, rather shaken by the story. A few minutes later, an explosion ripped through the tent, sending men diving for cover. When the lights went on, Lance Sergeant Walker was doubled up with laughter. After scavenging some chemical heating powder from an American ration pack, Walker had mixed it in a water bottle, replaced the lid and tossed it into the middle of the tent and waited for heat and pressure to take their toll on the bottle.

On the next operation, Lance Sergeant Walker would continue to act as Second in Command of the Platoon Commander's multiple, which meant working for his friend Sergeant Kirkwood. On the first Sayedebad, Kirkwood had 'been amazing' according to Captain Murly-Gotto. He had kept the platoon together and morale high, despite the Company's high casualty rate, through making a joke about most things. He kept his younger Guardsmen genuinely enthused and buzzing about the experience they were having. Older men knew what an anomaly this type of fighting was compared with tours of Iraq and Northern Ireland, or even some people's experiences of

Afghanistan. Professionally speaking, everyone going on these operations, despite the risks, was extremely lucky. Sergeant Kirkwood wouldn't let them forget it. His one concern before flying out on the second operation, he told me later, was that 1 Platoon would be in some way passed over for hard tasks because they were without an officer. He knew that he would have to prove the Platoon all over again.

In the final hours of Valentine's Day, Right Flank paraded in front of waiting coaches and drove to the helicopters. It was a freezing night. The mood in the coaches was sombre. Confidence that they knew what to expect had given way to concern. Five Scots Guardsmen and one interpreter had been very seriously wounded in the first week and now they were returning to the scene. The platoons got off their coaches and went into three fenced pens to sit and wait for their Chinooks in the cold.

After an hour or so Lance Corporal McGonagle's morale dropped off. 'The only thing that could possibly improve this situation are some chocolate éclairs,' he said, to no one in particular.

When a quad bike towing a trailer full of boxes of éclairs turned up a few minutes later, Lance Corporal McGonagle announced to an astonished Platoon that, 'Yes, God loves me!' This kind gesture by Rear Party couldn't take the edge off the waiting. Many men had a bad feeling about going that night. News came that two of the Chinooks had shown faults on pre-flight checks. The mission was postponed by 24 hours. The roulette of delayed flights had spun in Right Flank's favour.

*

After a slow day in camp, Right Flank were once again in the pens by the helicopters. After a short wait, the

Chinooks came in, picked them up and they were up and off at around 00:30 on 16 February.

After the familiar half-hour commute to Sayedebad, the platoons fanned out and waited in silence as the Chinooks returned to base. 1 Platoon remained on the large landing site providing security and cover for 2 and 3 Platoons as they went to investigate potential base compounds. Through night-sights, the main village of Sayedebad was just visible to their south while the smaller hamlet, almost a suburb of Sayedebad, that they would invest on this operation was away to the north. 3 Platoon led off on the one-kilometre march from where they'd been dropped. The ground was wet, boggy and freezing. When wearing night-vision monocles, basic depth perception fails; in combination with heavy packs and slippery thick clay mud, it was little surprise that men started to topple over on the march. 'It didn't look bad but as soon as you started walking in it, it went straight up to your knees and every step was a nightmare', remembers Lance Corporal Bradbury. 3 Platoon found their compound and occupied it. Once 2 Platoon dismissed their compound as unsuitable, the whole of Right Flank made for 3 Platoon's. One of 2 Platoon's Guardsmen had fallen into an irrigation ditch and was soaked through in freezing muddy water but had carried on marching. When he began to go down with hypothermia, his Platoon Sergeant bundled him into a sleeping bag and tried all the usual tricks to keep him from developing critical symptoms. As he started drifting in and out of consciousness, the decision was made that he needed to be Casevaced at once. Having used the landing site an hour earlier, it was to the RAF's credit that they came back for the casualty.

1 Platoon dragged themselves up from the all-round defensive positions they'd been lying in for several hours and got into their order of march. Crossing a ditch on a

ladder, Guardsman Stafford fell head first into an irrigation ditch and began to display the early symptoms of
hypothermia. He had to try and warm himself up along the
one-kilometre tramp to join the Company. As dawn
threatened to break, the whole Company got into the
compound. Looking out, Lance Corporal Bradbury
thought that 'It started to look really, really dodgy'. In
the distance, cars were dropping off young men who were
moving into compounds.

Inside the compound, conditions were more austere
than in Miyagi's Compound. Used needles littered the
floor, alongside other drugs paraphernalia. Sangars went
up in the corners, including one for Loder's Javelin, but
the compound was pinned in with trees making it much
harder to identify where firing was coming from. One
advantage of the trees was that patrols could push out
under cover and attempt to infiltrate insurgent lines.
Everyone had got pretty wet on the march and tried to
dry out as best they could, some removing boots and socks
and putting their feet in one another's armpits to try and
warm them up.

1 and 2 Platoons were immediately sent on patrol.
Sergeant Kirkwood realised his concern that 1 Platoon
would be overlooked because of the loss of Captain
Murly-Gotto was unfounded. Their task was to investigate a compound assessed as sitting inside an IED belt and
set up a cordon for a clearance. After sneaking out of their
new base, the patrol headed northeast. Almost immediately, Guardsman Jordan Wignall from 2 Platoon picked
up a double tone on his Vallon as he swept a safe route for
the patrol. Getting down on his belly, he began probing
the dirt. He quickly confirmed that the Vallon had picked
up an IED constructed around a mortar round. Concern
about dropping into an IED belt had been legitimate.
Major Lindsay-German's decision to move the landing

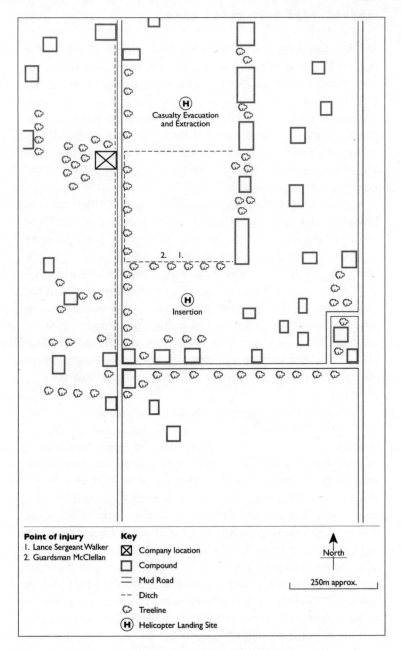

Point of injury
1. Lance Sergeant Walker
2. Guardsman McClellan

Key

⊠ Company location

☐ Compound

— Mud Road

-- Ditch

☘ Treeline

Ⓗ Helicopter Landing Site

North

250m approx.

Casualty Evacuation
and Extraction

Insertion

Second Sayedebad Mission

site further south than originally planned had been correct. The risk of clearing what could be a serious IED belt behind enemy lines wasn't worth the reward of recovering a few easily manufactured devices. The clearance was cancelled and the patrol made their way back to the compound cautiously. On the way back, Guardsmen kept expecting contacts that never came. Based on their previous experiences, and the carloads of men they'd seen moving about earlier, they were sure they'd be engaged but made it back without further incident. Guardsmen began to bet pizzas and crates of pop on when the first fight would start.

That afternoon, 1 Platoon was on patrols again. Kirkwood was ordered to take his men out to the southwest. As an additional complication, he was asked to take a two-man Sky News team with him. However, the pair had already made themselves popular amongst Right Flank. The cameraman was an old soldier and seemed professional, as did the journalist. More of a problem was the obese Royal Logistics Corps officer who had been sent to keep an eye on them by the Bastion Media Ops team. In an effort to ensure that embedded journalists are managed even on the front line, they are often assigned an escort. The escort, something of an aristocrat in Bastion as he occasionally gets to go 'out on the ground', is often from one of the areas of the Army traditionally despised by infanteers. Thus, the journalist arrives with the double handicap of being dressed in blue and an association with someone a Scots Guardsman will label a 'belter'.

Kirkwood pushed a few hundred metres to the southwest before being engaged with fire that riveted into the clods of earth at his men's feet. Taking cover, 1 Platoon tried to identify the firing points. Despite the gunfire, a number of civilians were still milling about between the two sides of the firefight. After getting a fix on the insurgents, the men briefly engaged and then moved on, only to be contacted again moments later. Civilians were still in the area.

'Sighted weapons only, machine gunners cease fire, sighted weapons only. Identify the firing points,' Sergeant Kirkwood hissed into his mouthpiece. Another issue was the Royal Logistics Corps escort officer. 'He was trying to get himself onto Sky News – being the big lad in a contact,' one young Guardsman remembered. When he started giving fire-control orders, Sergeant Kirkwood eventually had to tell him: 'Sir, wind your fucking neck in. My Guardsmen know what the fuck is going on, so shut the fuck up and stay down.'

After a few more minutes' shooting, a group of elders walked into the middle of the contact. Both sides stopped firing. The elders then walked up to 1 Platoon and asked to talk. Sitting with a slightly stunned Sergeant Kirkwood, one of the men identified himself as a Mullah and pointed out the insurgent compounds in the area. He then asked that no missiles be used in the fighting and said that the local people wanted a permanent Isaf checkpoint locally. He walked off. In under a minute, all the civilians in the area disappeared and the shooting resumed. The patrol moved back but got pinned down next to a bund line while the sangars began to take accurate fire. As 1 Platoon had moved about, the sangars saw minibuses dropping off unarmed men next to compounds along the path the patrol was likely to take. While everyone knew what the purpose of these battle taxis was, engaging them was clearly impossible.

Accurate single shots were now landing amongst 1 Platoon every 5–10 seconds from a trio of firing points. Realising his men were pinned, Sergeant Kirkwood took Lance Sergeant Walker back in the direction of the insurgents. The pair laid down as much fire as they could towards the enemy, drawing a smart response and allowing the platoon to draw back to the cover of the sangars. Walker and Kirkwood covered each other back towards the gate under fire. Ten metres short, a Javelin missile dropped over the wall and made straight for their heads. Leaping out of the way, they saw its rocket motor start and the missile cruise into a firing point, silencing the fire. Up in the sangar, Lance Sergeant Loder relaxed as the contact ended and conducted his post-firing checks. Looking up, he noticed a round that had worked its way through the wall, like a drawing pin through a corkboard. It had lodged where his face had been during the first part of the firefight. He looked back through the Javelin sight to see a white minibus drive up to the compound he'd engaged a few minutes earlier. It picked up what was left of the casualties from the Javelin strike. He thought about how many Casevac helicopters he'd seen shot at by insurgents and lit a cigarette.

In the Ops Room, Sergeant Kirkwood briefed the Company Commander on the patrol. Major Lindsay-German wanted to close down the insurgents' approach routes to their firing points by investing another compound in the way 2 Platoon had done on the last mission. He identified a compound out to the south-west that could be suitable and asked Sergeant Kirkwood to go out immediately and recce it. 1 Platoon set off again and made for the compound. The Javelin had clearly put any other insurgents in the area off engaging and the patrol was not shot at. Instead, it turned into a talking patrol, as locals approached to tell them about IED sites. They also said anyone on a motorcycle in the area was almost certainly an insurgent. This population-focused approach seemed much more like the sort of tour the men had trained for in Britain. The men had a quick look at the compound of interest, decided it was unsuitable and headed back. The afternoon was still warm and some stripped down to the 1 Platoon T-Shirts Sergeant Kirkwood had ordered before Christmas – 'SEEK AND DESTROY' was written on the back, 'THE FIGHTING FIRST' on the front.

What remained of the day was spent on a myriad of small patrols. The locals had mostly stayed in the area and seemed willing to speak to Isaf – one man who said that the Taliban had chopped off his hand providing a possible clue as to why. They also pleaded with Isaf not to fire indiscriminately. The terrain was difficult for foot-patrolling: irrigation ditches meant men had wet, cold feet most of the time and a never-ending succession of compound walls needed to be scaled in full kit to make progress. As it grew dark, the pace of patrols gradually dropped off. Those not tasked with a lurk put on their warm kit and crawled into the sleeping bags all had found room for on this operation. Guardsman Stafford had warmed up after his immersion in freezing water and slept through to morning. The Sky News team flew out that night.

*

After a peaceful night, Right Flank woke up cold on the second morning. Fires are started; the ritual first brew is served. By now, everyone knows how everyone else likes their tea or coffee so before you even ask 'Fancy a brew?' you've already got a Nato standard (powdered milk, two sugars) in your mucker's mug. As one gets the brews going, another boils a mess-tin of water and immerses foil-wrapped baked beans and bacon and looks for Tabasco sauce to give it some kick. The rations do their job and fleeces come off, replaced with the green camouflage smock that got you through training and courses in Catterick or Brecon. You take your ski hat off and run your hand through greasing hair if you're an officer, across a neatly shaved head if you're not. The desert scarf is next off, catching against the stubble you'll harvest next. Instead of leaves, the tree in the middle of the compound is wearing the drying clothes from yesterday's soaking march. Men approach it, shake hands with a limp sock, then decide to leave it another day. The insurgents have politely waited for you to finish breakfast. The first rounds sing over sangars and, rather unnecessarily, the sentries shout: 'Contact!'

'Here we go again,' everyone thinks.

Up in the sangars, Guardsmen could see men and vehicles moving about. Over their radios an intense game of prediction took hold as they tried to guess where the next shots would come from. The firing point most used seemed to be a line of compounds about 500 metres to the south, towards Sayedebad. At that range, the Kalashnikov rounds fired at the sangars were erratic. The insurgents may have been trying to tease out a reaction and figure out the exact whereabouts of all the Isaf call signs on the ground. In an effort to gain better visibility of insurgent firing points, engineers blew up trees and a nearby wall that was a potential approach route to the compound. Patrols went out to try and push against the insurgent front line. Young Guardsmen were as surprised by the reluctance of the insurgents to get into a contact as they were by the confidence the locals had in coming up and speaking to them. Those not on patrols were tasked with setting up a secure helipad for replens in a walled field adjacent to their living compound.

After their brief splash of comparative luxury in Bastion, men had once again to adapt to living 'light-scales' in the field. The smell of smouldering shit and plastic from the burns pit mixed with the waxy chemical odour of hexamine cooking tablets and that of unwashed men clung to the compound. The few rooms were now Ops Rooms, so everyone slept outside. Guardsmen Stafford and McHugh drew stag above the latrines and spent their nights spying on other Guardsmen going about their business, relaying live commentary over 'Radio Poo Ditch' to the other sentries via their radios. Lance Sergeant Walker found a stray chicken in the compound, improvised a leash and took it for regular walks around camp. There was general celebration when a Guardsman found one of her eggs in his bed space.

*

On 18 February, the third day, Major Lindsay-German wanted to follow up on the previous days' engagements and aimed to identify a suitable compound to put a platoon in overnight. He sent a patrol south in the morning. They weren't contacted and found a possible compound.

That afternoon, four multiples, two each from 1 and 3 Platoons, left their base and headed south across the muddy fields and through the deep, cold irrigation ditches. Their aim was to occupy the compound until nightfall, when they would be relieved by 2 Platoon. A section from 1 Platoon under Lance Corporal Little remained in the base compound on standby. 3 Platoon headed along the main road running south to Sayedebad, while Kirkwood kept his men in a large field east of the road. The patrol had been out less than ten minutes when 3 Platoon began to take sustained, accurate fire. Moving south through the field to support them, 1 Platoon was shot at from six points to the south and east.

'Davey, take the multiple up to that bund line. I'm staying here with the ANA and the others,' Kirkwood told Walker over the net.

Lance Sergeant Walker and ten others doubled the 200

metres under accurate fire. As they got into scant cover, Walker turned his head right and looked at his boys. 'Troops, keep your heads down,' he said. A moment later he was shot.

'MAN DOWN, MAN DOWN!'

'Davey Walker's been shot in the head!'

Kirkwood couldn't believe what he was hearing; no one could. Psyching himself up for the 200-metre dash across the field, he let out a roar and doubled across the open ground.

'MAN DOWN, MAN DOWN!'

'Davy McClellan's been shot in the chest!'

Kirkwood finished his zigzag run and reached the cover of the bund line. Rounds were still rippling through the air. He crawled along the cover out of breath and reached Lance Sergeant Walker. He saw the grey face and stood up. The whole world seemed to stop.

Later, it would emerge that Lance Sergeant Davey Walker died instantly. At the time, men grasped at the chance that there might be a flicker of life and rushed to get him to treatment. The medic did not declare him dead on the scene. A MIST Report went to Company Headquarters.

Sergeant Kirkwood turned to Guardsman Davy McClellan, who was lying back against the bund line with blood soaking out across his uniform.

'What's happened to you, then?'

'I've been shot in the chest, Kirky. Me fags are in the top pocket of me day-sack. I reckon I'm giving up on smoking.'

'Right, we need to get Davey back to the helicopters now. Get that stretcher out and let's fucking move. You lot stay here with this McClellan,' said Kirkwood.

The Afghan soldiers fanned out and started returning fire onto the insurgent positions. One of their snipers shot a man out of a tree, as Kirkwood and five others carried Lance Sergeant Walker back.

Lance Corporal Little's section were stood-to and ready when the first cry of 'Man Down' had come from the men in the sangars who could see what was going on but were too far away to help with fire. The report came through in pieces.

'Gunshot wound to head.'

That was a shock. That hadn't happened before.

'Davey Walker.'

Unbelievable.

'Another Man Down. Davy McClellan. Shot in the chest.'

Little turned to Guardsmen Rab McClellan and told him his brother had been shot. The section doubled out of the compound and made their way across the field.

Lance Sergeant Walker's Casevac group was struggling. They'd crossed the field under sustained fire but a five-metre-wide irrigation ditch slowed them down. The men were up to their necks in mud and water, sliding the stretcher across one another's helmets, doing everything to get the casualty back. The fire on them continued as they got back into the field and made their way on. Kirkwood demanded and got more supporting fire as 3 Platoon came on to targets, shooting armed men on motorbikes heading to join the fight. Little's section ran past Kirkwood and crossed the ditches and field under more fire. Guardsman Rab McClellan pushed through to the bund line and found his brother lying down, his eyes closed.

'Davy, Davy!'

He opened his eyes.

'Aye, Rab?'

'Don't fucking do that to me, Davy!'

He slumped onto the top of the embankment, aimed his

weapon at a compound and started firing away, shouting 'Bastards!' at the men who'd shot his brother.

Sergeant Kirkwood was still 300 metres short of Right Flank's compound and the stretcher carrying Davey Walker had collapsed. Inside the compound, Lance Corporal Harris grabbed a solid stretcher and a few men, and doubled out to help get the casualty to safety. After struggling over yet another wide irrigation ditch, the men finally got him back to the compound. Harris gave CPR. 'We're not going to stop working on him. As long as there's a chance, we're not going to stop working on him . . . He was dead before he came in the compound,' Harris said later. There can be no doubt that everyone did everything they could to try and get Walker onto the helicopter alive. The mark of the man was that his comrades wouldn't give up on him. Sergeant Kirkwood ran back out to lead the next Casevac.

Lance Corporal Little couldn't get the chest seal to stick on Guardsman Davy McClellan. There was too much blood seeping out of the wound. He decided to just clamp it on with his palm. The white valve used to let air out of the lung flapped between two of his fingers. Kirkwood returned to take control of the situation. Getting him onto the stretcher, Guardsman McHugh started the banter with McClellan to keep him talking.

'Ha-ha, check you out!'

'Aye, I'll be chilling out in Bastion while you lot are still stuck here.'

The going was incredibly hard but Guardsman McHugh said, 'It's not like some daft wee exercise. You knew you were going to have to carry him and jump in rivers. He'd been shot so nobody jacked it, everybody mucked in.' At the back of the Casevac party was Rab McClellan, looking over his brother, carrying his bloodstained body armour. They dropped him in the compound, where the medics took over and waited for the helicopter to fly in and pick up both men. Some of the men then headed back to the bund line to pick up their weapons, the casualties' kit and the rest of the section. Feeling naked without weapons, they zigzagged across the field and through the ditches and linked up with the men who had remained to cover the Casevac. Reunited with his rifle, Little launched grenades into firing points as Apache helicopters came overhead firing 30mm into compounds and jet fighters flew low over the firefight in deterrent. The men picked up blood-spattered helmets and weapons and pepper-potted back to the compound. Little gets in and finds a sandbag and a few bottles of water. He takes off his body armour and lays it on the ground, pours water and sand all over it and starts scrubbing with the sandbag: 'It's no good cutting about with blood all over yourself.'

As they headed to the helicopter landing site, rounds zipped between the Guardsmen heading to cover the Chinook. Behind the Guardsmen's shoulders, from a compound to the north-west, a man calmly walked out carrying something. A hundred and fifty metres from the soldiers he sat down and waited to be beckoned over. Looking through their sights, the men see that he is carrying a child covered in blood. They beckon him over. He walks up to them and shows them his eight-year-old son shot through the chest. One multiple is crashed out to bring the boy and his father in through the back door while another rush the two wounded Scots Guardsmen to the landing helicopter. They strip the child but find no exit wound. He is still conscious. The medic says that it looks like a tumbling Kalashnikov round has done the damage. He is rushed back out too, as another Mert comes in. The boy seems OK when he is put on the helicopter. Guardsman McHugh finally slumps back into the compound.

'That's probably the hardest I've worked!'

1 Platoon gathered themselves in their corner of the compound and tried to think positively as the day faded. About an hour later, Lindsay-German called the Right Flank together and they gathered by sunset. He struggled to clear his throat.

'Unfortunately, Sergeant Walker died,' he said. 'He was pronounced dead on arrival at Bastion. Let's just bow our heads and reflect for a minute.'

The silence was broken by Scots Guardsmen showing that while boys might not cry, men most certainly do. Even the medics, who were sure that Lance Sergeant Walker died instantly but had worked on him until handing him to the helicopter crew, were still shocked by the finality of the news. Sergeant Kirkwood gathered 1 Platoon around and hugged them close.

'Let's go and sit around the fire and talk about Davey,' he said.

They talked about all the good things: the joke, laugh and song Davey had for each of them, and they composed moving tributes to their mentor and friend. News came back that Davy McClellan 'should' pull through, a worse assessment than Right Flank had held when they put the smiling and conscious Guardsman on the Chinook. The news was broken sensitively to his brother Rab. The wounded Afghan boy had died on the operating table at Bastion. Major Lindsay-German sat next to the radio and struggled to dictate the eulogies over the radio net. He had cancelled the evening's lurk, so the deep orange glow of Illumination rounds from the Grenadier's mortars lit the night as men struggled with sleep.

★

The next morning, Sergeant Kirkwood sought out the Company Commander and told him that his men were ready to patrol and that the loss of a man wouldn't stop them. Fortunately, it was 1 Platoon's turn on guard so the offer could be declined with honesty. The insurgents had clearly worked Right Flank out by now. They knew where they were and had taken their time setting and executing a successful ambush the day before. The insurgents also realised that by being drawn into a static fight around Sayedebad with a unit who looked to have no long-term ambition in the area, they were ceding vital ground in Kawshhal Kalay and Marjah to forces who would remain. Those who elected to stay around Sayedebad on 19 February harassed Right Flank with sporadic fire from a distance, especially after a pair crawling towards the compound through a field of dead poppy had been picked up by the Javelin and killed. When another insurgent began hitting the wall around the Javelin position, Major Lindsay-German and the US Marine Fire Controllers got on the wall, were guided onto the shooter through the Javelin's thermal sight and put a round through his head. Lance Sergeant Loder used his laser range finder to measure the distance – an utter fluke at 867 metres with a little 5.56mm round – and the men on the wall claimed a sixth of a kill each. The ongoing contacts in the area made recovering the body impossible for the insurgents that afternoon. Eventually, the local elders came to the compound and asked Lindsay-German for permission to recover the body for burial. He told them to bring him the body and weapon first. They agreed, borrowed a stretcher, and brought the dead man into the compound. He was forensically searched and biometrically photographed and his weapon and ammunition were kept before the body was handed back for burial. He was the only 100 per cent definite kill from either operation. Word came that Right Flank would fly out the next night.

★

The Company flew out of Sayedebad for the second and final time just after dusk on 20 February. If much of significance happened that day, few could remember it. When I interviewed Right Flank about the second Sayedebad mission, their recollections, even months later, were solely focused on the events surrounding the casualties. The enormity of the loss had telescoped their minds. After collapsing the defences and getting out to the helicopters, 1 Platoon and Company Headquarters got out first. 2 and 3 Platoon got on their knees ready to go and waited. Then they waited a while longer. No one had told Right Flank about a change of plan that meant they were getting picked up in two waves. The men left in the field felt pretty exposed. After 20 minutes the Chinooks came and the men were up and off.

1 Platoon tramped into their tent. The first bed on the right had already been stripped. Everyone looked at the void as they walked past. Lance Corporal Little turned to Lance Corporal McGonagle: 'Listen, wee man, I want you to move into that bed space because they're just going to keep looking at an empty bed space and keep thinking about it.' McGonagle put his kit on Davey Walker's bed and sat down. Twelve hours later Right Flank, less those who stayed to carry Lance Sergeant Walker onto the plane home, left Camp Bastion in their Warriors for Patrol Base Pimon. It had been a unique start to a tour.

★

Operation Moshtarak, of which Right Flank's two operations had been a key part, would shape Isaf operations in Helmand for at least the next six months. On every Herrick there used to be at least one large Brigade Operation. Some have a specific target: getting the famous, and still uninstalled, turbine to Kajaki Dam, for instance.

Others, such as Operation Panchai Palang, are about clearing a space on a map previously marked 'here be monsters'. Operation Moshtarak was a larger operation, reflecting the greater resources the US Marines were bringing to bear in Helmand. Its effects were so great that building on its success – and it was tactically successful: routes were cleared, Marjah was taken – would take a long time. 4 Mechanised Brigade, of which 1 SG was a cog, had the sense not to throw together a Brigade-scale operation, and instead focused on reinforcing Moshtarak's legacy. While the Scots Guards wouldn't touch Sayedebad again, their tour would stand or fall on their ability to hold areas like Kawshhal Kalay that had been initially cleared at cost during Moshtarak. They would then hope to build enduring success in these areas in partnership with the Afghan Government. The key factor in the coming battle would be gaining the local people's support or otherwise.

Range days

The coach to Otterburn Ranges takes an hour and a half from Catterick. Up the A1 and then through snow-clad hills.

At the front of the coach I'm chatting to Lance Sergeant Dale McCallum as the miles tick past. He's a Londoner, originally from the Irish Guards but now firmly a Scots Guardsman. As a teetotaller and the only black member of the Sergeants' Mess, he could be a man apart but certainly isn't. In his prime he ran the 100 metres in 11 seconds for the Army team and is an excellent sniper. He's done two tours of Iraq, including the invasion in 2003. When he returns to London he doesn't wear his uniform, 'in case someone tries to beat you up'. Anyone who tried that with McCallum would be pretty stupid. 'Even Dale's muscles have muscles,' his guys say. He's engaged to a girl he met in Germany eight years ago and there's a wedding planned for December, when he's back from Helmand. He's delayed the wedding until after the tour, 'in case something bad happens to me out there, and as an extra something to look forward to when I get back: another reason to stay alive'.

The journey draws to a close.

'This place is worse than Sennelager,' one voice comes from the back.

'Aye, at least Germany was flat,' agrees another.

'Eh boys, have you heard about the Celtic fans who've sent 50,000 strips to Haiti after the earthquake? The Haitians sent them back and asked for Rangers shirts,' says another, to cheers (mostly).

The next day the Fire Support Group men are huddled against the wind. We're all mummified in layers of warm kit under the heavy body armour our backs are getting used to. In batches of five, the men go forward to zero rifles. I wait with the others in a loose circle as men swap opinions and wait their turn on the range.

'That Jade Goody goes and dies and gets 19 pages of OK Magazine . . .'

'Aye, no other girl who dies of cancer gets that.'

'. . . and the day she dies, four lads get killed in Afghanistan.'

'Don't understand it. The media likes reality. Boys are getting killed in real time . . .'

'That's reality.'

'They should do a Squaddie Big Brother . . .'

'Aye.'

'Shopping list: fags, Stella, bread, eggs. Ten weeks of egg banjoes and beer.'

'Send in ten squaddies and ten nurses . . .'

'They'd be putting cling film on the toilet seats . . .'

'And drawing pins on each other's beds.'

'And be wanting a webcam.'

'Why?'

'Squaddies would be saying: "If you can look at those girls taking a shower then I want a look too."'

And talking about what to expect:

'My missus was gaen to buy me a two-hundred-and-fifty-pound watch. I says: "Don't do that, I might have nae arms in a year."'

'My missus is going to be nine months pregnant by the time I get back from this tour. She's buying the nappies and I said: "Buy loads, I might be needin those too.'"

'My kid's just out of nappies, but I'll be back in them soon.'

'Time I get back I could be the size of my little wean.'

'On your skateboard . . .'

'Your missus saying: "Eh, wean, take your father for a walk.'"

'*Jock Guards – no sympathy.*'

We rotate onto another range, where a pair of vehicles is parked. One has a squat-barrelled Grenade Machine Gun mounted on its back. The boys take turns aiming it at markers 100, 200 and 400 metres away and then firing a few coke-can-sized paintballs at them, layering the snow with orange powder. Every few minutes, someone is up on the .50 Calibre Heavy Machine Gun. It makes a satanic rattle, then we watch the rounds ricochet off concrete pillboxes and into a reluctant grey sky. 'The Taliban don't like this weapon,' a recently returned Welsh Guards officer comments rather superfluously – who would? At day's end, bored Scots privates drive us back to barracks in ancient Bedford trucks.

That night, a round ricochets into Guardsman Jason Kernaghan's leg on a live firing exercise. A helicopter flies in to take him to hospital in Newcastle. As he's being stretchered off, high on morphine, Sergeant Tony Gibson is running next to the naked Guardsman screaming, 'Don't think you're getting out of Afghanistan because of this!' It is probably the best training the Company does that week, and the Guardsman does indeed make Afghanistan.

Back in the grim barrack block the Company holds a conference. I sit in the corner and struggle to keep up with new acronyms, names and faces. 'What is it with Left Flank? It never rains but it pours,' says Captain Hamish Barne, who is running things while the Company Commander does his recce of Lashkar Gah. Sergeant Lee Paxton walks in and does an immaculate impression of a young Guards officer.

'Hi, how's it going?' he asks.

Will Tulloch, a Second Lieutenant who left Sandhurst in August and joined the Battalion just before Christmas gets a call.

'You're joking,' says Company Sergeant Major Neil Lawrie when he hears that the ringtone is the Regimental Quick March, Heilan' Laddie.

'Hi, how's it going?' Tulloch starts the call – bringing another laugh for Paxton.

It's Charlie Pearson, another Second Lieutenant, on the line. He flew with the casualty to Newcastle.

'All well with them?' Barne asks Tulloch.

'Yeah. The Commanding Officer's already called Pearson,' says Tulloch.

'Fuck,' says Barne.

Platoon Sergeant Major John Lilley, who commands the Fire Support Group and is a B Company man, comes in next.

'What a shower of fannies Left Flank is. Shot in the leg. I'll bask in yer glories but when you do something stupid – steal a pistol, start shooting each other – I'm nae part of you.'

The mood darkens briefly when they hear news that Sergeant Tam O'Donnell has been shot in the leg for real in Afghanistan with Right Flank. He is back in Camp Bastion and his condition is stable.

'The back of the leg? That means he was either running away or the Company Sergeant Major did it,' says Lilley. (Jock Guards – no sympathy.)

'Or the Afghan Army.'

'Never rule out the obvious – if it's an old rusty bullet.'

'Or Right Flank have had an ND.'

'Or a ricochet like us.'

'Right, we've got the "fun" part tomorrow,' says Barne, bringing the conference to order. 'After platoon compound assaults, we're heading up that hill and overnighting in the mock base which we'll then defend. Then it's a Company Operation the next morning, so we'll have built up from section to platoon to company attack over the week. Can we try to shoot the targets rather than each other from now on, please? And the Company Commander's coming back from his recce at some stage too, I think.'

After another day on the ranges we make our way up a long hill in the back of trucks and arrive at the base just before last *light. Everything is damp from the foggy drizzle that is enveloping the summit as it gets dark. We're advised to avoid the back of the base, where various chunks of explosives are waiting to blow up, simulating incoming mortar fire. There are tents for some, shipping containers for others. With boil-in-the-bag dinners inside us, there's little to do but stand outside smoking and waiting for the inevitable training exercises to start.*

Out of the gloom Major Rupert Kitching, Officer Commanding, Left Flank, emerges and we are introduced. He has the air of man who has just walked out of a Max Weber essay on charismatic leadership. He's finished his recce in Helmand and made it home in time for the birth of his first child: a daughter called Florence. He married last year and ran a marathon at the North Pole by way of honeymoon. He's come up to Otterburn for the night but wants to let the boys get on with it. By this stage of the training there shouldn't be anything he can teach them. It sounds like Left Flank is due a varied tour. Two platoons will be split across several checkpoints in a fairly calm area called Basharan, while another platoon gets to stay in Lashkar Gah on call to support other units' missions that need back-up. They've lucked out.

The fog puts paid to the live-fire base defence package and the helicopter can't fly fire missions. The Exercise Controllers (Excon) let off the dummy mortar rounds anyway, so there's lots of lying in puddles pondering the origin of the term 'soak period'. Missing the defensive part of the exercise is no drama really, as everyone has heard how the insurgents no longer go for out-and-out gunfights on bases, as they know they'll lose – that was the old Helmand. This tour will be all about winning the locals over and avoiding IEDs.

The Company is up before first light for the deliberate operation exercise. It has been a horrific night on the moors and the unfortunates in unheated metal containers nearly froze. There's more drizzle, so the much-heralded helicopter is out of action again. The platoons set off into the valley and the Fire Support Group drives off onto a spur to support the advance. I bounce after them in a Land Rover with an Excon who talks me through what's going to happen. The platoons come under contact but before the Fire Support Group can do their job, they get ambushed from behind. Metal plates jump up 50 metres from their sentries, who start putting down a rate of fire. The back door of one of the Excon Land Rovers that has been sitting forgotten swings down and a man rolls out covered in blood and missing a leg. The soldiers look at each other, realise the man is from Amputees in Action (a charity that pays amputees to go to training areas and simulate the horrors of war) and get on with treatment. Platoon Sergeant Major Lilley needs to get the casualty away, so he rushes back to the base and that's his men done for the day. I wander into the valley to follow the rest of the assault.

Platoon pushes through platoon as they wade up a freezing stream and through mock IEDs, Casevacs and ambushes. A Brigadier has joined in for the day as an observer, so Barne is under even more scrutiny and he thanks God he filled his magazines when Tac are ambushed, plates flipping up at close range. The helicopter might not be flying but damp won't stop the artillery and mortars that conduct their own battle against a barren hillside for hours on end. Excon walk a few hundred metres behind the platoons, pressing buttons to make more targets jump up and down and pass comment on how Left Flank are getting on. The exercise ends with a horrific Casevac back through the stream and then across a bog. 'STOP, STOP, STOP! Unload,' Excon finally announce. The boys pant through exertion and cold and are then told to march back up the hill to the trucks that will drive them to the administration area.

Back in hastily swabbed barracks and ready to go, the

Company Sergeant Major comes over. 'Afraid it'll be a while yet,' he says. 'The civvy coach drivers need an hour break after the 90-minute drive from Catterick.' The news is met with incredulity and bodily threats against the drivers. All that noise in broadsheet letter columns about the civilian/ military divide in society is brought to life by the delay. As they file on the coaches an hour later, the Guardsmen thank the nice Yorkshire ladies who are driving them home – after all, they're only obeying policy – and then fall sound asleep.

CHAPTER FOUR

'It was nice at times to get out and just go for a wander about'

February to May 2010

'What on earth is a Babaji Pear?' thought Major Rupert Kitching, re-reading the email from Helmand. 'Company Sergeant Major, can you bring a map in here, please? Plan's changed again,' he said.

On his recce to Helmand in February, Kitching had covered the ground his company were, he was promised, going to hold for their tour. Major Alex Cartwright of The Queen's Company Grenadier Guards gave Kitching a positive appreciation of the area. The most pressing concern was the Forward Line of Enemy Troops to the east, which some of his checkpoints would rub up against. Behind this line was bandit country – unknown to Isaf and rumoured to be full of insurgents. The eastern end of Operation Moshtarak changed all that. D Company 1st Battalion, The Royal Welsh had broken into the southern half of this ungoverned space (known, due to its shape on military maps, as the Babaji Pear) but, unlike in Right Flank's operation to the south-west, they had been ordered to hold the ground and begin digging in. Left Flank would relieve them. The long-term ambition in the area seemed, from the information available to Kitching back

114

in Catterick, to be all about a route named Mars turning into a route named Trident.

Like all of 1 SG (see Chapter One), Left Flank had been linked with many different jobs. Wiser heads had realised not to listen too hard to any briefs until their actual handover/takeover in Helmand. Even so, everyone had to pay attention and try to gather as much information as possible about the latest place they were meant to be heading. The pressing question was what their address in theatre would be for the vital parcels and letters sent from home by loved ones. Left Flank were now going, it appeared, to Lashkar Gah Rural (North). The other headline was that they were going into a 'new' area, so were starting a process from scratch, as opposed to around Tapa Paraang where, a year after Isaf had moved in, the insurgents had largely melted away, the locals had accepted the Afghan Government's presence and the British troops were concentrating on schools rather than snipers.

What gaps there had been in training over the past eight months had been spent by many on interminable qualification courses. Mastiff Drivers, Jackal Commanders, Vehicle Gunners and All Arms Search Teams had to appear from the wreckage of the fully trained Armoured Infantry Company, which returned from exercise in Canada in August 2009. A 32-strong team from B Company bolted onto Left Flank as a Fire Support Group to add snipers and Javelin to the mix. Those elements of C Company not folded into mentoring roles then merged into Left Flank's platoons to boost numbers. Finally, Company Sergeant Major Neil Lawrie came over from Right Flank, meaning the Company had men from across Battalion.

New platoon commanders, lean but still toddler-like in experience, finished the Infantry Battle School in Brecon, then arrived at Battalion before Christmas to meet platoon sergeants who had been getting on rather well without the interference of officers. Guardsmen fresh from training and a stint in front of the Palaces of London were thrown into platoons that became unrecognisable from a few months before. Only in February, on the final Mission Rehearsal Exercise on Salisbury Plain, were the platoons complete. That exercise, though, had become a beauty parade for visiting VIPs and for a team of trainers who were sent to teach the rudiments of house clearances in case Left Flank were called upon to support Strike Ops from their base in Lashkar Gah. (Though, of course, everything had changed between February and their deployment, so Left Flank hardly saw Lashkar Gah.) Some of the Guardsmen did, however, manage to pinch a few flash-bangs from the training team with which they terrified the ex-Gurkhas paid to play the insurgents when they assaulted the mock base on the last night of the exercise. So began yet another lengthy disciplinary email chain.

The Company travelled down the M1 in early April. On arrival at the reception centre in Brize Norton, Left Flank checked in for the Sunday morning flight to Kandahar. Later that night, they were told that the plane due to fly them was grounded so they'd be split in two, with the first lot flying as scheduled and the second half left kicking heels in Oxfordshire. On Monday, the leftovers were put on a plane. Some of them fell asleep as the engines began to tick over prior to take-off. They were then woken up and told to get off as the plane was grounded. This second fault meant that half the company eventually flew out on Tuesday morning, 72 hours after leaving Catterick. In Kandahar, they were split into various queues, one of which was delayed a further 24 hours in the sprawling mess of Kandahar Airfield – a distinctly seedy destination.

I flew through Kandahar a while later – once the general

election was over and the Ministry of Defence's ban on Dictaphones in the Helmand Valley had been lifted. Everything about the airfield is brown, including the air, which smells of sewage. Amongst the endless pre-fab accommodation blocks rests the Boardwalk, a raised wooden circuit surrounded by a ring of mostly shut fast-food restaurants. It had recently been hit by rockets, possibly to the grim satisfaction of General McChrystal, still god in Kabul, who had ordered many outlets shut. Circling the Boardwalk is a constant procession of personnel. Belgian Navy, Romanians with Kalashnikov variants slung across their bulging shoulders, Canadians in mock-Jock Tam O'Shanters and many, many Americans, every third one seemingly wearing a rather self-defeating 'Special Forces' shoulder flash. All pass in a dull khaki rainbow of national camouflages. Flirtation takes place over decent coffee at the French Café between off-duty servicemen and women, though the Assault Rifles both parties carry must affect the frisson of a first date. There is a steady roar of jets taking off to go to the aid of men on the ground somewhere; at night their afterburners glow white and lift them into the sky as meteors in reverse.

On eventual arrival in Camp Bastion, the men had a night in bed and then launched into training the next morning. It was still pleasantly cool in the evenings, but the days were hot after the cold British winter of 2009–10. Men were marched back and forth through the heat to ranges, to zero weapons, and to tents to attend lectures for nine straight days. The dummy IED lane commanded complete attention, especially for the young Vallon operators who topped up their knowledge of the system with the latest information from men who had been out on the ground with live devices days before. No matter how good the training can get in Britain, the knowledge that filters through is often out of date and occasionally delivered by men who have not been to Helmand. The in-theatre training package, along with slicing nine welcome days from a six-month tour, bridges the gap between past and present conditions and is a final opportunity to make mistakes.

As training came to an end, Major Kitching called his men together to deliver his briefing on the area.

'This area is Loy Adera and this is Route Mars, which runs through it,' Kitching began. 'Our aim is to hold this ground from seven checkpoints, protect the communities around those checkpoints, learn about and influence the communities away from our checkpoints and disrupt the insurgents in depth in the contested areas throughout our area.

'The reason we are strung out so laterally is the road – Route Mars – and fellas, it's all about the road. Route Mars is a rural principal route between Lashkar Gah, the provincial capital to our south, and Gereshk, Helmand's second town to our east. The problem is, it's been shut for the last two years because of Loy Adera and we reckon it's IED central. The Provincial Governor, Gulab Mangal, has asked us to open this route and keep it open to facilitate Freedom of Movement for the Local Nationals. It is one of the governor's "key priorities". The only way we're going to do that is watching that road, driving it and patrolling around it. As the tour moves on, an upgrade to the road will come in from the west and the east of our patch, hopefully meeting up before we leave. Route Mars will then become Route Trident. So expect to hear a lot about the Trident build, especially as it's one of Brigade's main efforts for this tour.

'To facilitate our mission, we're going to be partnered by Afghan National Security Forces at every level. That means living with them and possibly fighting with them, or should I say, beside them, every day of this tour. As you know, this is a nascent area. Before Operation Moshtarak, the Forward Line of Enemy Troops was in the western half of our area. We now straddle their lines – half to the west and half to the east. We know the eastern area, behind their lines, to be a previous insurgent transit and logistics hub. It's where insurgents used to do what you've just done – train – and where they used to go for R&R. They are beginning to respond to Isaf's presence in Loy Adera but the poppy harvest is ongoing, so we can wait out for something bigger.

'The area has also been the insurgents' in terms of the people. Guys, I cannot stress this enough: for us and for the insurgents it is the people who are the key terrain in this campaign. We have to convince them that they are better off with the Afghan Government and the Afghan forces in the long run and with us in the meantime.

'There is a lot of work to be done. We will not solve all the problems Loy Adera has in our six-month tenure. Our success, or failure, will be based on the condition in which we leave this place for the people, for the Afghan Government and the Afghan forces, and for the guys who will be sitting where you are sitting now in six short months' time.

'As I've said, our area is new and it is a priority. We're going to be given a lot of support to make this happen but the tough slog is always going to be on the 141 of us. I would wish you luck if I thought you needed it.'

In Loy Adera, Second Lieutenant Will Tulloch was on a foot patrol with the Royal Welsh Platoon Commander whom he would succeed the next day. The Royal Welsh had enjoyed utter freedom of movement in the six weeks they had been in the area. In the last week, Tulloch had whizzed up and down Mars, being given hurried words of advice from the officer: 'This blindspot here is Bravo

Foxtrot 3. Vallon if anything looks out of the ordinary but the atmospherics seem pretty chilled round here.'

On the final patrol a Mastiff had hit an IED followed up with small arms. They responded robustly, fire pouring from their Mastiffs. Sitting below the turret, Colour Sergeant Paul Cody put the empty bullet cases into ammunition tins as they fell around him. The Welsh gunner looked down at him. 'Fucking Guards!' he said. 'Only you lot would start tidying up in a firefight.' It lasted three hours.

Lance Sergeant John Cardwell looked over at Tulloch as the contact ended.

'Sir, that's more rounds fired in anger than I've seen in four operational tours with the Jock Guards,' he said.

April

The different elements of Left Flank filtered into Loy Adera over a week (see map, p. xxix). The Fire Support Group had the most taxing journey in the Jackals they drove from Bastion to their new home in Checkpoint North, at the western edge of Left Flank's area. Combining an armoured underbelly with the manoeuvrability of a 4×4, the British-built Jackal was designed to meet the needs of Iraq and Afghanistan and is the obese great-nephew to the vehicles the Long Range Desert Group used in the Sahara during the Second World War.

Leading them was Platoon Sergeant Major John Lilley, 39, from Easterhouse in Glasgow. A Warrant Officer from B Company, Lilley had spent much of his time in the Scots Guards in the Close Observation Platoon in Northern Ireland and then the Reconnaissance Platoon when 1 SG went armoured. Like a recce platoon, his men were split into two semi-independent multiples. The second was commanded by Colour Sergeant Alan Cameron, who had served with Lilley in Northern Ireland. Their job had been to quietly get close to suspected terrorists, watch them for weeks without compromising their hideout and then leave behind nothing when they departed. This meant eating cold rations then shitting in the foil packets and carrying them back to base. Lilley and Cameron clearly knew and trusted each other. Both had also served with Major Kitching during his misspent youth when he had commanded the Recce Platoon, so he was happy to let them get on and run the western extremity of the Company's Area of Operations. Company Sergeant Major Lawrie was probably pleased that these 'gypsies' from B Company were well away and wouldn't give his impressionable young Guardsmen any bad habits.

Checkpoint North was built around a complex of existing Afghan compounds leased from their owners. The Grenadiers who had been there over the winter had clearly had a tough time. There was water damage to the compounds and the place was crawling with camel spiders. Even an ever-expanding population of wild cats and the occasional snake couldn't keep up with the rats that infested the compounds, while the orchard that formed part of the complex was replete with sand-flies whose bites carried Cutaneous Leishmaniasis, a flesh-eating disease that ended one Guardsman's tour.

The men set about fixing the place up. Raiding parties led by Lance Sergeant Dale McCallum went to Tapa Paraang on ostensibly social calls to Right Flank, who had deployed to that area (see Chapter Five). Carrying empty packs, the men would wait for Right Flank's quartermaster to be disarmed with a brew and then set about looting his shipping containers of anything not nailed down. Next, poisonous spray came through the logistics chain to deter rats and a *Ghost Busters*-style backpack stuffed with insecticide arrived to wage war on the sand flies. Kittens were drowned in the brook that ran through camp. Guardsmen who knew a spot of carpentry put in a kitchen between endless rotations of stag and patrols. Within a month or so, Platoon Sergeant Major Lilley had his base to a standard he was happy with. 'You give a Guardsman shite and he'll make gold with it – it's just one of those things,' he explained to visitors.

Checkpoint North lay on Route Orion, a branch route from Mars. About two kilometres down Orion was Checkpoint South, manned by 10 Platoon and sitting practically on the banks of the Helmand River. Commanded by Lieutenant Ivar Milligan, supported by Lance Sergeant Dale McCallum's Fire Support Group multiple, Checkpoint South's primary role was to keep Route Orion open and watch the utterly ungoverned space that lay to their east up Route Medusa towards the village of Kunjak. Orion had been opened at some cost to the Welsh Guards in the summer of 2009 when Checkpoint North and South had been built, thereby pushing the Forward Line of Enemy Troops east into Loy Adera. Platoon Sergeant Major Lilley up at Checkpoint North would keep a close eye on 10 Platoon to his south – one of the men there was his son, Guardsman John Lilley, Junior.

The rest of the company were strung out along Mars itself. Right in the centre of the area lay Checkpoint Said Abdul, garrisoned by 11 Platoon. Second Lieutenant Charlie Pearson, aged 24 and six months out of Sandhurst, commanded, while Sergeant Tony Gibson, a 28-year-old with 12 years of Army life already behind him, ran the 29-strong platoon. Gibson was from the undisputedly straight-talking school of sergeants, something he had made clear to Pearson when they met just before Christmas. He was also fiercely competitive and pushed his men to their limit in training and on operations. Outwardly hard, everything he did rested, at an emotional level, on love for the men in his care and the view that only by demanding the best of them would he maximise their chances of survival in Helmand. It was sometimes difficult for an 18-year-old Guardsman on the end of a verbally succinct talking-to to appreciate this approach.

Unlike Checkpoint North, Checkpoint Said Abdul was newly built by the Royal Engineers. The Royal Welsh had only been in for six weeks, so had little incentive to make the place their own, knowing that home was fast approaching. The Engineers had laid a curtain of Hesco barriers – the four-and-a-half-foot-high textile-and-steel-mesh sacs that have largely replaced the sandbag – two high and then put in a super-sangar of tubular steel scaffold. It would be permanently manned by Guardsmen for the 4,000 or so hours of the tour. Apart from a well, the 80 by 70 metres patch inside the walls was dirt, which was gradually ground into inches-thick dust by the wheels and tracks of vehicles. The dust would begin clinging to you almost as soon as you had washed in the refreshingly cool well water – a nightly treat. The Platoon Sergeant who Gibson took over from left on the helicopter Gibson arrived in, so there was no chance of a proper handover. There was little to actually handover: two sunshades, a container each of ammunition, drinking water and rations, a plywood dining table, no vehicles and no tents. Between familiarisation patrols close to the base, Gibson set 11 Platoon to building a latrine block, gym and kitchen with whatever they could find.

The hub of Left Flank was Patrol Base Nahidullah, though it hadn't been built when Company Headquarters and 12 Platoon flew in to relieve the Royal Welsh. They moved into local compounds instead. The 20-minute flight in gave the men their first proper look at Helmand. Bastion could have been anywhere, and reminded some of

the seemingly endless Contingency Operating Base outside Basra they'd spent so much time in during the last
decade. Afghanistan was clearly different – especially the
lush Green Zone they were coming into.

'It actually looks quite nice,' said Lance Sergeant Christopher Leyden once the helicopter had flown off. 'I didn't
expect it to be so green. If you didn't see the compounds,
you'd think you were flying over Britain.'

'Nah, shithole,' thought Lance Corporal Joe Nickson.
'It fucking smells and all.'

As the tireless Royal Engineer Field Troop got to work
on Patrol Base Nahidullah, half of 12 Platoon drove up to
the Vehicle Checkpoints (VCPs) that watched the final
three kilometres of Left Flank's section of Route Mars.
The other half remained with Headquarters. The plan was
to keep a half-platoon sized multiple in the Patrol Base to
conduct patrols and act as a Quick Reaction Force, while a
second multiple would man the three VCPs and patrol out
from there, manpower permitting. Second Lieutenant
Tulloch would lead one multiple and his Platoon Sergeant, Lee Paxton, would run the other. The multiples
would swap roles intermittently to keep the men fresh.

*

'Partnering' was a new reality for Isaf in 2010. Due to their
various changes in role pre-tour, Left Flank had hardly
touched it in training but was expected to live it on the
ground. In the past, large groups of Afghan forces, perhaps company-sized, would deploy on the ground with an
Operational Mentoring and Liaison Team (Omlt) of
roughly eight Isaf soldiers. In the vicinity, an Isaf company would also operate and the two would attempt to
execute plans jointly. This had not worked consistently
and a feeling emerged that the Afghans – thrown into the

fight in various states of readiness – were not developing once deployed, as a ratio around 1:15 was not conducive to teaching. This produced the new orthodoxy of partnering. In it, Afghans and Isaf live amongst each other, commander-to-commander and section-to-section. The theory runs that good Isaf practices will rub off on the Afghans, strong personal relationships will develop between men who live and fight together, and the Afghan forces will undergo an accelerated development, allowing Isaf to head for home. Preferably this will all happen before political will in Western capitals evaporates or the insurgency achieves some degree of strategic success in the campaign. In Left Flank's VCPs in April 2010, this meant a ratio of one Guardsman to two Afghans.

It was too late to break up some mentoring teams already in theatre when partnering came into fashion, but a team of Scots Guardsmen was split off, re-designated 'Advisors' and sent to Left Flank to act as day-to-day liaison with the Afghan National Army Company co-headquartered at the Patrol Base with Major Kitching. The team was Second Lieutenant George Cowdry and Lance Sergeant John Thorpe. Thorpe's first reaction on hearing he was working with Afghan soldiers was 'Oh shit!' A Blackburn man with a self-confessed short fuse, he was worried that his temperament wouldn't suit working with the Afghans, especially in the light of various horror stories filtering out of theatre – chiefly the tragedy of the rogue Afghan National Police Patrolman who had killed three Grenadiers and two Royal Military Policemen in November 2009. Thorpe knew he would have to learn to bite his tongue and try to avoid the sort of confrontation that could end in him getting 'reveille' from a disgruntled Afghan soldier.

Out on his first patrols, Thorpe learned that the Afghans were reasonably competent, if slightly wild. On an early

joint patrol a soldier found an IED next to a wall. The Isaf
process then kicked in – a report was compiled by Second
Lieutenant Cowdry and sent to Brigade via Left Flank and
Combined Force Headquarters; Brigade tasked a counter-
IED team to deal with the issue, helicopters were sought,
an estimated time of arrival was sent back down and given
to the Afghans. One of their sergeants didn't fancy a wait
so he went round a corner, picked up a brick and threw it
on the bomb, which detonated. Thorpe rushed round the
corner expecting to see one less Afghan. The Sergeant was
emerging from the rubble, smiling. Apart from a burst
eardrum, he seemed happy. The counter-IED team were
stood-down.

★

The British Infantryman is primarily trained to close with
and kill the enemy. General McChrystal's July 2009
Counter Insurgency directive stated that 'support and
will of the population' and not the enemy was the campaign's centre of gravity. In light of this, the importance
attached to figuring out who exactly the people are became
a higher priority than it had been. McChrystal also pronounced: 'We will win this war.'

With a 'new' Area of Operations, Left Flank had to get
out amongst the people and figure out who their new
neighbours were. Loy Adera is a strictly agricultural area.
The main crops are poppy (carpeting the land and ready
for harvest when Left Flank arrived), wheat and maize.
Mostly, the ground is decently irrigated. There is no
industry, no regular employment nor regular income.
The people are subsistence farmers, though a few may
run improvised shops. The 20th century had filtered into
Loy Adera through the Kalashnikov, the 1.5 volt D Cell
battery and the occasional ride on or in something made by

Toyota; the 21st through the Nokia mobile phone. Apart from these few developments, Loy Adera, like much of rural Helmand, is in a similar state to the Highlands in 1744.

The people are a mixture of landowners, tenants and squatters. The issue of who owns what would develop into a key issue as Left Flank developed their understanding of the area. Another dynamic was the tribal mix with Barakzai, Noorzai and Balooch, who were the main blocks. The Company Intelligence Officer, Warrior Sergeant Major Dave Brettle, an immense Brummy from the Irish Guards and the last person on earth any suspect would choose for an interrogator, was told in training to expect tribalism to be the key to understanding any area. Yet, in Loy Adera, an area with little to fight over, it seemed the tribes got on, often lived in mixed *kalays* and intermarried, though in certain areas frictions were very evident, especially at the hyperlocal scale the campaign in Afghanistan is waged at.

Across Loy Adera in April 2010, there was a vortex of governance. Major Kitching described the people as 'ginger step-kids', as far as the Afghan Government was concerned. Nearby towns exerted some gravitational pull on the people. Those in eastern Loy Adera might look to Gereshk, those to the south to Lashkar Gah, while in the west people might consider themselves part of Nad-e-Ali. The problem was none of these districts wanted to take responsibility for the people of Loy Adera, despite Governor Mangal's directive to open the road through the area for the benefit of all Helmandis. In contrast to this indifference, the insurgents had treated Loy Adera as home turf. In order to keep Mars open, the insurgents would have to be pushed away from the route, which Left Flank could do overnight. Keeping them away would involve winning over the locals and showing them that governance would be better for them than insurgency; that it would not, as in the past, amount to corrupt Afghan forces and token gestures from the Provincial Governor. Major Kitching's secret weapon in achieving this was going to be a mechanic from Anglesey.

'I like the Jocks, I really do. But the racism . . .'

Being the only Welshman was always going to be hard for Sergeant David Jones, known universally as 'Taff'. Jones was a mechanic with the Royal Electrical and Mechanical Engineers in Cyprus six months before he arrived in Afghanistan. After years of garrison soldiering, Jones, 32, decided to go operational. His transition to sole representative of the military's newest unit, the Military Stabilisation and Support Group (MSSG), in Loy Adera happened 'sort of by mistake' after he volunteered for a job in Pakistan but ended up in Andover instead. The three-month training course he attended there was the strangest of his career. As a tri-service group, the MSSG attracts Royal Navy mess waiters, infantry sergeants-major and RAF flight lieutenants. In three months, those that need it are taught the basic patrolling skills that will keep them alive and ensure that they are not laughed out of Helmand. But the core of the course for every student is a download of what the international aid industry has been trying to get right since the Red Cross began in 1863, in order to teach students how to get the people in their area onside in order to defeat an insurgency. The military's arrival in this area has not put noses out of joint in the NGO sector. It has smashed them.

Sergeant Jones's first encounter with Left Flank was a meeting with Major Kitching in Bastion the night before they both flew to Loy Adera. They agreed that going into a 'new' area, it would be best to start small – wells rather than schools – and that the first priority would be meeting the people. The man he relieved in Loy Adera the next day

had been on three footpatrols in six weeks. 'Still,' thought
Jones, 'that's more than I've been on in my career.'

★

'No, John, you go down to Checkpoint South now and see
John Junior, and Gaz and me'll go on the patrol to the
north this afternoon. He's your son, man, go on,' said
Colour Sergeant Cameron on the morning of 13 April.

'Cheers, Hairy Back. I'll see yooz all in a couple,' said
Platoon Sergeant Major Lilley as he left Checkpoint
North's Ops Room. He threw on the body armour, which
was getting easier to wear each day, and his day-sack,
which certainly was lighter after he'd chucked half the kit
they'd had issued in Catterick, then he headed out the
gates and to the south. The poppy seemed to have grown
since they'd arrived a few days earlier. The insurgents had
a standing agreement with the farmers not to fight until
the harvest was in, which worked out well for both parties,
as it kept the locals happy and, through the cut the
insurgents would take, the poppy would help finance
another fighting season come May. Everyone felt sorry
for the poor squaddies coming next summer when Governor Mangal's Eradication Programme kicked in. This
April, at least, the locals had seemed friendly, even the
ones in the remoter parts of the locality who hadn't
encountered Isaf before. They'd seemed a bit surprised
to see the British soldiers, but were keen to talk. It was
only a few days in, but on all the familiarisation patrols the
whole area had seemed, well, nice.

After an uneventful few hours in fields and ditches, the
patrol walked back into Checkpoint North and stripped
out of their armour and combats. It had been good to see
John Junior, even if he did stink of the cigarettes Lilley
had told him to avoid. When Junior first joined Battalion,

everyone had asked him if he was Lilley's son; a year later they were coming up to Lilley and asking him if he was Junior's father, so the boy was clearly making a name for himself somehow and everyone's got to be a Guardsman once.

'Have you got the brews on then, Cammy? It's time for scoff,' said Lilley.

Colour Sergeant Cameron headed out the gate after lunch and Lilley made his way into the Ops Room. When the explosion came, about an hour later, it sounded to Lilley like it was right against the wall. In fact it was about one kilometre north and two men's lives had just changed forever.

Colour Sergeant Cameron's patrol was pretty routine. The eight men had cut across dry fields and finally reached the corner of a mosque right up on Route Mars. A local had approached Cameron and told him about an IED around the corner. After the lead man, Lance Sergeant Gary Jamieson moved forward to investigate with Cameron sticking inside the safe lane swept by the Vallon. When Jamieson trod on the IED before the one the local had pointed out, the blast took both his legs and an arm. The shrapnel from the device went straight into Cameron's head. Behind him, Lance Sergeant Ben Martin was unscathed. The three Guardsmen watching at the back of the patrol were on their first patrol in Helmand, on their second day away from Bastion. Something took over – later they mentioned Amputees in Action – and they got to work with tourniquets and dressings. Both casualties were responding, Jamieson mumbling incoherently, Cameron trying to rip the bandages from the gaping wound to the side of his skull. On such a small patrol, taking two casualties, especially two commanders, and then treating them, effectively ends any pretence at soldiering – security is forgotten and the men have to take the risk that the follow-up shoot they tell you about in training won't kick off and that compassion is the right response to what you hoped you'd never see.

In the Ops Room, Platoon Sergeant Major Lilley couldn't believe it was Cameron. After everything they'd been through together it seemed inconceivable that his friend would get hurt so badly so quickly. Not for the last time on the tour, Lilley looked at a Zap Number identifying the casualty and couldn't believe his eyes. The urgent task was to get men out to the patrol at once. Lance Sergeant Cammy MacDougall was already on it and out the gate, reaching the site less than ten minutes after the explosion. By the time MacDougall arrived, Lance Sergeant Martin's small team had largely dealt with the situation.

Updates came throughout the day. Both men had survived. Platoon Sergeant Major Lilley knew it would take a while to get morale up. That night at Left Flank's evening radio conference, Lilley gave the Company a consolidated report of what had happened.

'Two Zero Alpha – thanks for letting us know your side. The doctors up at Bastion want to know which Combat Medical Technician treated the casualties, over,' said Major Kitching.

'Seven Zero Alpha – that was just my young Team Medics here, over,' replied Lilley.

'Two Zero Alpha – Roger. Well, the doctors will be pretty surprised by that. Say well done to the guys who treated. They saved two lives today. We'll discuss TRiM in the morning but clearly getting to you along Route Mars isn't an option. Out to you.'

After the conference, Major Kitching went back to his laptop. Mars was clearly sown with IEDs and he'd have to devise a company-sized operation to clear and open it. 'After what happened today though, what the fuck are we going to find up there?' he thought as he returned to the endless email chains.

★

The IED had exploded on a spot on Mars that cut Left Flank in half. To the east lay 11 Platoon, 12 Platoon and Headquarters. West sat a devastated Fire Suport Group and 10 Platoon. Troops east of the choke-point were reliant on helicopters for all resupply and any link up between the two halves would be on foot. The dangers of that had been shown by the IED on 13 April.

Due to these risks, it was vital that foot-patrolling continued. To sit in defensive positions might protect Guardsmen in the short term but would cede ground to the insurgents rather than seize it from them. As always, the truly vital ground was the people of Loy Adera. Sergeant Jones, the Welsh stabilisation representative, set up a weekly *shura* at Patrol Base Nahidullah and after the Company Commander had introduced himself, Jones told the assembled locals that he was the man to see to sort out compensation. He then started getting out of his base and seeing what the people needed. At first, a foot patrol carrying full kit was a culture shock for the mechanic.

Jones's main initial effort was trying to identify possible Cash for Works projects in the area. A quick and relatively cheap win in terms of influence, Cash for Works is designed to fix or provide pretty basic amenities to the locals. Much of it can be done by the locals, but some projects, such as drilling for wells, require contractors from elsewhere in Helmand. Only two projects were in production when Left Flank arrived in Loy Adera.

An early area of success was around Checkpoint Said Abdul. Second Lieutenant Pearson had quickly organised a *shura* through his interpreter in the local mosque. There, the three leaders of the area made themselves known. These men were the elders of their *kalays*, which were named after them. The people who choose to live in these *kalays* do so as feudal tenants of the elder, agree to respect the elder's voice, and all work done is for the elder, including any small stabilisation projects. Pearson outlined what Isaf and the Afghan Government had to offer and the locals appeared informed about this, especially the stabilisation side. They wanted to know what the local security plan was and what the outsiders would bring to the neighbourhood. Pearson asked them what they'd like and promised to tell Sergeant Jones and get Cash for Works projects moving. Sergeant Gibson stood beside Pearson. He looked around the room and tried to figure out which of the men were insurgents scoping their new opposite numbers.

Within a few weeks, Sergeant Jones had agreed a Cash for Works plan for Said Abdul. Contractors from Lashkar Gah would drill eleven wells for the use of the whole community and three mosque upgrades alongside a community centre would get funding, pending approval from the relevant bureaucrats in the Afghan Land Registry office in Lashkar Gah. The three main landowners in the area would be paid to dig new irrigation ditches across their estates and good bridges put across existing channels for improved access. The local shopkeeper agreed to three new micro-shops opening in the area to sell elementary necessities. The hope was that once Route Trident was fully functioning, these shops would renew the local economy.

Up in the Vehicle Checkpoints, 12 Platoon also got on with getting to know the people. The risk of leaving six men in a small outpost caused much concern. Like any innovation, the system had its detractors. It seemed that the further people were from the Vehicle Checkpoints, the more worried they were. The men living it just got on with the job. Major Kitching accepted that it was risky, and the rumour that the Taliban's Quetta *shura* had said that a strategic aim for 2010 was a checkpoint overrun in Helmand didn't help. 'But there's a significant element in Counter Insurgency that is taking risks to get things done,' he explained to detractors. These were usually mollified after seeing the Vehicle Checkpoints for themselves and speaking to the sanguine young men who manned them. To mitigate the risk, the Vehicle Checkpoints were given a Mastiff to act as a mobile reserve rather than relying on crashing men out from Nahidullah in a hurry, but the best way of getting around the risk was getting out on foot patrol and winning the people over.

At first, the people around the tiny bases weren't quite sure what to make of Isaf troops. The platoon had relieved a group of soldiers who had lacked sufficient resources to mount regular patrols. As this meant that the area had not been dominated by Isaf, the men in the little bases found themselves in an area rich in IEDs. While the unofficial ceasefire during poppy season might have kept the area quiet in terms of small arms, the area's insurgents were happy to sow bombs for their new guests. At first 12 Platoon went around the edges of the poppy fields to keep the locals happy but when they found a number of new IEDs emplaced on these routes, they started to go through the fields. After a few days, they found IEDs in the fields. Clearly, the insurgents were in the area and watching the patrols but choosing to stick to the ceasefire. The response to this was to try and get the message across that Isaf had more to offer than simply bombs, a number of which would claim the lives of civilians over the next six months. One quick win was offering medical assistance. Tannoys broadcast messages to the locals that any sick or injured civilians would always find help at the excellent Medical

Centre established in Patrol Base Nahidullah and staffed by Sergeant Paul Brader, Royal Army Medical Corps, Lance Corporal Jimmy Moffat, Scots Guards, and others. In six months, this small team would deal with over 600 incidents of every imaginable permutation. The stabilisation message also got out and locals were coming to the gates of the Vehicle Checkpoints most days with suggestions for schemes. Sergeant Jones approved a number of mosque upgrades consisting of amplifiers, carpets and copies of the Koran, as well as a few new wells. Further foot patrols went out, sometimes two kilometres from Patrol Base Nahidullah, sat down with locals and explained the plan for the area, then politely asked them who they were, the name of their *kalay* and what they might like in the future. The closer villages were to the outposts, the better they seemed to respond to these overtures. The *mirab* (the man in charge of irrigation in the area) living in the *kalay* next to Vehicle Checkpoint Pirooz, for instance, was a regular visitor. All this information was then fed back to Warrior Sergeant Major Brettle's Intelligence, Influence and Human Terrain Cell, to map the people further, and then to Sergeant Jones's list of possible Cash for Works projects. The money, after all, wasn't going to spend itself.

Getting used to their housemates had taken some time, not least because of the language barrier. Some interpreters were good, while for others, the Guardsmen felt they needed an interpreter for the interpreter. Cultural differences also presented a barrier. The first group of Counter Narcotics Police took a novel approach to counter-narcotics operations: consumption on a heroic scale. This made them by turns lethargic and skittish. On Thursdays, the younger men would dress up in feminine clothing and put flowers in their hair. The smallest member of one group wasn't even allowed on patrol and was, in the pungent opinion of Lance Corporal Campbell, purely deployed forward for 'stags and shags'. These excesses would have to be confronted if Left Flank was to succeed in the partnering side of their mission.

Despite being the other side of the line of acceptable behaviour in the British Army, the Counter Narcotics Police (CNP) were good at stopping and searching vehicles – their primary role – and were used to Helmand ways since they had been policing the province for six years. They also provided a link with the local population.

'They say on the news that partnering puts an Afghan face on it, which it does, but this place gets all the best intelligence from the locals through the CNP. Loads of people won't talk to us because this is just the Crusades to them: white Christians in their land. But they'll talk to the CNP. All the intelligence we get is through the CNP Commander because he knows the locals in the area by name. If he wasn't here, they wouldn't call us at night and they wouldn't come in during the day because they'd be seen. By which time, we could have walked over and trodden on the IED the informer would have told a CNP Commander about,' said Lance Corporal Paul Ramsay about the area around Vehicle Checkpoint Rabiullah when I caught up with him.

A quiet start to the tour had given 12 Platoon the opportunity to get used to the heat and the weight of patrols. The fields had been flooded for the poppy, so even short patrols became doubly exhausting, as men dragged themselves through cool mud. Early apprehension, especially about the IED threat, meant that the patrols were doubly slow, as Vallon drills were carried out meticulously. Three-kilometre patrols could take as long as five hours and always ended in exhaustion. For commanders, patrolling was mentally gruelling as well – always trying to think where the likely choke-points for IEDs or ambushes were and attempting to think a few steps into any possible scenario. The slow start had also meant that the men had got to know each other very well, especially in the Vehicle Checkpoints, where there was little choice other than to get on and find something, anything, to laugh about. Life in the little forts could be stifling, though.

'It was nice at times to just get out and go for a wander about,' said Lance Corporal Kenny Wallace.

However, while the poppies were undoubtedly beautiful and the people seemed friendly enough, this wasn't the tour they'd expected. Guardsman Dodd spoke for many when he expressed disappointment in how the tour was going.

'I thought it was going to be stuff like Ross Kemp – where they're fighting and all that, but it's boring, to be honest,' he said.

'Guys, I think you really need to be careful what you wish for,' said Second Lieutenant Tulloch.

It was an attitude I'd encounter a few times in Helmand – and one I succumbed to. Running into a group of men who had been through the wash a few times, the refrain was they'd be happy not to fire their weapons again. They'd proved themselves and were counting down the weeks, talking about home. A group who had just arrived in theatre were keen to get out and have that first brush. The old term 'blooding' is wrong; it's more about testing and tasting. I had no idea how I'd react – unarmed, largely untrained and with a habitual fear of cricket balls (let alone Kalashnikovs). The aspect that most worried me was, bizarrely, 'What are you actually going to do in a firefight? Everyone else has a job, as they have a weapon. You have a notebook. What are you actually going to do?' What boyish vanity, to focus on not looking like an idiot rather than one's competence to survive. Perhaps that particular thought process was a displacement activity of note. The

desire was also there to put one's mind at rest and say
afterwards: 'Yes, I've been shot at; I can sort of handle it.
Fuck me, I wanted that? Jesus, man.' Afghanistan provides an answer to the question many had been asking
since we picked up that first toy gun.

2–13 May

Major Kitching had almost planned the operation to clear
Mars. The only niggling concern was leaving the area
around Patrol Base Nahidullah, which was finally reaching completion, and the Vehicle Checkpoints pretty undermanned for the ten days of the operation. The area did
seem pretty permissive, though – a bazaar, some weeks
800-strong, was thriving outside the Patrol Base, the
Sunday *shura* in the base was well attended, Sergeant
Jones was making good headway with about half a dozen
local elders and no one had attacked the Vehicle Checkpoints. They would have to look after themselves for the
duration of Opertion Zamaray Zeya, which would begin
on 2 May. The plan was to move into the area where the
IED had detonated a fortnight earlier, seize a compound
and turn it into a permanent base, robbing the insurgents
of a key piece of ground. With the choke-point isolated,
the counter-IED team would begin a painstaking two-
kilometre search from Checkpoint Said Abdul westwards
to the new base, which would be called Checkpoint
Inzargul. The operation would take as long as it took
the counter-IED team to defeat each device they encountered. Kitching now realised that the area Colour Sergeant
Cameron had patrolled into was the insurgents' key defensive position from the old days when their front line
faced west towards Checkpoint North and Tapa Paraang.
To seize it and then turn it into his base would be a blow to

the insurgents in Loy Adera. In doing this he would be continuing the work of one of his predecessors and friends, Major Sean Birchall of the Welsh Guards.

Major Birchall had brought IX Company Welsh Guards to Basharan in March 2009. Insurgents contested their presence but Birchall had seen an opportunity to create a protected community at Basharan, a few kilometres south-west of Loy Adera near Tapa Paraang. He had pushed the front line out onto Route Orion, creating Checkpoints North and South to keep the insurgents away from Basharan. The centrepiece of his plan was Basharan School, which had been closed by insurgents. Birchall sensed an appetite for education in the area and began work to get the school reopened. On a regular patrol along Orion, Birchall's Jackal struck an IED and flipped, killing him. He left a widow and a son. The school was eventually opened by The Queen's Company Grenadier Guards and continued to educate in the summer of 2010. By then, Basharan had become the model Birchall had sought to create and Right Flank were capitalising on his success, sinking wells and proceeding with further stabilisation work rather than fending off insurgents. Within a few weeks of arriving in Checkpoint North, the Scots Guards had been approached by an ex-Mujahedeen. He had told them the local insurgents' numbers and hideouts and pointed out a number of IEDs similar to the one that Lance Sergeant Jamieson had struck. Asked why he was helping Isaf, the man simply said: 'These Taliban offer nothing but trouble. If the bombs are cleared and you get rid of these men, my son can get to the school in Basharan.' This demonstrable example of what became known to the Scots Guards as the 'Sean Birchall Effect' showed how smart consent-winning projects would yield security for all much more effectively than bombs and bullets. If Left Flank could begin to replicate in Loy Adera the success

Birchall had created in Basharan, then their tour could be considered a success. The first step to doing this was clearing Mars.

*

Before dawn on 2 May, men were on the move towards Inzargul. The counter-IED team and a search dog had flown into Checkpoint North the night before, along with Tac and some of 11 and 12 Platoon who had trained in Vallon work to a high-enough standard to qualify as an All Arms Search Team. This was commanded by Company Sergeant Major Lawrie and worked to the counter-IED specialists and the dog's nose. Going in with them were eight men from 10 Platoon under Lance Sergeant McDougall to garrison Checkpoint Inzargul. Jackals from the Fire Support Group were out on high ground providing support if the insurgents tried to take the 35 men on.

The patrol into Inzargul went well. The village itself was deserted. To Warrior Sergeant Major Brettle, it seemed like an exercise.

'It was like we had moved into Copehill Down on Salisbury Plain. It was very quiet.'

The plan of punching into the choke-point from an unexpected direction and then holding it had achieved surprise. Once Left Flank's search team had cleared the compound chosen to act as Checkpoint Inzargul, Tac moved in and began fortifying it with makeshift sangar positions. The search teams then turned to Mars.

For Guardsman Maclachlan his experiences as Vallon man in 12 Platoon had been pretty dull so far. In the poppy fields, he would get the occasional tone saying his detector had found something, would dig around and inevitably not find anything. When he got a double tone on his Vallon on the morning of 2 May outside the ruined mosque on Mars, he paid a bit more attention. He was yards from where the IED of 13 April had exploded. Dropping onto his chest, he kept his eyes on where the Vallon had been when it started beeping. He drew his bayonet and began conducting his IED confirmation drill through the rock-hard ground. He was careful not to disturb the suspected device that could end him. After a few minutes, he could see the Pressure Plate designed for him to stand on and called over the Advanced EOD Operator to deal with it.

A few minutes later, a bearded bald man appeared suddenly out of some bushes, surprising Maclachlan and the specialist.

'Who the fuck are you?' shouted Maclachlan.

The man smiled and gestured that he wanted to cross the minefield.

'No. No. No cross. IED. IED. Stop,' said Maclachlan, using what he hoped was the international body language for 'blow up'.

'No IED, no IED. OK,' said the man.

'There's an IED right there. You're going to blow us all up. Stop!' pleaded Maclachlan.

'No IED,' the man said again.

'All right. Wait a minute,' said Maclachlan. He pulled back to what the experts assured him was a safe distance and waved the man on. The man got onto Mars and then nimbly walked right through a minefield that would yield six low-metal-content IEDs that day.

With the choke-point at Inzargul cleared, an exhausted search dog, along with the counter-IED team and the Left Flank search team, headed back to Checkpoint North for the night. Inside Isaf's newest outpost, the garrison kept an eye up and down Mars to prevent any reseeding of the route. Over the next few days, a number of locals started coming into Checkpoint Inzargul saying they were the villagers who had lived in the nearby compounds. The insurgents had kicked them out two years earlier to turn the village into a defensive position. Inzargul itself had been the insurgents' headquarters, they said. Major Kitching offered to assign search teams to their compounds once he had cleared Mars. One of the locals then offered to help Left Flank with this. Under cover of darkness the night before the search teams (now flown to Checkpoint Said Abdul in order to begin the clearance east–west to Inzargul) began the operation's second phase, the local walked down Mars. In his hands, he carried some stones that had been sprayed yellow by a Guardsman. Whenever he walked past a site where he suspected there was an IED along the one-kilometre route to Said Abdul, he dropped a stone. He dropped 14 stones.

This coup not only speeded the mission up but certainly saved lives. All the devices recovered under the painted stones by the counter-IED teams were built by a single talented bomb-maker and were low-metal-content, meaning that they would have been more difficult to detect. The clearance was still painstaking work.

The teams were out of the gates of Checkpoint Said Abdul before dawn and back at dusk after long hot days of nerve-shredding work. At night, the weather was the worst of the tour, with dust storms and rain eating into the few hours of sleep the men could grab. After the shock of losing a key base at the start of the operation, the insurgents began to fight back on the first day of this second phase. A pattern of shoots onto Checkpoint Inzargul from the north began and a sharpshooter took on the search teams. Taking fire while clearing IEDs is not ideal. The teams would hear a high-velocity single shot over their heads, get down and wait for ten minutes and then start work again. After a few minutes, another shot would sing out. The day was very frustrating. After some time, a Scots Guards sniper identified the shooter and killed him at 600 metres. The shots stopped. The Afghan National Army's contribution to the operation was also wearying. Try as Second Lieutenant Cowdry and Lance Sergeant Thorpe might, the Afghans refused to soldier past lunchtime and invariably abandoned their part in the outer cordon for the search teams at around noon. This meant Guardsmen had to be dragged away from searching to bolster the infantry screen for the bomb specialists. Some days, the counter-IED teams would clear only 100 metres of ground. Even though the devices had been pointed out to them by the local, every inch of Mars had to be fingertip-searched (literally) in case he had missed any. What slowed the search down even more was that the amount of shrapnel along Mars set the Vallons off constantly. Each tone had to be fully examined with bayonet and brush. At times, the search teams must have felt like combat-archaeologists unearthing rusted scraps of war from a road that had clearly been fought over many times in Afghanistan's history.

In Catterick, Guardsman Wannuwat, 12 Platoon's Thai Guardsman, was a store-man – hardly the most glamorous role in the Scots Guards. In Helmand, he was a lead Vallon man and had already helped find two IEDs near the Vehicle Checkpoints before the Mars clearance began. On Mars he found another three, one less than Guardsman Menzi Bhembe, who had six by the end of the operation. Each time one of them shouted 'Find!' to the counter-IED specialists, the other would add it to the tally and calculate how many he was behind or in front of his rival. Bizarrely, many men picked as Vallon-operators were possessive about their dangerous new job.

'I was shaken up with the first one I found, then I was all right and I got used to it. I'm glad to find one because I've saved a lot of people's lives – and my own as well. You get excited afterwards, when it gets blown up. It makes it worth it,' Wannuwat said.

The rest of 12 Platoon labelled Wannuwat a 'ninja' because of his Vallon skill. No one had suspected the store-man had it in him.

On the first day of the second phase, Second Lieutenant Will Tulloch in Patrol Base Nahidullah had been tasked with getting a Mastiff crew together and providing fire support in case trouble brewed up on Mars.

'Sergeant Wood, we're heading out for the day and probably a night on over-watch. Could you get a Mastiff ready, please?' he said.

'Aye, sir. Nae dramas,' replied Lance Sergeant Steven Wood.

With a Guardsman driving, the Mastiff headed along Mars to the spot west of Said Abdul where the counter-IED teams were working. Luckily, Lance Sergeant Wood had read between the lines of his orders and anticipated that once on site, the Mastiff would be stuck until the operation ended. A week later, they returned to Patrol Base Nahidullah with mangy beards.

Lance Sergeant Wood had packed fags, water, rations and shit bags to keep them going for a week, so the basics were sorted. Beyond that, Second Lieutenant Tulloch brought paper to write home with, a few magazines, some board games and a Perudo set, which failed to get much traction with Wood or the driver. Their job was to ensure that the route stayed clear overnight. 'The insurgents have a good stock of IEDs and access to plenty of components and they're easily made. We could go out and clear IEDs all day, but unless you've got permanent eyes-on afterwards, the area will just be reseeded, probably the following night,' explained Warrior Sergeant Major Brettle to Tulloch before the operation began. This meant long nights on stag for the three men in the Mastiff. Four nights out of the seven they spent out there were in the same spot, about 500 metres from Inzargul and Said Abdul. The men would do two hours on stag and then four hours off. In front of them were dense reeds, to the left a treeline and on the right a stream with bushes along its bank. 'Oh, for fuck's sake!' thought Lance Sergeant Wood as he looked through his night-sight and tried to make out any movement hour after hour, night after night.

During the day, one of them would be on the gun scanning for insurgents and providing intimate support for the search teams. After a week, their world had become this little metal box – reeking of fags and a bin bag full of empty rations sachets and full shit-bags.

'It sounds shit, but it was actually all right. The week flew by,' said Lance Sergeant Wood.

The Guardsman who had driven them had a different opinion. A few weeks later he went home on R&R. At the end of his fortnight, he failed to show up for his flight back.

Clearly life on Mars wasn't for everyone.

*

The Royal Engineer Field Troop finished the build on Patrol Base Nahidullah and left Captain Barne to move what was left of Headquarters and 12 Platoon into the large fortified position. The sappers then split and while some went to Checkpoint Said Abdul to construct an external sangar to keep eyes-on Mars in that area, another team went to Checkpoint Inzargul and began a super-sangar. Twenty feet high, the watchtower would command Mars west to the junction with Orion and east towards Said Abdul. Its completion coincided with the arrival at Inzargul of the search teams who had found a total of 16 IEDs. On 13 May an opening ceremony was held at Checkpoint Yellow 14 and local media cameras recorded an Afghan Commander cutting a strip of mine tape strung between two steel pickets. Afghan soldiers provided a cordon while Major Kitching and Right Flank's Major Lindsay-German smiled and let the Afghan face get front and centre. The compounds around Checkpoint Inzargul were then searched for IEDs and the locals moved in. Lance Sergeant MacDougall was tasked to remain in Inzargul for the first month. He was told to keep the good will of his new neighbours.

Left Flank's Jackals spent the followings days tearing up and down Mars to make the point to the locals that the route was open. The message quickly filtered through. The bazaar outside Patrol Base Nahidullah started to tail off until eventually just one man with a cart of melons turned up but didn't find any customers. The initial assessment was that insurgent intimidation had stopped the locals going to a bazaar so close to an Isaf base, but then Mars became busier as people made their way to the larger and cheaper markets of Lashkar Gah and Gereshk.

'That operation was a massive fuck-you to the insurgents, boys – we've cleared your IEDs and we've got your compound and now we hold it. Look at this fucking road now; it's busier than the M-fucking-25. Well done, troops,' said Lance Corporal Ramsay a few days later as he looked out from Vehicle Checkpoint Rabiullah. What he also noticed on the top of the vehicles were tubs of freshly harvested opium resin. Ramsay was a Scots Guards original – loved by the men he commanded and listened to, though a taste for drama had kept him in junior rank. A scar on his cheek spoke of a bottling and his latest demotion was due to a legendary incident on a stop-over in Houston Airport on the way back from Belize. A few drinks had turned into a few too many and he'd attempted a joyride in a car dropping off passengers at the terminal.

He spent six weeks in the County Jail wearing an orange jumpsuit. The story doesn't relate quite what the other prisoners made of the Glaswegian.

'Army didnae even pay for ma flight hame,' he'd tell everyone.

None of that, of course, mattered in Helmand because he was a first-class soldier.

While freedom of movement for locals was the main aim of the operation, what mattered most to the men of Left Flank was the supply column that rolled down Mars bringing everything they had lacked for the past six weeks. Mars open also meant trips down to the Main Operating Base in Lashkar Gah for the soldiers. Here they could stock up on cold juice, real cigarettes and a decent meal followed by a gorge on Facebook. One disadvantage of a run to 'Lash Vegas' was the obligatory haircut and sideburn trim before men left Loy Adera. Another disadvantage was what happened after you got back to Left Flank. Lance Sergeant Wood was one of the first who got down to Lash. After his week in the Mastiff, the steak, chips and fresh vegetables all looked brilliant but he could hardly finish his plate. Fresh milk in his tea tasted wrong after the powdered whitener he'd been using for a month and a half. When he got back to Patrol Base Nahidullah, he was violently sick.

The discrepancy between life in the main bases and out in the platoons was brought home whenever men transited back from Loy Adera. Lance Sergeant Leyden was called back to Camp Bastion. In camp one day someone asked to borrow his knife.

'Aye, help yourself, fellah,' said Leyden.

'It's pretty blunt,' the man said, running his thumb against the blade.

'Sorry about that, I've been cutting up plastic bottles,' said Leyden.

'What for?' asked the man.

'To make plates and cups,' said Leyden.

'You fucking what? Do you have nae plates?'

'No. Been waiting for a supply column for six weeks. We've improvised,' said Leyden.

★

Major Kitching was happy with the clearance of Mars. It was the sort of operation he would struggle to mount again as the R&R plot kicked in and his boys started filtering out of theatre. The focus for the past three weeks had been planning for, gearing up to and executing the operation. This had left the area around the Vehicle Checkpoints undermanned and unable to patrol in depth in their neighbourhoods. The insurgents had noticed.

11–27 May

The seven men looked a bit dodgy and it was no surprise when one of them raised a Kalashnikov at the evening foot patrol mounted near Vehicle Checkpoint Rabiullah on 11 May. Darting for cover, Guardsman Christopher Blackburn struck an IED. Quite how he got off the ground with all his limbs was anyone's guess but 'fucking lucky' was the assessment at Guardsman level, a possible partial-detonation caused by poor bomb-making the official line. The patrol had gone out to conduct an assessment on a compound that had been lit up with RPGs by the Counter Narcotics Police in Vehicle Checkpoint Rabiullah two days earlier.

The Afghans had been out on Mars picking up supplies when their commander had seen something suspicious down the route running south-east away from the base. Grabbing his machine gun, he had sprinted off, followed by his men, and begun spraying a treeline. A few rounds had come back towards the Vehicle Checkpoint and the men in the sangar responded. Two days later, on 10 May, three bursts of inaccurate fire flew over Rabiullah and the Counter Narcotics Police responded with four RPGs. It was to investigate the damage done that the patrol went out on 11 May.

The armed, or 'kinetic', side of activity around the Vehicle Checkpoints and Patrol Base Nahidullah was only one part of the picture. With so many troops around Inzargul, the insurgents had moved into the nascent protected communities and began intimidating locals. The number of elders turning up to Sergeant Jones's Sunday *shuras* began to drop off. The *mirab* near Vehicle Checkpoint Pirooz was badly beaten one night because of his frequent interaction with Isaf and Afghan forces. Even with the opening of Mars accounting for much of the drop-off in the use of the local bazaar, reports of verbal threats about an attack on the bazaar filtered into the Intelligence Cell, further confirming the feeling that the locals were being heavily intimidated.

When Second Lieutenant Tulloch returned from his sojourn in the Mastiff on Mars and began foot-patrolling again, he noticed the change in the area. Where once locals had come up and talked pretty freely, now they scattered for their compounds and kept battened down as his patrols walked through. The poppy was also down. On 17 May, Tulloch took a large foot patrol to the south of Vehicle Checkpoint Ranaa. Platoon Sergeant Lee Paxton led a second multiple and they were coming to the end of the patrol when they came across a man in a field carrying a mirror and a copy of the Koran. Paxton, his interpreter, Lance Sergeants Leyden and Dodds and Guardsman

Mears went over to him. They were then joined by Lance Corporal Jones from the Royal Military Police. He began questioning the man.

'Guys, the atmospherics are really going south here. I reckon we should wrap things up with the fella in the field and head off now,' said Tulloch over the radio.

'Aye, roger, sir,' replied Paxton.

The man had said he was just a farmer, and they turned back and started walking towards the road where Tulloch's men were.

'The boss really needs to calm down. This has happened before and nothing's developed,' thought Lance Sergeant Leyden as he walked back.

The first burst of machine gun fire rippled out from the treeline and threw them all to the ground. Lying in the open, they looked for cover in vain. Tulloch's team dropped into a ditch as they took fire from another direction in a classic scissors-shaped ambush.

'Two Five Alpha – contact: wait out,' he said onto the Company net.

Then he started to try and figure out what to do. He looked around and saw his Guardsmen all looking at him with expressions that said, 'What are we going to do now, then?' Though he'd been in contact with the Royal Welsh in April, this was the first time he'd had to command. Through his earpiece he heard Paxton.

'Right! Lance Corporal Jones reckons he's been shot.'

'Roger.'

In the field, a round from the second burst had sliced through Lance Corporal Jones's ankle, neatly bisecting the area of flesh between the bone and Achilles tendon. The other men were pinned down. Each time they tried to take a knee to identify the firing point, they received a burst for their trouble. Even if they could have spotted the gunmen, the men with SA80 rifles all had stoppages as soon as the contact began. They would fire one round and then have a stoppage, have to cock the weapon manually, then fire another. Everyone started shouting 'stoppage' at once. It was unbelievable. Luckily, Guardsman Mears's machine gun was functioning, and he could suppress the treeline, which was only 50 metres from where he was lying. He then saw a gunman at the corner of a compound and killed him. Further fire came from the treeline.

'Sir, you're going to need to start suppressing here. I need to get this casualty extracted back to you,' said Paxton.

'On it. Guys, extract back with me to the bund line and then rapid fire on that treeline,' said Tulloch.

He was rather amazed at his Guardsmen. At Sandhurst and the Infantry Battle School at Brecon, everyone was an officer in training and, as such, rather enjoyed questioning your orders to show the Directing Staff that they had a tactical brain. Here the Guardsmen would move where he told them, shoot where he told them and do it all rather calmly and quietly.

Once the friendly rounds started pinging the treeline, Sergeant Paxton could make his way to the casualty with Lance Sergeant Leyden. At first they couldn't find him. Lance Corporal Jones, justifiably terrified, didn't even want to put his arm up to tell them where he was. Eventually his shouting led them to his prone body.

'We will get you out of here. Where have you been shot?' asked Paxton.

'Ankle,' said Jones.

'Oh, right. It looks all right – not too much blood but we'll have a dressing on. Chrissy?' said Paxton

'Aye, Pax. Do you want morphine?' asked Leyden.

'No, I'm all right. I'm just fucking scared.'

'Good lad. How much do you weigh?' asked Leyden.

'Fifteen stone.'

'Reckon you'll be doing some crawling then, fellah,' said Leyden – 15 stone, plus three stone of kit and their own meant the pair would be carrying over ten stone apiece.

'Chrissy, we'll take his kit to the bund line where Mr Tulloch is and then come back for him. Corporal Jones, we'll be back in a mo. Try crawling to the bund line as much as you can. Doddsy, Mears: rapid fire. Right then, Chrissy,' said Paxton. The two of them stood up, picked up Jones's rifle and kit and started walking backwards, putting single rounds into the likely firing point as Jones crawled back. They then turned and dashed back the 50 remaining metres to the bund line, dropped the kit and ran back to Jones. Grabbing the shoulder straps of his webbing, they dragged him face down through the mud to cover.

'Pax, I've been shot in the leg,' said Lance Sergeant Dodds on the radio.

'Fuck's sake! Can you move?' replied Paxton.

'Yes.'

'Get on with it, then. Bring Mears, too.'

Dodds and Mears crawled for the bund line under cover.

'Where have you been shot? There's no blood,' said Lance Sergeant Leyden.

'In my leg, I think,' replied Dodds.

'Can you walk?'

'I reckon so.'

'Right, you take Corporal Jones back along the road. The Mastiff's pushing down and will meet you,' said Paxton.

'He's left his fucking pack in the field,' said Leyden.

'Aye, I know,' said Paxton.

'Right, dirty dash time,' said Leyden, stripping off his day-sack.

'Grenade launchers – on the treeline now, rest of you chuck any smokes you've got too. Rapid fire once

Chrissy breaks cover. All right?' asked Paxton.

'Aye,' said Leyden and set off into the smoke.

'Rapid fire!' shouted Paxton.

Less than a minute later, Leyden came back through the smoke with the pack – it contained sensitive kit that, had it fallen into the wrong hands, could have assisted the insurgents. As he ran, most of the fire was going towards the insurgents, he later said, modestly. But they'd put a fair few rounds his way, too.

'Sergeant Paxton, we'll start extracting now. The Mastiff has the casualties. I reckon we need to get out of the road and into that stream. It's 800 metres to Ranaa,' said Second Lieutenant Tulloch over the net.

As the patrol pulled back, the insurgents followed, harassing them all the way as they fought against a stiff current in the stream. It took 40 minutes to get to Vehicle Checkpoint Ranaa. Inside they found Dodds stripped off. His thigh was bruised black. A round had passed through his map pocket, just grazing the skin. The impact, he said, had felt like being hit hard with a cricket bat. Discussing how the contact started over bottles of warm water, Second Lieutenant Tulloch and Sergeant Paxton came to some conclusions: the man in the field was possibly a come-on, as he'd been praying to the east (away from Mecca) while watching them and his mirror was bound to attract attention. The insurgents had probably hoped they'd continue the patrol towards the treeline – further into the ambush's killing zone – once the Isaf commander took the bait and went to investigate who the man was signalling to. Tulloch's instincts on the atmospherics had been right and it was lucky they'd turned round when they did. 'More fool me!' thought Leyden when he remembered thinking Tulloch too cautious.

★

The next day, Major Kitching put out a pair of large fighting patrols drawn from 11 and 12 Platoons mixed in with a multiple of Afghan soldiers to clear the areas north of Vehicle Checkpoint Ranaa. The patrol turned into a rolling four-hour gunfight only a few hundred metres from Patrol Base Nahidullah. The fight began with hundreds of rounds fired in the direction of the two patrols while they were moving along Mars.

The troops had learned from Guardsman Blackburn's experience the previous week and lay in the open rather than dive for obvious cover where a bomb might lurk.

'It's completely against your human nature. Instead of crawling somewhere to safety you have to stay in the killing zone. They might be firing at you but they're firing over your head and you might dive down and that's where they want you to go – next to the wall where there's an IED,' said Lance Sergeant Leyden.

'It's not pleasant being pinned down with rounds flying everywhere and you're the one who has to come up with the plan to get people out,' said Second Lieutenant Tulloch.

The options open to Tulloch were constrained by the British Rules of Engagement. Card Alpha, the Rules of Engagement that the Scots Guards deployed under, retains soldiers' 'inherent right to self-defence' under British Law. However, as General McChrystal lay down in his Counter Insurgency directive: 'We must fight with great discipline and tactical patience. We must balance our pursuit of the enemy with our efforts to minimise the loss of innocent civilian life. Every Afghan civilian death damages the strategic effect of our operations.' This means that the initial action on having found the enemy through taking incoming fire (firing back with vigour in order to suppress the enemy and figure out what to do next) is tempered, as soldiers must identify gunmen before returning fire. This is very difficult during daylight when dealing with murder holes and men moving along rat-runs and treelines.

With the enemy found, the next idea in the commander's head will be to fix him in position with fire support – mortars, artillery and air-support are the traditional options. However, in Helmand, the commander must think, 'Can I, should I, must I?' before requesting fire support (which will have to be approved by Brigade if it is anything heavier than an 81mm mortar round).

Lastly, a Brecon-trained commander will want to strike the enemy, possibly by sending one section left or right flanking, then assaulting the position with the remainder of his men and plenty of smoke for cover. In Helmand, with the possibility of an IED field between the ambush site and the ambushers, a commander has to think very carefully before doing this. An additional complication produced by partnering with Afghan forces on foot patrols where the individual order of march alternates between Glaswegians and Tajiks, is how to coordinate a section attack considering the communication issues and range of abilities.

Faced with these conditions, many commanders choose to simply 'break contact' and withdraw after inflicting what damage they can on the insurgents within the constraints Counter Insurgency places on them.

Many contacts in Helmand, therefore, occur on ground and terms set by the insurgents, who have confidence in Isaf Rules of Engagement and hem them in with the IED threat. The fight then ends with both sides heading home for the night and cleaning their weapons before the next engagement. McChrystal's 'great discipline and tactical patience' translates into lying in a field, looking for a near invisible enemy and relying on his shoddy marksmanship and the effectiveness of your camouflage to keep you alive.

This is what is meant by 'courageous restraint' and it is very demanding for the men on the ground. It is, however, Counter Insurgency, and marching in good order into enemy fire is something Scots Guardsmen have been paid to do for several centuries. It also shows how such a conflict can only be won by appealing to the people. Endless fights with the insurgents, thrilling as they may be initially, will not win the campaign. Civilian casualties, besides the obvious human tragedy, will damage Isaf's campaign at a strategic level. Insurgents know this and will try to tease out overreaction – using their enemy's superior firepower for their own ends. It is a cunning tactic that has somewhat neutered soldiers' ability to call in heavy support. For commanders to get their men to understand this is demanding. As the resources available to Left Flank ramped up over the tour, the ability to absorb insurgent fire and then strike back surgically increased and courageous restraint made more sense. Throughout the tour, though, the tactics dictated to the men in the rifle platoons put them at significant risk.

Unlike on the day of Lance Corporal Jones's wounding, what Second Lieutenant Tulloch and the other Isaf troops did have out with them that day were enough Afghans to get them out of trouble. The Afghan National Army have a more relaxed attitude to Rules of Engagement and are happy to fire at will in the general direction of the insurgents and win the firefight through weight rather than accuracy of fire. This makes them very popular with Guardsmen in a contact. Some of them are also undoubtedly courageous and skilled soldiers. Lance Sergeant Leyden saw the Afghans around him using their grenade launchers and rockets to great effect. Without even flipping up the sights, they were able to place rounds accurately into likely firing positions. Intelligence later suggested they killed four insurgents that day. Their casual attitude to safety was the only concern the British soldiers had about their partners in contact, especially after they saw some soldiers cutting around camp with faces blackened with the back-blast of RPGs.

'The ANA are awesome. They're a bit crazy like, but they're good with the Vallon and the ground-sign and will find IEDs. The firepower they've got – you're never going to lose a firefight. Any patrol, I'd go with them without a shadow of a doubt,' said Lance Sergeant Wood.

The Afghans' fire control was cavalier, perhaps callous, considering the civilians in the area. Left Flank tried everything to get them to check their fire in fights but, as ever, it was their country.

For Lance Sergeant Thorpe, the Afghan National Army's Adviser, patrolling with them was hard work, especially trying to make them stick to the utter fundamentals drilled into British soldiers in training, such as sticking inside the lanes marked safe by Vallon men. Afghan soldiers would regularly wander off from a patrol, perhaps to pick up a watermelon from a field. If they did step on a device, the blast and shrapnel could injure other soldiers in the patrol – Afghan and British.

'Listen, it might not happen this time, but next time you might not be so lucky, so stay in the Vallon lane,' Thorpe told the Afghans through his interpreter. The Afghan's wild ammunition use also threatened stocks in camp and put stress on their disastrous logistical operation – something Second Lieutenant Cowdry and Lance Sergeant Thorpe spent a lot of time trying to sort out.

Eventually the fight dried up. Vehicle Checkpoint Rabiullah had also been contacted throughout the day while the men on the ground had been involved in a dozen separate contacts. Somehow, everyone got back into Patrol Base Nahidullah. Kitching had been told earlier that, due to certain circumstances beyond his control, there would be severely limited scope to pick up any casualties by helicopter that afternoon. Having assessed the tactical necessity of the patrol, he had made the tricky judgement call to continue pushing his men on. His discretion was proved correct on this occasion.

*

After these two days of fighting, Major Kitching realised he had lost contact with the people on his doorstep. The intimidation of locals meant that they were less likely to engage with what Isaf had to offer them. Kitching decided to mount large fighting patrols through the Chah Bagh area near Patrol Base Nahidullah to clear the firing points and tackle the fighters. The patrols were 70 or so strong – notionally enough to dominate and handle anything that develops.

On 27 May the second of these patrols went out. The locals seemed quite happy to see the troops and opened up their compounds to searches. One hastily abandoned compound was stuffed with drug-making paraphernalia along with some potential IED components such as battery chargers and copper wiring. Nearby, a man acting suspiciously was arrested and then began trying to delete numbers and pictures from his mobile phone – a possible indication that he was acting as a 'dicker', or observer, for the insurgents. He was taken back to Patrol Base Nahidullah and entrusted to the tender care of Warrior Sergeant Major Brettle's Intelligence Cell. The patrol, by now a long snake of tired Guardsmen mixed in with Afghan soldiers, got into a deep stream to mitigate the IED risk and made their way upstream for the final 400 metres to Vehicle Checkpoint Ranaa.

'It was good craic that day – guys falling off logs and getting soaked,' said Lance Sergeant Wood.

He was almost at the back of the line behind Second Lieutenant Tulloch's Multiple and Sergeant Paxton. They came to a pair of logs across the stream. The terrain was very close and it was impossible to see more than a few men ahead. Most of the 70 men had crossed over the logs rather than going round them, following in the safe path of the Vallon man. To the right there were wet bootprints going around the logs, so Wood got up and out of the stream to get his bearings and then jumped back into the water. Lance Corporal Ramsay behind him hurdled the logs and then turned to help Lance Corporal Wallace get over and followed Wood. Guardsman Watson got out and followed the boot prints round the logs. He turned to help the next man up from the stream.

An explosion.

'What the fuck was that?' shouted Guardsman Masters to Lance Sergeant Wood. The noise was a few metres behind them.

'I don't know,' Wood replied and then got on the net. 'Two Five Echo: Contact – Wait out.'

Wood ran back with Lance Corporal Ramsay. The first thing they saw was Lance Corporal Wallace, his face tattooed with dust, looking into the water.

'Where's my gat? Where's my gat? Where's my gat?' he was repeating.

'Clearly oot the game. Fucked but a'right,' thought Wood, as he moved past Wallace. 'Two Five Echo: Contact – IED,' said Wood.

Guardsman Baba, the last man in the patrol, was trying to get his top half out from the water.

'Oh fuck! – he's lost his legs,' thought Wood, but then saw Baba free himself from the logs that had been blown from the crossing point by the IED.

'Right face out with your weapon and watch for follow-up,' shouted Wood at the shocked Guardsman.

Guardsman Wannuwat gets out of the water and turns to Wood. His face is covered in specks of blood but otherwise intact. He made eye contact with Wood and immediately burst into tears.

'Wannuwat – face out and watch those fuckin' arcs!' shouted Wood as he waded up and came to the casualty. Guardsman David Watson was floating face up. Despite the fast flowing water, there was a pool of blood around him. His eyes had filled with water and turned black.

'Oh fuck! He's dead,' thought Wood.

'Paul, where are we going to fuckin' drag him?' Wood said to Ramsay.

'Crater – there'll no be an IED there any more,' said Ramsay.

'Aye. Fuckin' drag him up with me,' said Wood.

The two men dragged Watson into the crater and realised the extent of his injuries. Both legs gone from the knee down, just leaving swordlike shards of shinbone and flaps of skin. Right arm mangled below the elbow. Mouth and chin smashed in by a body armour plate and weapon. His eyes beginning to dart from side to side – alive.

'Tourniquets now, chuck me your tourniquets!' screamed Wood. Catching Guardsman Baba's, he starts on the left leg to stop the flow of blood. Lance Sergeant Leyden has run back and starts work on the other leg while Ramsay is on the right arm. Wood gets a second tourniquet on the left leg – there's that much blood – and really takes his time screwing it in. This brings Watson to and he starts crying out in agony from the tourniquet's pressure.

'Do you want morphine?' asks Wood.

'No, I'm all right,' says Watson.

'Are you in pain?' asks Wood.

'I'm all right,' replies Watson.

Sergeant Paxton and Lance Sergeant Thorpe get back with Lance Corporal Moffat – the medic.

'It's Watson. He's hit an IED. He's lost his legs,' said Paxton on the radio to Tulloch, who gets on with passing up the vitals that will launch a helicopter. Watson was beginning to really come round. The bleeding had stopped.

'Don't look down, don't look down,' says Ramsay.

'You've got your balls,' says Moffat.

Watson realised that he didn't have his legs.

'Paul,' he says to Ramsay. 'Watch.'

Watson begins to push his teeth out one by one on his tongue and then spit them high into the air.

'Watson – look on the bright side. At least you cannae get any more bangin' than you are right now,' says Wood.

'My parents aren't going to be happy about this,' says Watson. 'I've enjoyed my time in the Scots Guards, though.'

'This is fuckin' surreal!' thinks Wood and he tries to keep the 20-year-old's spirits up. He looks up to trees decorated with the Guardsman's kit: bandana, bits of clothing, ammunition, kneepads – all suspended.

Lance Sergeant Thorpe pulls out his foldable stretcher that snaps rigid and will take Watson away from his legs. Thorpe realises that he'd walked inches from the IED a few minutes earlier.

'That's how easy it is to ruin your life,' he thinks.

Six men get under the stretcher and start carrying Watson. The water is so deep that Guardsman Masters is submerged under his burden. Second Lieutenant Tulloch's multiple has Valloned an emergency landing site. They clear a safe route back from Ranaa to where the men are struggling in the water. They push Guardsman Watson onto the bank; flaps of bloody skin smear their body armour and hands. They rush the last few hundred metres. As he waits for a helicopter, Watson asks for a cigarette.

Lance Sergeant Wood has kept an eye on Guardsman Wannuwat, kept him busy with checking pulses and carrying smashed kit. When they get to the landing site, Wannuwat kneels next to Company Sergeant Major Lawrie then tries to pull his trigger. They take his rifle from him. His face is a palette of blood and tears. Lawrie knows battleshock and when the Mert arrives for Watson, Wannuwat flies too, his sensibilities saved with a designation of 'back injury' on the casualty report card. Both casualties are in Bastion 28 minutes after the explosion. The poppy is down, the wheat is in; Left Flank is only just beginning its fight for Loy Adera.

How you get to command 1st Battalion Scots Guards

A 22-year-old with sandy hair is sitting in front of a television. His intense blue eyes are watching the Berlin Wall getting hacked away. With small deliberate circles – everything he does, even at this age, is deliberate – he is polishing a pair of black boots for a parade. He has been at Sandhurst for two months. This time has already transformed him from a graduate into the young man who will pick up the Sword of Honour and pass out top of his intake. He's joining the Scots Guards, so needs to get the sheen just right.

In a year, he'll be woken in the middle of the night, in a tent, in a desert, and told to take two sections of Guardsmen forward. They'll replace nine dead and eleven wounded British soldiers who've just been shot up in a friendly-fire incident halfway through the 100-hour ground war to kick Sadaam Hussein out of Kuwait.

Next he'll start the first of his three tours of Northern Ireland. In three years time, he'll be a Captain and be made ADC to a General. Here his boss, who reminds him constantly that 'small points turn into big points', will reinforce his love of detail.

In five years' time he's back with his regiment and given in succession the two jobs that tell a captain that someone has picked him out for management: first Operations Officer for a tour of East Tyrone and then Adjutant. He fits in getting married to the sister of a brother officer and having two children too. Next he'll try Selection for the SAS. He'll get to the end, be thanked for coming and go back to the Scots Guards.

At a loose end, he'll apply to run a military training team in Sierra Leone. He'll walk into a coup. Holed up on the roof of a hotel on the edge of Freetown, he'll fight off a stream of rebels who want to overrun the hotel. In the basement are hundreds of ex-pats who have been unable to flee the capital. After a few hours, he'll receive shrapnel wounds from an RPG and will leave a British mercenary to continue the battle alone. As a Lebanese gynaecologist in the hotel's basement tends him, his wife will learn that her husband has serious head injuries and is missing. The Red Cross broker a ceasefire and he escapes to a waiting US Navy vessel dressed as a civilian. He collects a Military Cross from the Prince of Wales a few months later.

He'll be sent to Australia for a year to recover and returns as a Major to take over a company in Northern Ireland. After Staff College, he'll help draft the military side of the Downing Street Declaration and hope that his Northern Ireland days are behind him.

They are. He'll return to Iraq for the second war, this time as a Company Commander in Basra in 2005. It is four months before he speaks to an Iraqi. He'll bring his Company back to Germany and will be made Battalion Second in Command for six months before going to the MoD to work in the Resources and Plans department for two years.

He'll return to Iraq for a third time, on this occasion as a Military Assistant to the Deputy Commander of all international forces in the country. Here he'll see General Petraeus up close, and see how the Americans view the British. It will be a sobering and instructive experience. At 42, he'll get the job that officers stay in the army to do and that all his previous experience has groomed him for: taking his battalion to war. This time it will be Afghanistan.

But at the moment, 22 year-old Officer Cadet Lincoln Jopp is just polishing his boots and watching the world change as a wall comes down.

CHAPTER FIVE

'These are diplomatic skills I've never had to use before'
May to October 2010

There were 200 packets of peanut and wheat seed and roughly a thousand farmers, so 27 May was always going to be a headache, especially for Sergeant Major Tony Devanny. He was Right Flank's stabilisation representative in Basharan, their new Area of Operations based around Checkpoint Tapa Paraang. Fortunately, deciding who got what had already happened. Turning 800 or so disappointed Afghans away was the job of Tajik security guards from the north. I watched them threaten the farmers with car aerials and swear at the sun. In the vehicle park, computer-savvy Afghans from Lashkar Gah matched names from their database with those on identity cards, took photos and ticked farmers off the list. Two large white Zimbabweans oversaw the operation. The whole enterprise, contracted out to an NGO these men worked for, was part of Governor Mangal's Food Zone Programme, itself a part of his Poppy Eradication Programme, which would begin in earnest in the spring of 2011. The farmers contributed Afs 1,000 for the seed but the majority of the cost was borne by Mangal's coffers. The effort was all to keep farmers on the side of the government and 'the offer'. The term relates to what Isaf, Afghan forces and then the Afghan Government can bring to people in a particular area. First comes the break-in, then a gradual increase in security through joint Isaf and Afghan forces' presence backed by low-level stabilisation work. Finally, once security is established around the protected communities, and the Afghan Government are willing to commit, larger projects such as schools begin. The seed distribution is a typical piece of the third and final stage of the process. Four kilometres to the north-east of Yellow 14, and on the same day, Guardsman Watson lost three limbs in a typical sign of the first stage of the process.

Inside Checkpoint Yellow 14 – a dust bowl built around a police station – Right Flank's 2 Platoon sat in whatever shade there was and let the afternoon take care of itself. The British have been told to let the Afghan face be front and centre during the distribution process; it is important that locals associate the largesse with Mangal, not Isaf. Right Flank had arrived from the north three weeks earlier. Between the Sayedebad operations and now, they had been around Patrol Base Pimon. In that time, five members of Right Flank had been seriously wounded and four Warriors had been blown up by IEDs. Around Tapa, they had relieved B Company, Scots Guards – now on the 601 Highway to the south-east. They in turn had taken over from the Royal Welsh, who had taken the area on from The Queen's Company Grenadier Guards. In six weeks, four companies had gone through Tapa. This flux was in fact a sign of the place's stability. If there had been a fight, Brigade would have plugged the hole on the map with one static company. As the area was considered calm, it could be treated like the last square on the Rubix cube while Staff Officers tried to get the laydown right and the Commanding Officer fought and won a battle to get his old company under his command for the tour. Against this stood Sergeant Major Devanny, the only Isaf continuity in the area. From 3rd Battalion, The Yorkshire Regiment, Devanny was a bright and personable Warrant Officer who took to stabilisation work and Afghans naturally. He knew they were trying to rob him and they knew that he knew this, so stabilisation work in the area went with a smile and a wink rather than accusations and arguments. Locals arrived at the gates of Tapa most mornings asking for 'Sergeant Major Tony'.

The seed distribution is the end of ten weeks of wrangling with tribal elders about which faction gets how many packets of seed. One of the theories prevalent in Counter Insurgency is using human jealousy to attract people to the offer. The one piece of Pashto lore known to all British officers is the phrase: 'I don't care that my cow is dead but that my neighbour's cow is still alive.' In theory, the seed distribution would convince the 800 disappointed farmers that they should side with the government and reap its rewards. On the ground, it had created anger amongst those who had switched from poppy but had left the seed distribution empty-handed. Even those who had received seed remained out of pocket – they'd be earning more with poppy based on today's prices. The majority of subsidised wheat seed in Helmand is going to areas that haven't made the switch in order to convince them to do so. The people of Basharan had seemingly been penalised by the offer. It would be the Guardsmen who would have to soothe this feeling on many foot patrols in the coming weeks. Satellite imagery compiled by the Provincial Reconstruction Team would show an 11 per cent decrease in poppy cultivation across Helmand during Herrick 12, so perhaps the Food Zone Programme did have some impact.

Once the distribution is concluded, Devanny and I sit down to lunch with Commander Israel, the Police

Commander in the area. Israel was highly regarded by Isaf and seen as a near-model commander. He was born in Left Flank's area, so is fairly local to Basharan. The reasons for him not still being in Loy Adera are opaque. Sitting with Devanny and Israel is Hasti Gul (name changed to protect identity), a local tribal leader and ally of Israel who has jockeyed successfully for 70 of his people to receive seed. Dipping flat bread, Devanny soaks up juice from the lamb slaughtered and roasted for this occasion. When the feast ends, Israel and the Yorkshireman trade banter about one another's perceived corruption. Devanny jokes about the chests of cash he sends home to Britain each week. I tell Israel that I've been sent out from Britain to help Devanny count the money – there's that much floating about. Israel laughs. Serious business begins and Devanny agrees to look into an Afs 50,000 contract to paint the police station and the possibility of building a small jail to keep detainees in. This larger contract will have to be cleared in Lashkar Gah.

After lunch, I head to the other side of camp where 2 Platoon's commanders shelter between patrols in the Ops Room, a small Hesco square filled with radios and maps. There are three patrols a day and stags for the Guardsmen, but the main enemy here is boredom, as insurgent activity is thankfully minimal. The TV is broken and the fridge is heading that way, so Lambert & Butler, teabags, UHT milk and *Nuts* magazine keep the Platoon together. Lieutenant KHC fights time typing out annual reports on Guardsmen with whom he fought through Sayedebad and then Pimon. Others work on Operations Badger and Massive (suntanning and bodybuilding) as the afternoon boils away. Days, months perhaps, are lost amongst one another.

'This is not something we're really used to,' Guardsman Wignall tells me as we look out from his sangar position.

'A bit of quietness. It's good to – I wouldn't say relax because no one is ever relaxed, but not be on edge the whole time.'

We head out on a 90-minute foot patrol around the local village. Once back in camp, a sandstorm blows in and shuts down movement. My return ride to Tapa, where my kit is stashed, is cancelled and I overnight in a howling tent with a bundle of sandbags for a bed and an unwashed mouth for company. Lieutenant KHC loans me a pack of Marlboro Lights and I am eternally grateful. Making best use of the time, I realise again that checkpoints are an interviewer's paradise. Locked together for months, with little real contact with the outside world, the men usually welcome a new character's arrival. With hours spare between patrols, the guys are happy to sit and talk. Every interview ends with, 'So, what's the book going to be called and when's it out?' Soldiers, mostly, like being written about and I, mostly, like writing about them – it's a pretty even deal. Being Guardsmen, 2 Platoon all have immaculate manners and I'm inundated with offers of tea and coffee and someone sorts me out a ration pack. As always, I'm surprised by quite how good these are – though I'm not doing six months in theatre and the hunger produced through patrols would make most things edible. The contrast with the old ration packs is palpable. Someone's gone to town devising the new packs, throwing in mini-bottles of Tabasco and sachets of energy drink. The only casualty of the change that I lament is Kendal Mint Cake – how that town must have howled when the MoD cancelled that contract. There's enough variety in the new ration packs to keep the palette vaguely awake and pre-pping a boil-in-the-bag requires near-zero effort in an environment where even simple tasks are a chore thanks to the heat. There are some old standbys – corned beef hash, bean-heavy breakfasts, lamb curry – but newer dishes, too.

Beef with cassava is the most random menu item I sample, with sweet and sour chicken and three bean salad coming in second and third. Tearing open yet another Vestey Foods packet, I reflect that if anyone's going to make a bundle of cash on the rations, it may as well be a company run by old Scots Guardsmen.

★

Non-kinetic Counter Insurgency still worked 2 Platoon's men incredibly hard. The rapid turnover of their predecessors meant there was some mistrust from some locals towards Isaf. This was compounded by a tribal dynamic of haves and have-nots that also had to be negotiated. Commanders spent a lot of time in conference with elders and Commander Israel. On top of this were the peculiarities of living alongside Afghan National Police partners. These ranged from petty theft and drug taking to what some delicately called 'cultural differences' (paedophilic buggery to you and me). All in all, much like life at a British public school, I thought. For the soldiers, though, it was all a long way from the certainties of fighting through Sayedebad. Even in the short time 2 Platoon have been here, some steps have been made in getting these issues addressed. When I return to Yellow 14 two months later, it is clear that Lieutenant KHC's men have engaged with Commander Israel's and, mostly, confronted excesses, sorted the place and the partners out before they handed over to the next unit. These sorts of incremental steps – grinding, tiring, frustrating steps – are a true measure of success in this campaign.

Checkpoint Yellow 14 sits on the junction of two main routes from Lashkar Gah to the south and Mars, which makes its way east, across a canal and into Left Flank's area. Across the canal are settled people living on irrigated, green land who are Gul's tribesmen. To the west are squatters who try to eke out a living from compounds built on sand. From Isaf's arrival in the area, Gul had bet that cooperation with them could be his route to becoming the area's apex elder. His people had followed him and embraced the offer. According to Commander Israel, 'his enemies hate him'. He wears a 'Support the Scots Guards' charity bracelet. At his home on 7 July Gul is shot twice in the stomach but survives. No one appears to know if he was shot in a robbery that went wrong or was targeted for assassination. The lawlessness of the area points to one conclusion, the tribal dynamics another.

Complicating the picture in Basharan was the rivalry between Commander Israel and his uncle, Mira Hamza, also a police commander. Mira Hamza was based out of Checkpoint Tapa Paraang, which was built around compounds belonging to one of his cousins. He had also left Loy Adera in unclear circumstances. The commanders and the local factions they commanded 'won't speak to each other, patrol with each other or sit down with each other', said one British officer. When Israel did visit Tapa one day, a perceived slight of honour led to a 'Mexican standoff' between the two; fortunately, a Scots Guardsmen cooled the situation down and neither pulled a trigger. Mira Hamza was also from Left Flank's area and both men were desperate to lead their own men back there. Israel was adamant that the reason Left Flank had such a fight on their hands was the absence of his policemen.

'They [the Afghan National Army and Counter Narcotics Police] are from Kabul and don't know the guys who are insurgents and who are not. They don't understand. We must recruit police from their own local area so they are able to provide better security in there.'

Isaf thinking was coming round to this view. In many

areas the locals remembered the police as a malign force and were unenthusiastic about their return. Simply put, they had been the local bullies empowered by Isaf backing and firepower. One corner was turned in 2010 when the Afghan National Police became bank-paid at the same level as Afghan National Army soldiers. This eliminated the temptation for police officers to steal their patrolmen's pay – something that had resulted in their men seeking alternative revenue streams. The second reform was the improved course at the Interim Helmand Police Training Centre. Still woefully short at eight weeks, the course did, in the words of a senior British officer in Lashkar Gah, give recruits 'the understanding that being a policeman doesn't just involve sitting on a polyprop chair and nicking money off punters as they drive past'. The quality of the training centre's graduates was obvious to 2 Platoon when they went on joint patrols.

'They were keen to go out on patrols,' said Lance Corporal Kieran Bradbury. 'They didn't prat about – they searched vehicles and stopped people. It worked out quite well.'

Regardless of the quality of Patrolman, the tribal rivalry between their commanders in Basharan undermined the local campaign.

*

'Almost certainly nothing will happen,' Colour Sergeant Paul Bailey told 1 Platoon. 'They'll see the Warriors and piss off – that's even if they're there. Q Bloke's squared us away with some sausages and cake, so let's go and have a barbie.'

Bailey had been working at Sandhurst in February when the Commanding Officer phoned him and told him that Captain Murly-Gotto was wounded. Bailey had to take over 1 Platoon as he was Warrior-qualified, unlike many of the young Scots Guards officers who had slotted straight into Afghanistan from their infantry training. He'd put on some bagpipe music and got packing. Bailey treated 1 Platoon well and they worked hard for him in return. He knew that they'd been through a tough start to their tour and still felt the loss of Lance Sergeant Walker very keenly. A barbecue at Checkpoint ANP Hill was a perfect way to break the routine of life in Tapa, and Bailey invites me to come along. Unlike the rest of Battalion who I'd met in training, Right Flank was new to me. Company Sergeant Major Johnstone had told me 1 Platoon were the men to focus on. I'd begun to hear about Sayedebad and would spend the coming days grabbing interviews whenever possible, chain-smoking as I listened to their stories. With the back of their tour broken, they had that mature air of men who've been through it in Helmand. From their faded combats, nicknames and in-jokes, I immediately got the sense of a strongly bonded and experienced family.

The Warriors arrived on top of ANP Hill an hour before dusk. The Checkpoint was one of Mira Hamza's and an informant had said it was going to be attacked that night. Some of the policemen were pretty stoned when 1 Platoon dismounted and lit a fire. The Warriors leaguered along the three-foot-high dirt rampart bund line. From the brow, much of Helmand was visible as the edge of the day's heat faded and farmers pulled recalcitrant water buffalo towards compounds. Guardsman Stafford got cooking. After everyone had finished their sausage baps, banoffee cheesecake appeared from somewhere – no one quite knew how the Q Bloke did it. Some of us sat on the ramparts, watching as the sun vanished over Helmand. Colour Sergeant Bailey poured rubbish on the fire and then threw spare hexamine fuel on to stoke it. 'Hexy pyros

– there's always one,' someone said. There was a popping sound. 'Why's the Hexy exploding?' I thought and then looked up. The red tracer glided some feet above our heads from the west. Everyone realised someone was trying to kill them and our helmets and body armour were where? The change of gear was almost comic, as we scattered to the Warriors. An infernal chuckle broke out from a few as they realised they were going to get to grips with the enemy again and sprinted to collect rifles and missiles. Others jumped to the Warrior turrets. A second firing point now opens up from another direction. Tracer rounds pour over the ramparts and dip down, bisecting the space between the Warriors and sending men diving for cover as they make their weapons ready. I'm lying at the back door of a Warrior as Colour Sergeant Bailey leaps over my prone form and invites me in.

'That was all a bit sudden.'

'Yeah. I'm going to fight from here. Would you mind closing the door?'

I shut the door as he crawls into the turret. Guardsmen in Tapa Paraang and Yellow 14 sprinted into sangars to get a good view of what would come next.

The 30mm cannon on a Warrior, when twinned with a thermal sight, is a reckless weapon to take on as a foot soldier. The gunner is quite able to pick you out and then coolly end you with clinical accuracy. This is what happened to one of the insurgents, while another was badly injured but crawled away. The pair over to the east fired from a spot out of the Warrior arcs and then disappeared. Sitting in the back of the Warrior, the cannon parps softly enough. I feel utterly secure and start laughing at the recollection of us all dashing about amidst the tracer. The back door opens and a Guardsman asks if I want to have a look round. I jump out and we shuffle along, keeping our heads below the rim of the bund line.

'We've been engaged from both sides – there are a couple of machine guns. There's a few of them.'

'The rate of firepower . . .'

A non-commissioned officer comes over.

'Listen, there's numerous fucking firing points coming from the west. Stu and Stevie, push up to the fucking bund line, reinforce the guys in the sangar, you stay here the now. Observe to the south and south-west. Max, you just stay with Stevie. Any firing happens, you want to be on your beltbuckle.'

'Yep, beltbuckle – got it.'

'No eyes over the bund line.'

There's no more firing, so a while later we're back in the Warriors. We talk through it on the trip back to Tapa.

'That was a pretty rapid change of pace,' I open.

'Aye – one minute barbecue, next minute shooting. That will go down well in book. Will make for good reading, will that.'

'Did you see how close it was to where we were sitting up there on the bund line?'

'Dash of death.'

'We were sky-lined there.'

'We were figure tens.'

'There were fucking rounds coming through the opening.'

'That's never happened to me before,' I say.

'When you just hear the whizz, it's not too close.'

'It's when you hear the crack . . .'

'There weren't that many cracks that time; there were a couple. With tracer, it looks closer.'

'At least they had the decency to let us finish our sausage sandwiches.'

'Police probably rang their mate up: "Start firing now, the party's over."'

'Aye, I know. Weird like. Broke the night up kind of nicely that did.'

The policemen didn't fire a round, despite some vocal encouragement from the Jocks.

Back in Tapa, Colour Sergeant Bailey called his men round.

'Big well done there, we were on the back foot. They let us finish the barbecue though, which was good. I doubt they'll try that again.'

He leads them in a round of applause.

'Bap and a contact – perfect,' says Lance Corporal Billy Stuart.

Some of them hadn't fired their weapons since Saye-debad; the whole experience was almost therapeutic.

The insurgents could have been a group of fighters transiting through the area and keen to make a point. Equally, there may have been a tribal dynamic – possibly an attempt to discredit Mira Hamza in the eyes of the latest Isaf company to come through Basharan. The spot-on intelligence pointed to something local, which was surely confirmed when 3 Platoon went up ANP Hill a few weeks later on an identical tip-off and also had their evening interrupted. The use of tracer was also atypical of the insurgents, though ammunition security is so fluid between Afghan National Security Forces and insurgents that it is foolish to draw anything other than circumstantial conclusions from its use that night.

★

Trying to work it all out was Captain Chan Monro, Right Flank's commander while Major Lindsay-German took well-deserved R&R. There was a basic three-sided relationship between the locals, the Afghan forces and Isaf. Commander Israel said that the reason the area was calm was 'because Isaf helps the local nationals and the locals help the police'. For Monro, increasingly aware of how opaque the true situation in Basharan was, there was a simple choice. He could delve into those complexities and possibly discover unpalatable truths about a fourth side of the local picture – the nexus between insurgency and tribal feuding linked with the local Afghan Government forces. Alternatively, he could allow these undercurrents to work themselves out with an Afghan solution to an Afghan problem. Stirring things up and causing friction could lead to increased violence in the area, fundamentally threatening Right Flank's aim of helping the local people and minimising risk to them.

'These are diplomatic skills that I've never had to use before,' Monro conceded.

These complexities could fascinate, and while it was important to ask why Basharan didn't go 'bang' on Herrick 12, the most important fact was that it didn't. Whatever the intricacies of the situation, Isaf units that passed through Basharan worked around them for the benefit of some of the local people. Foot patrols established locations for 80 new wells, which Sergeant Major Devanney had contractors drill despite insurgent intimidation. At Yellow 14, a medical engagement treated many local nationals and two veterinary engagements treated hundreds of animals. The school in Basharan established by Major Sean Birchall, Welsh Guards, remained open; another school was refurbished at a cost of $50,000 so that it could educate girls. Irrigation schemes were extended. Under the gaze of a Warrior, a major causeway and bridge crossing the canal outside Yellow 14 was also built as part of the Trident upgrade. It was all very different from the start of Right Flank's tour and indeed from their previous trip to Helmand in 2007–08. 'There's more to Counter Insurgency than closing with the enemy,' Lance Corporal Andrew

Bennett from 3 Platoon said. 'The previous tour was extremely kinetic – company manoeuvres, Warrior assaults. That's a very straightforward job for us: we'd turn up and they wouldn't want to know; basically the whole Company was kinetic. This time we're extremely restricted because of the courageous restraint side of it, but it worked because we engaged with the population. We were a lot more hands-on with the population and, as opposed to raiding some place and leaving, we'd actually stay in and put the pieces back together. It was a lot more satisfying for us because you're seeing the job through, as opposed to just turning up and making a mess – which there was a lot of earlier, more kinetic Herricks. Taking ground and not holding it – what are you doing it for? It was good to be able to follow up and actually get some results for what we were doing.' In a long and tiring final few months of their tour, Right Flank learned how complex relatively non-violent Counter Insurgency operations could be in Helmand. If the British campaign in the province is to be a success, then nights like the one on ANP Hill, when basic soldiering skills are rapidly dusted off, will have to be as rare an aberration as possible.

★

'What's the checkpoint like, Sergeant Chappell?' asked Lieutenant Jonny Clayton over the telephone.

'Great, sir. Swimming pool and SLAM accommodation. We'll be fine,' the Sergeant lied.

When he arrived at Checkpoint Dre Dwahl on 5 May with the rest of 1st Troop, Fondouk Squadron, Queen's Royal Lancers (QRL), Clayton appreciated the joke. The base's name translated as Three Walls, though one had fallen down since the Household Cavalry Regiment had occupied it in February as part of Operation Moshtarak.

Luckily, Clayton's troop had three armoured Scimitar reconnaissance vehicles armed with 30mm cannons to deter any assault on the outpost. His men slept in hutches improvised from unfilled Hesco barriers and the Ops Room was a poncho slung from one of the two remaining walls. It would be an uncomfortable six months for 1st Troop in the Bolan South Desert west of Lashkar Gah.

The Scots Guards had trained with four different sub-units, each of which, they were assured, would be the one that would come under their command in Helmand. Fondouk Squadron, QRL, only found out they would be working with the Scots Guards when they arrived in Camp Bastion, slightly delayed by the Icelandic ash cloud. In their training, they had been told to expect a Scimitar-based tour disrupting insurgents in the unpopulated desert with occasional forays into the Green Zone for major operations. Now they would be ground-holding along a route cleared by Operation Moshtarak – another example of how that operation's legacy continued to echo through Herrick 12. As with Left Flank, their tour was going to be about a road: Route Elephant. This connected Marjah in the south with Lashkar Gah and Gereshk. This fitted with the new imperative of freedom of movement for local nationals, as requested by Governor Mangal. Elephant was reputedly the most mined road in Afghanistan before Moshtarak and keeping it clear would fix the QRL along the route in five checkpoints. Their Squadron Headquarters was further east on the outskirts of Lashkar Gah. The young troopers were unconcerned about being up to seven kilometres from their Squadron Leader, Major Jim Walker. As a reconnaissance unit who could trace their ancestry to 17th-century light cavalry regiments – the men wore a capbadge with skull and cross bones over the 'Death or Glory' motto of the 17th Lancers – the idea of being forward and independent came naturally. A troop, perhaps only 12-strong, is trained to work far ahead of the Army's formalised structure. It relies on mutual trust, leading to a true family ethos. This spirit was reflected in the relaxed mood I found in Dre Dawal in May and nicknames dominated between all ranks. Lieutenant Clayton, from Blackpool, was older than many troop commanders at 28, having meandered into the Army via Oxford and a few years in accountancy. Sergeant David Chappell, the Royal Armoured Corps boxing champion, had spent much of his career in Challenger 2 tanks, as had Corporal Gavin Revel, a veteran of the 2003 invasion of Iraq. Sergeant Andy Jones was an animated Welsh Royal Engineer with a dozen years served, though Afghanistan was '. . . the first time I've ever done any of the light role sort of stuff. It's been good.' The troopers were mostly English and the group had a very different feel to it compared with the Scots Guards on their flanks. The troopers were smaller though slightly sharper than most Guardsmen, their individuality most pronounced in Trooper Andrew Howarth, a third-generation cavalryman aged 20 from Dorset whose inability to be smartly turned out gained him the affectionate nickname of 'Steptoe'.

There was a fundamental tension in Fondouk Squadron's mission on Route Elephant. The Afghan Government had requested the road clear and keeping it so was the QRL's main job. Sweaty troopers on stag would count vehicles on the road and the stats would go to the Battlegroup Headquarters. These would then go onto a larger PowerPoint slide for the Brigade Commander. This then fed all the way up so that the Liaison Officer briefing General McChrystal in Kabul could say that Freedom of Movement had increased across Regional Command South West compared with the previous week. This was certainly the case. In January 2010, an average of 200 vehicles were recorded each day on Elephant.

Through constantly 'proving' the route to Local Nationals by vehicle patrols along it and observation of the route from partnered Vehicle Checkpoints, this increased to an average of 1,400 vehicles a day, with up to 2,000 on market days and 3,200 during Eid. Night use increased from nil in January to some during the summer, though the Afghan way of life usually limits movement to daytime. Significantly, the only two IEDs encountered on Elephant during Herrick 12 were both planted during periods when, due to circumstances beyond the QRL's control, patrolling was impossible. Such periods are always noticed and exploited by insurgents. One of these devices killed two police Patrolmen. The situation was so good on Elephant that Governor Mangal was happy to drive to Marjah in April.

'Freedom of movement is important,' the Commanding Officer would remind people, 'because if the state ain't giving you stuff where you live, you need to be able to get to the places where they are.'

Hard work throughout the tour from the troopers achieved this part of their mission. The tension for the QRL was, having inherited an area cleared during Moshtarak and then held, they now wanted to complete the third part of the doctrine of Counter Insurgency and build. To do this, they needed the support of the Afghan Government in Lashkar Gah, who controlled cash for large projects. The problem was, the Afghan Government had almost no interest in the people surrounding the cavalrymen.

The farmer would show his file to anyone who visited his compound. He had been to Kabul eight times in the last two years to try and secure ownership of the land he lived on and farmed. Each visit to the capital's ministries would garner more signatures and instructions to go back to the Land Commission in Lashkar Gah. Entering this building, according to one senior British officer, 'was like walking onto the set of a *Harry Potter* movie: shelves and shelves of paper frozen in time 30 years ago'. Before then, in the time of the Shah, land had been parcelled out to tribes and families who were registered with the Land Commission and helped feed the Kingdom's taxation system. The Soviet invasion had brought warfare but also attempts to realign the countryside along ideological lines then fashionable in Kabul. Then the Civil War had come, followed by the Taliban, who reportedly made those farmers who had retained their Title Deeds eat them in a particularly Year Zero play.

An additional complication was that those Deeds that were presented would read along the lines of: 'the land from X stream to Y compound is owned by Ahmed Barakzai, grandson of Ahmed Barakzai'. The bureaucrats were also unwilling to leave Lashkar Gah to see the ground and their capacity to map their people was near nil. Sorting out to whom what parcel of land belonged was like sifting Campbell from Campbell in Argyll without the use of an Ordnance Survey map while remaining in Oban. Corruption was also perceived to be part of the problem. The registration issue also compounded issues related to compensation payments from Isaf to locals (see Chapter Nine). In some areas, families had managed to hold onto their land and the Afghan Government acknowledged this. The people following Hasti Gul in Basharan were one such group and they were therefore entitled to pro-grammes such as the seed distribution. In the QRL's patch, just a few kilometres away in the Bolan South, the additional complication was that this arid land had never been divvied up amongst the tribes of Helmand. It remained, technically, government-owned and the people who had fled there in the 1970–'80s from fighting else-where in Afghanistan were seen as squatters. Without land rights, the government refused to recognise the people of Bolan South or to provide them with basic state provisions such as schools or health clinics. Also, without subsidised wheat seed, the farmers were even less likely to turn away from poppy. The political class was also unwilling to take ownership of the people, as they didn't own land or contribute taxes or vote in anything like the numbers that could be found in the towns. So the Bolan lay in a vacuum between Nad-e-Ali and Lashkar Gah. Without political representation the people couldn't lobby for the most valuable commodity of all: water drawn from the Helmand River to irrigate their subsistence crops. And when water is scarce, which durable crop will Helmandis turn to? Poppy.

The people of the Bolan South were very much have-nots and the symptoms of 'Accidental Guerrilla' syndrome were present in abundance; what the QRL did over their tour ensured that these did not rise to the surface. At a Squadron level, Major Jim Walker told his men to focus on the people and allowed his junior commanders to devise their own plans. The scouting ethos of a light cavalry unit worked in the hyper-local environment of Bolan South. (The people of one *kalay* might not know their neighbours only 200 metres away if separated by a small stream.) The local people responded well, especially those who lived within sight of Isaf bases. In the past, they had met with indifference from their government and venality from the Afghan National Police, who had notional control of the area before Moshtarak. Now the people were policed by relatively competent Afghan National Civil Order Police Patrolmen and, see-mingly, governed by friendly troopers with cash-in-hand.

Walker decided to engage first with the people's reli-gion. This was an area Isaf had been fearful of addressing. Clearly a focus of the people they now lived amongst, the

QRL tackled the issue. I attended a mullah *shura* held in the middle of Bolan South on 26 May. It was attended by 60 or so of the local clerics, who sat in the shade and listened to Major Walker outline his vision of 'the offer'. Eight holy men who had previously engaged with Isaf were given Afs 9,000 ($180) for mosque refurbishments. Despite an illusion of transparency created by thumbprints and mug shots, the RAF stabilisation representative conceded that there was no way of checking the money would in fact be spent on amplifiers and carpets.

'Some of them, perhaps, will invite us to see what our money has bought,' he said as he handed the cash over.

I sensed that the real commodity being bartered was influence and this was more important for Isaf than what the money ended up being spent on – dollars are bullets, as General Petraeus said in Iraq. Watermelon was then sliced out and Padre Colin MacLeod engaged in a theological discussion with the group's sole Haji. They swapped quotes from the Koran with similar lines from the Bible to emphasise common ground. Meanwhile, I was introduced to a man who claimed to be 110 and to have fought the Soviets. Like many of the people in Bolan South, he came from elsewhere in Afghanistan. His reason for leaving his own area was sharp.

'I killed the local *badmash* in my village. Split his head like a watermelon with my knife. I was 60 years old when I did this. I had to flee.'

Rather an advanced age for homicide, I thought, but this is Afghanistan, as the man from the RAF reminds me. The *shura* was built on when the British Army's Senior Imam visited a second *shura* in Bolan South, which one observer described as a 'Mullah Off'. The Imam then handed out first-rate copies of the Koran and went into Lashkar Gah to lead the city's Friday prayers.

Ramadan was another opportunity to show locals that

Isaf was making an effort to understand Islam. Two officers in Squadron Headquarters fasted on the first day and had a 'horrible, horrible' time in the heat. The police there – a distinctly seedy bunch that kept a 12-year-old boy with a permanent intravenous line hanging limply from his forearm to serve them – laughed at the two *ferengis* and told them that Ramadan began the next day. On the Night of Power, a festival during Ramadan celebrating the anniversary of the revelation of the Koran to Muhammad, a scripture reading competition was held between the local Mullahs and their novices in an Isaf base. To mark Eid, a fortnight later, containers of food were collected from a police kitchen in Lashkar Gah and distributed to the QRL bases. Troopers then went to their neighbours' compounds, sat down and were eaten dry. The Civil Order Police were also drafted into the process of religious engagement and gently encouraged to go into local mosques and pray with locals at the end of evening patrols. This matrix of influence projects was designed not from some desperate intellectual curiosity about the nature of Islam in rural Helmand; it was a smart military tactic to undermine the insurgent argument that they alone have religious authority in Afghanistan, that Isaf are infidel and their uniformed Afghan partners are un-Islamic.

Religious engagement was a good way of shaping perceptions in the area, but the best way to win over the locals was through their pockets. The Household Cavalry Regiment had splashed cash around the area 'like they were on a night out in Chelsea', according to one QRL officer. This had bought local consent around their outposts. Lieutenant Clayton and 1st Troop built on this and immediately contracted some locals to build up one of Dre Dwahl's collapsed walls. The southern wall still needed reinforcing, so when I came through, periods

when patrolling was impossible were spent filling sandbags. Sergeant Jones brushed off his Royal Engineer basic
training and supervised proceedings. When each layer was
complete, he'd jump to the top of the rampart and neatly
tap the bags square with a pick handle. His enthusiasm
turned the event into a strangely enjoyable team-building
exercise. Filling sandbags was better than the couple of
dumbbells that passed for a gym or even the interminable
games of Risk we killed the hottest period of the day with.

1st Troop had been in Dre Dwahl for enough time to be
quite restless by the time I got to them. They took me on
my first foot patrols. The assumption I had from training
was that the place would be laced with IEDs and the
people determined murderers. The reality was quite different; the troopers relaxed me and we trudged happily
around, getting back to the checkpoint towards sunset.
Clayton had asked all the right questions of the locals and
the troopers were all on top of their drills – a feeling they
confirmed the next night when we went on a long night
patrol through Lashkar Gah's suburbs. The darkness
increased the tension of patrolling through tight alleyways, as dogs barked and figures scuttled into doorways.

The troopers were set for a long tour based on the hard,
draining graft of Counter Insurgency. I could tell they
itched for the chance to put the more prosaic aspects of
their training to use – one of them describing their
operational posture as little more than 'hugging' the locals.
It was a game of expectations that I was also learning to
play. The mental assumption you have to work on before
deploying, and the one hammered at sub-unit level in
training, is you'll land in something approaching war
fighting. It's not going to be Burma in 1945 – unless your
officers have massively cocked up the area and alienated all
the locals – but there will be regular firefights and 'serious
incidents' amidst the all-important stabilisation work.

When the force lay-down lottery throws you to a see-mingly benign area and the moments you've trained for don't pitch up, there can be a natural sense of disappoint-ment. This is explicable – we expect the most aggressive members of our society to join the teeth arms of the Army and behave bravely. The generous charity boxes marked 'Afghan Heroes' I watched the troopers rifle through were one example of what we civilians generically think of soldiers. Keeping spirits up and men motivated and alert through mundane patrols and hours of stag, as Lieutenant Clayton and Sergeant Chappell did, takes reasoned leader-ship. However, it would be a foolish man who bets against involvement in at least one serious incident in the course of a six-month deployment. The fundamental quality anyone in uniform outside of Camp Bastion must have remains the ability to deal with a kill-or-be-killed situa-tion. This five years into the campaign.

With his defences in some sort of order, Lieutenant Clayton began putting in small building and irrigation projects to win over local farmers. At first he seemed to have limitless money to burn and projects under Afs 25,000 ($500) were hardly questioned by the stabilisation teams, meaning that he could authorise schemes that took around 100 man-days (assuming there were no other costs such as building materials). As the tour went on, it seemed that this pot began to run dry at the troop level. With little to offer in terms of stabilisation support, Clayton began to notice a difference in the attitude of the locals, especially away from Dre Dwahl.

'By the time your vehicles had driven through some crops and had damaged some of the irrigation systems and you got off and asked them, "What do you want?", some-times they'd be like, "To be honest, we just want you to stop coming round," ' Clayton said of the local stance.

Many would also complain that the more the soldiers

came round, the more the insurgents would turn up and intimidate them.

For larger projects such as schools, the QRL ran into a blockade in Lashkar Gah unwilling to spend in the Bolan South. Requests from the locals would go through the stabilisation chain to the British-led Provincial Reconstruction Team of Department for International Development and Foreign Office officials who would then work with the Afghan line ministries in Lashkar Gah such as the Ministry of Education. While the funding for these ministries was very much international donor-based, local bureaucrats had a great deal of autonomy in how they spent it and refused to splurge on the people of the Bolan South. One workaround was the euphemistically labelled 'Community Centre' built in the north of the area with stabilisation funds. The small two-room building acted as an informal madrassa, school and *shura* hall for the locals. At Sergeant Chappell's suggestion, Lieutenant Clayton tried to put in a keystone project around Dre Dwahl – a small school to teach boys in the morning, with a football pitch next to it to encourage them to stay and have some fun with Isaf troops in the afternoon. It was exactly the sort of hearts-and-minds project that Major Walker had asked his men to come up with. Clayton arranged a water supply for the pitch and grass seed was found from somewhere. Unfortunately, the plan had occurred to Clayton during the stage of the tour when funds had begun to dry up, so he couldn't hire a construction firm. Luckily, it seemed, a local contractor was working on Route Elephant as part of a massive multi million-dollar upgrade paid for by Britain's Department for International Development. Chappell approached the man and asked if he wouldn't mind lending his machinery for half a day to level the pitch. The man quoted a ridiculous price. Chappell asked if he'd consider doing it free for the local community.

TRAINING

Left. Salisbury Plain in a blizzard – ideal training for a summer tour in Helmand (Photo credit: Max Benitz)

Below. Lance Sergeant Jamie Simeon rushes to treat an 'Amputee in Action', Otterburn Ranges, February 2010 (Photo credit: Max Benitz)

RIGHT FLANK AND OPERATION MOSHTARAK

1 Platoon, Right Flank line up in Camp Bastion prior to the first heli-assault into Sayedebad. Lieutenant Murly-Gotto is centre with black band on helmet (Photo credit: A member of Right Flank, Scots Guards)

Lance Sergeant Davey Walker 1 Platoon, Right Flank and friend (Photo credit: A member of Right Flank, Scots Guards)

Sergeant Colin Kirkwood, 1 Platoon, Right Flank, commanding his multiple through the ditches around Sayedebad (Photo credit: Lance Corporal Mick Little)

Lance Corporal Mick Little (left) and Guardsman David McHugh look out over
Sayedebad (Photo credit: Sergeant Colin Kirkwood, Scots Guards)

Basic conditions in Mr Miyagi's Compound
(Photo credit: Sergeant Colin Kirkwood, Scots Guards)

LEFT FLANK IN LOY ADERA

Major Rupert Kitching, left, in conference with Sergeant David Jones, Stabilisation Adviser to Left Flank (Photo credit: Max Benitz)

Sergeant Tony Gibson, 11 Platoon, Left Flank, on the quad he used to pick up so many casualties. Note 'WANTED' poster of rogue Afghan soldier Talib Hussein on grey door (Photo credit: Max Benitz)

Above left. Lieutenant Will Tulloch, 12 Platoon Commander (Photo credit: Max Benitz)

Above right. Guardsman Ritchie Carr, 18, in the sangar at Checkpoint Said Abdul (Photo credit: Max Benitz)

Left. Lance Sergeant John Thorpe, Afghan National Army Adviser to Left Flank (Photo credit: Max Benitz)

Below left. Lance Sergeant Tom Morris pauses in a cornfield near Vehicle Checkpoint Naeem (Photo credit: Max Benitz)

Lance Corporal Paul Ramsay, centre, lighting cigarette, holds court at Vehicle Checkpoint Rabiullah as Lance Sergeant Steve Wood, right in chair, smiles on (Photo credit: Max Benitz)

Patrol Base Nahidullah under attack at night. Insurgents were able to mount co-ordinated shoots on all of Left Flank's locations simultaneously (Photo credit: Max Benitz)

Guardsman Ryan Gowans, Lieutenant Charlie Pearson and Guardsman Steven Fuller (left to right) fix bayonets as they enter Popolzai (Photo credit: Max Benitz)

A local boy stares down the barrel as gunfire ripples out over Loy Adera (Photo credit: Max Benitz)

An Explosive Ordnance Officer on a live IED on Route Mars (Crown Copyright © MoD)

Another day at Checkpoint Said Abdul: Lance Corporal Izzy Henderson, centre, treats a dying member of the Counter Narcotics Police (Photo credit: Max Benitz)

Above. Piper Fraser Edwards takes a smoke break. A Battle Casualty Replacement, this was the young soldier's first day in the field (Photo credit: Max Benitz)

Left. Platoon Sergeant Major John Lilley and Guardsman John Lilley meet up on Fathers' Day (Crown Copyright © MoD)

Colour Sergeant Alan Cameron
(Crown Copyright © MoD)

Lance Sergeant Dale McCallum
(Crown Copyright © MoD)

Corporal Matthew Stenton, Black Horse
Squadron, Royal Dragoon Guards
(Crown Copyright © MoD)

Lance Corporal Stephen Monkhouse
(Crown Copyright © MoD)

THE QUEEN'S ROYAL LANCERS IN BOLAN SOUTH

Padre Colin MacLeod surrounded by local holy men at the Mullah *shura* on Route Elephant. The QRL were keen to engage with local religions network (Photo credit: Max Benitz)

Sergeant Andy Jones, Royal Engineers, centre wearing T-shirt, directs the men of 1 Troop, Fondouk Squadron, Queen's Royal Lancers in a spot of sandbagging. (Photo credit: Max Benitz)

Trooper Andrew 'Steptoe' Howarth, Fondouk Squadron, Queen's Royal Lancers, keeping his rifle clean, Checkpoint Dre Dawal. (Photo credit: Max Benitz)

RIGHT FLANK IN BASHARAN

2 Platoon, Right Flank and their police partners on a joint patrol near Checkpoint Yellow 14 (Photo credit: Max Benitz)

Mayor Daoud cuts the ribbon declaring Stabilisation Bridge on Route Trident open. It was the Mayor's only trip to the rural areas of his District on Herrick 12. Lieutenant Israel, in spotless blue fatigues, looks on. The interpreter's face is obscured for his own safety. (Photo credit: Captain Malcolm Dalzel-Job, Scots Guards)

B COMPANY ON ROUTE 601

Colonel Satir, right of central standing man and Major Hugo Clarke, right of Satir, conduct a *shura* at Checkpoint Attal. The interpreter next to Major Clarke has had his face obscured for his own safety. (Photo credit: Max Benitz)

Taj Babi, aged three, is carried by her father to a waiting casualty evacuation helicopter. Despite being very seriously wounded by fragmentation from an Afghan National Policeman's rocket-propelled grenade, Taj Survived (Photo credit: Max Benitz)

HELMAND'S FUTURE?

'I found them, you found them, we all found them.' Colonel Kamullidin talks the Commanding Officer through his men's successful operation. Note female police officer and local media on hand to spread the word (Photo credit: Max Benitz)

A happy cow and a happy boy after a vet engagement in Basharan
(Crown Copyright © MoD)

HOME AGAIN

Above. First night back in the Officers' Mess and Lieutenant Tulloch is in high spirits as Major Martin French looks on
(Photo credit: Max Benitz)

Left. Guardsman Rab McClellan back on the Bucky, St Andrew's Day
(Photo credit: Max Benitz)

Below. Major Kitching, remarkable black wig, leads Left Flank to triumph in the Tug o' War
(Photo credit: Max Benitz)

1st Battalion Scots Guards on parade to collect their Operation Herrick medals, St Andrew's Day (Photo credit: Max Benitz)

After much persuading, the man agreed. The appointed morning came and he never turned up. Likewise, the small school Clayton tried to get built by the local community next to the pitch failed to gain traction. If the people weren't going to be paid, they refused to help, even if Clayton provided the building materials. Eventually, enthusiasm for the scheme died in the Troop.

'Why should we bang our heads all day for people who clearly aren't interested, sir?' the troopers asked Clayton.

Perhaps the locals were spoilt by Isaf's previous largesse and loath to do something for nothing. Perhaps they genuinely couldn't afford a few days of 'Big Society' style volunteering, even though the harvest was in. Perhaps they grasped the transience of something put up without government support. Whatever the reasons, the grass seed stayed in its sacks.

As in Loy Adera, the lack of political boundaries further complicated matters, though by the end of the tour Nad-e-Ali's District Governor had taken ownership of the northern end of the area. Route Elephant also lay on the extreme western edge of the QRL patch, meaning that they couldn't cross the boundary into another Battlegroup's Area of Operations without good reason. When they did go west, the QRL inevitably got into gunfights for little reward other than the knowledge that their soldiering skills remained sharp. To their east lay a vast hinterland they were notionally responsible for but couldn't effectively patrol due to heat and weight – the constant enemies during a summer tour. Eventually, as the months went on and cash dried up, ambitions were sensibly curtailed. There was little point getting into gunfights in the west in areas they would not hold, and to the east they were only putting people at risk of intimidation from insurgents. Rather than going into these areas to 'provoke, lose and leave', as the Chief of the Defence Staff parodied poorly executed 'clear, hold and build' counter-insurgency doctrine, the QRL focused on the ribbon of stability they could create along Route Elephant. They hoped that their occasional goodwill gestures would keep the people of the Bolan South from blaming them for the Afghan Government's conspicuous absence. In either direction there were certainly insurgents, and QRL patrols still went out to fly the flag. It felt to everyone, though, that they were fighting ghosts in Bolan South. There was also the very real possibility that one day something would go wrong.

'If anyone died for no matter what reason or got injured, it would be bad,' Sergeant Chappell said to me in Checkpoint Dre Dwahl in May. 'But if someone got shot, I think it would be much easier to deal with than if someone stands on an IED. It's one of those things we'll have to deal with at the time.'

The unfortunate truth of Bolan South may have been that the people there were so dirt-poor and un-influential that neither Kabul nor the insurgents could be bothered to court them. For the duration of Isaf's commitment to Helmand, they might benefit. But what then?

'How much of this stuff will be undone within a month or two of British absence?' asked Lieutenant Clayton, 'The sad fact of the matter is. Almost all of it.'

R&R

'I've just got back from Afghanistan and I will gouge your fucking eyes out.' It was a pretty good line to defuse a nightclub fight and the drunken civilian backed away. *R&R* was a tricky one. A fortnight at home from the moment your flight landed in Oxfordshire. There wasn't time to truly readjust before the inevitable countdown began.

The journey home was a headache and started with a helicopter ride to Bastion. A white Toyota pick-up truck from the Scots Guards Bastion team greeted Guardsmen at the helipad. At all hours there was a group of guys sitting there dressed for war and waiting on a helicopter to take them. After a shower at the accommodation area, men would set out for food. The vastness of Bastion, an ever-expanding logistical bacterium on the desert, was a shock after life in tight checkpoints. With no high ground, it was impossible to establish scale during the long walk back from Pizza Hut if you didn't fancy waiting for the bus. (Bastion is large enough to have a bus service.) Men would walk round the next corner and hit another empty field of desert ringed with concrete walls and ditches. By Herrick 12, Bastion was on its fourth upgrade and the contractors were already muttering about plans for Bastion 14. Men felt odd without a weapon, especially at night.

'I was walking to my tent and it was pure dark,' said Guardsman Campbell, 'and I seen a car coming and I felt different – I've never been out in the dark by myself since I've been on tour so I thought, "This is dodgy, this is dodgy." I had to get back into my tent.'

The next day the pick-up truck would take men to the main flight line for the hop to Kandahar.

At the start of Herrick 12, the flight shed at Bastion was a British affair. Movement Controllers dredged from the three services and a few RAF Policemen ran the place. By July, when R&R was in full swing, the US Marines had also taken residence. Giant flat screens showed Major League baseball's version of 'Match of the Day'. Their Gary Lineker appeared to have a fridge nestling underneath his box-cut black suit. Instead of adverts, occasional messages flashed up from a US Army Chaplaincy Colonel. Through security, a small concession served drinks, British Forces Broadcasting Service showed films or Sky News and a graveyard of abandoned books pleaded to be read. Predictably, Chris Ryan novels led the market though I spotted a copy of Barchester Towers *and even a complete set of Dirk Bogarde's autobiographies. Reading material was limited in theatre. The Army talks about being a learning organisation and Potential Officers are grilled on current affairs. Across the shops in Bastion only* Zoo, Nuts, OK! *and* Rugby World *are carried. All those senior officers in Bastion must get their wives to send them* The Economist *by Royal Mail. Eventually, the flight is called or cancelled with a weary, 'Sirs, Ma'ams, Ladies and Gents – there has been a problem with the airframe,' from the Movement Controller.*

In Kandahar, eventually, the wait for the next TriStar can involve long hours in a shed trying to sleep on top of cinder blocks. To help pass the time a quick readjustment video is shown to soldiers while some of them change into civilian clothing for the first time in months. The video even includes a short section telling soldiers not to talk to journalists, here portrayed as stubbly geezers hanging out in pubs to get quotes for 'The Con' newspaper from gullible squaddies. Final cigarettes, then a sweaty bus ride to the plane in the dark (all the flights in and out are in the middle of the night for security). Helmets and body armour back on, then up and out of Afghanistan for two weeks.

The RAF began the 'Beers for the Boys' scheme in 2007. It was possibly an apology for the dreadful food ('Beef Cobbler – Exp. Date 09/14') served on their planes, which was genuinely worse than anything in a ration pack. It was a great idea but the reality of being woken up at 05:00 by an aircraftman in a pink flightsuit proffering a warm Grolsch was slightly strange. Then down to Cyprus, the blue Mediterranean broken up with white horses. By July, the air bridge was knackered so troops were cutting away from RAF Akrotiri and getting civilian flights home (easyJet's PR team figured out what was going on and offered last-minute reduced flights to men in combats).

Flying into Oxfordshire, one had the feeling that nothing bad could ever happen in its green fields. Some had family waiting for them but most took a bus to Oxford and then a train on. My break from Helmand would be slightly longer than most, at seven weeks while I waited for another embed slot. I slumped at the bus stop outside Brize Norton after the shocking journey. An old woman came over. She'd spotted my helmet and body armour.

'Well, I don't think any of you should be over there,' she said.

Instant internal rage and a polite smile. Guardsman Wilson had the opposite experience while sitting on a train in standard class in his desert combats, snoozing as the ticket inspector came through.

'I'm afraid you've got the wrong ticket,' he said.

'But I got it from the machine!' said the Guardsman, really not needing this now.

'I know but there must have been a mistake. Your ticket should read "First Class". Come with me, please.'

The station pub in Birmingham had a strong flow of Scots Guardsmen through it that summer. Some got so stuck in they missed train after train north, blaming the long queues for a drink each time and getting progressively more steaming.

At home, things taken for granted in previous lives took on new significance. 'For me,' said Trooper Aidan Carter of the Royal Dragoon Guards, 'when you get home you've got all the luxuries. Tap water. You can run it all day when you're in your kitchen and you see people using their hosepipes on their cars. In Afghanistan, you throw a half-litre bottle of water outside and you've got two kids scrapping over it . . . it's madness.'

Others struggled to readjust. Guardsman Wannuwat spent time with a friend who had been in the Army. Walking down the street, his mate stopped him. 'Pal, you're not in Afghanistan and you haven't got a Vallon on your forearm. Stop sweeping your arm left to right – the pavement hasn't got any IEDs in it.'

Second Lieutenant Tulloch was walking through a supermarket in London, tossing things into a trolley for supper. A bottle of wine hit a bag of salad, bursting it with a little bang. Tulloch was on the ground screaming, 'Where's my fucking rifle!' at confused afternoon shoppers until he remembered he was a long way, physically, from Loy Adera.

Alcohol was a big part of R&R for many.

'Just drinking, basically,' said Guardsman Campbell. 'Having fun, chilling out a lot too. It was good anyway. It was just weird – different. I was out on the piss kind of thing and someone hit a balloon. I was just like there was pure something had blown up. You hear noises and you're pure tripping . . . And it's weird walking down the street and you don't hear helicopters.'

Many made the trip to Selly Oak or Headley Court to see wounded comrades. Sometimes Commanders would get phone calls from the Adjutant – 'Kitch, it's Guy. There's been an incident at Said Abdul . . .' – and reality would crowd out the temporary illusion of normality. Some attended funerals during their break from Helmand.

The men who had it toughest were the Commonwealth

soldiers who couldn't head home. Guardsman Murray from South Africa was luckier than many. In the time it had taken the Army to process his recruitment papers, he'd worked in a hotel in Scotland. The owner took him in for R&R and gave him the run of the place. The Fijians generally headed to Catterick for some heavy drinking in their company lines. British soldiers like Guardsman Maclachlan who lived in married quarters in Catterick had the constant reminder of war in the background.

'You can hear all the fire from everybody on the training area so it was just like being in Afghanistan. You'd hear it and just crack on with your dinner sort of thing. It was quite weird.'

Family men needed their R&R the most and got much more out of it than a two-week hangover. Whenever patrols paused in Helmand, Sergeant Al Dowd would perform little magic tricks for the Afghan children. R&R and the chance to be with his own kids were clearly longed for.

'First thing I did was take my watch off when I walked in so I wouldn't clockwatch,' said the Merseysider. 'Then I just enjoyed being a dad again.'

Time ran out.

'The first week goes,' said Guardsman Campbell, 'and then on the second week you're just thinking about Afghan and how you need to go back in a week. You should get R&R but you come back and you've forgotten everything – you feel a wee bit like a civvie again within two weeks. So you have to get your soldier head back on basically.' The traumatic flight process is reversed. Maybe 72 hours after leaving Britain, men were dropped off by the white Toyota pick-up at the helipad in Bastion. Dressed for war, they'd wait for a ride to take them back home.

CHAPTER SIX

'We're promising, the insurgents are demanding'

May–October 2010

23 July

Lance Corporal Greg Staunton, 30, of the London Scottish TA slashes his stomach on some razor wire. With a section of men, he's been hammering iron picket posts into knee-deep dirty water and stringing the wire all morning. This denies another drainage culvert under Route 601 to the local IED cells. Staunton walks over to Private Stacey French, a little 19-year-old from Accrington in the Royal Army Medical Corps. French cleans up the wound and Staunton goes back to the mud.

Private French and I are travelling up the 601 to her new post at Checkpoint Attal. B Company, 1 SG set it up in May to act as one of two permanent Isaf patrol hubs on the tarmacked route that connects Lashkar Gah with Kandahar to the east and Gereshk to the north. Work on the culvert finishes and a Mastiff drives down from Attal to pick up French. The medic she is relieving explains that her kit is in Attal ready to go when French arrives. French hands over her medic bergen and we jump in. The exhaust chokes and the Mastiff heads east.

Five minutes later there is a sound of wild gunfire and the Mastiff halts. French rolls her dark brown eyes back and replaces her too-large helmet. I smile and do the same. The topcover, Trooper Aidan Carter of the Royal Dragoon Guards (RDG), shouts down what has happened. An Afghan National Police convoy led by a white Toyota had overtaken the Isaf vehicles. An IED aimed at the Toyota had missed its mark but blown the back window out and the rear bumper was hanging loose. I opened the rear roof hatch and popped my head out to have a look round. The patrolmen had dismounted and headed towards a belt of compounds 250 metres north of the road, firing from the hip as they went. They shout that they were shot at after the IED, but Isaf heard nothing. Rough fields of stubble mark where wheat stood before the harvest but the area is mainly gravel. Mosque speakers on wooden polls mark the centre of the *kalays*. An RPG detonates.

Taj Babi would have woken up that morning unaware that the day was cool for July – at three she was too young to remember last year. The RPG fired by the police fragmented across her father's compound and ripped her abdomen apart and shattered her left arm.

'They're coming back,' I say, looking through binoculars. 'One of them is carrying something. Oh, fuck. Take a look.'

I pass the binos to Carter. He scans.

'It's a child, isn't it?'

I dropped down the hatch and told Private French.

The Afghan National Police Patrolman walked back across the fields carrying Taj. That was what really struck me. Why not run towards help when holding a dying girl? He placed her next to the back of the Mastiff. Private French, who realised she only had the minimal medical kit carried in the vehicle to save the girl's life, dismounted. She replaces the girl's guts and wraps up the abdominal wound. The first field dressing is too big for Taj's little body and arm. I force myself to watch – if the soldiers have to see it, I have to see it. Captain Spike Lee, RDG, jumps out from the Mastiff.

'What's happening?' he asks.

'Some little girl just got fragged by the ANP,' someone says.

Guardsman Christopher Gallacher from Renfrew comes over.

'That's not fair,' he says to me when he sees the girl, then turns away. 'You see things out here that will scar you for life and make you realise how lucky you are, sat at home in front of the telly.' Pause. 'What do you think of our new sharpshooter rifle then?'

The traffic diverts off the road to the south and avoids the convoy. Word comes that a helicopter is inbound. Taj's eyes are open. She isn't crying or making any other noise than her struggle to breathe. Private French squeezes her good hand, as the girl kicks her legs.

The police bring the girl's father, Qadar, to the Mastiff. He looks resigned. The Patrolmen are wild-eyed, panting for water, one has hair raised in an exclamation of shock towards the overcast sky. Qadar asks to take his daughter home and let her die in peace. He is told she can be in a hospital within 15 minutes of the helicopter landing. He agrees to go with her and is searched. A few cigarettes, some scraps of paper and a pencil are all he carries. Purple smoke grenades pop on the 601. The Pedro swoops down. Qadar carries his pale daughter to the helicopter. It is a time machine that flies them from rural Helmand life to the 21st century's finest trauma hospital. Taj lives.

Private French gets back in the Mastiff. I hand over a pack of wet wipes. She takes one for the blood, then another and another for a few tears. We both chain-smoke to Checkpoint Attal. I couldn't believe I'd been so naive, having not expected and prepared mentally for a scene like this, though catastrophically wounded toddlers don't feature in pre-deployment training. How could they?

*

Four of B Company's six multiples had moved up Route 601 towards the end of May, leaving two multiples to cover Lashkar Gah city. They were bolstered by 27 Dragoons in their Mastiffs. They would be the first permanent Isaf presence along Route 601, relieving an itinerant mechanised infantry company of Americans. A pair of multiples would remain in two checkpoints. Checkpoint Bamba Serai, nearest to Lashkar Gah, was manned by two multiples commanded by Captain Neil Gow and Sergeant Joel Burnside. Company Headquarters and a further pair of multiples were based in Checkpoint Attal further east. They would partner with the local police at every level. It was virgin Counter Insurgency territory and the largest company Area of Operations in Helmand. The aim was to secure the route by engaging with the locals and bringing the police on but it was primarily 'all about the road', as Sergeant Craig McAlpine put it. A safe road meant Lashkar Gah's economic mini-boom could continue to be fed by convoys of contractors coming in to service local businesses, Afghan Government/Isaf and NGO projects and the markets would be kept fed. Apart from the 601, the area was of no strategic significance – just a flat arid waste with a dropping water table and a scattered population of subsistence tenant farmers.

The two groups of people B Company would focus on were the road users (26,000 a week in June) and the road dwellers. For the users what mattered was keeping the road free of IEDs laid by insurgents and corruption led by policemen. For the dwellers, B Company hoped to engage them, improve their lives, build some trust between them and the police and – vitally – separate them from the insurgents. The people were achingly poor farmers.

'When I first got out here, I felt really sorry for them,' said Trooper Carl Pierce, aged 20, a voluble Merseysider serving his first tour with the RDG. 'The younger kids are waving at you and they do not know what goes on – Taliban, nothing at all.'

Lance Sergeant Matt Hay, a Mortar Platoon veteran originally from South Africa, realised the people's predicament.

'They're sandwiched in the middle: the insurgents on one side, us on the other – we're promising, the insurgents are demanding.'

The Afghan National Police at Checkpoint Attal were quartered in a two-storey former schoolhouse. B Company moved into a tiny, whitewashed compound nearly next to it and waited for the Royal Engineers to perform a characteristically thorough and swift Hesco base build around them. Facilities slowly improved once the defences were up. Troops made their tents as comfortable as possible, with shelving and sun loungers improvised from spare material. A sandbag-lined volleyball court was put in; plywood shower, and latrine blocks were erected. It was fortunate no one was occupied with *Zoo* magazine when a helicopter dropped several tonnes of supplies on the latrines a few days after their completion.

Men got into their routine. Three days were spent on standby or patrols and a fourth day on guard, with at least eight hours on stag.

'Each day rolls into the other. You lose the days until

you lose track and it continuously rolls until one day the tour ends,' said Guardsman Gallacher, 28. 'Everything feels like hard work. To get a shower you have to go and fill the bag from the well, leave it in the sun to warm up, take the bag to the block, hook up the bag and wash. Then you go and refill the bag and lay it out again.'

On the whole somewhat older than the men in a rifle company – Sergeant McAlpine, for instance, had been a Guardsman in now Company Commander Major Hugo Clarke's Platoon during the *first* Gulf War – the men brought a degree of maturity to their task. This would come in handy with their new Afghan partners.

The 313 Afghan National Police patrolmen of the 2nd *Kandak* (Battalion) were strung along Route 601 in 17 checkpoints.

'Personally, my first impression was that they were legalised Taliban,' said Sergeant McAlpine.

Outside Checkpoint Attal, Patrolmen could be seen stopping the vehicles loaded with melons and nicking the produce, further eating into the farmers' meagre profit margin. Others were seen abusing prisoners. Drug use was rife. 'They go up in twos and threes fully dressed and then come back absolutely shit-faced,' said Guardsman Scott McGregor from Kilmaurs in Ayrshire. 'It's funny to talk about but three or four hours later you're going on patrol with them and you hope they're compos mentis.'

Working with these men would be risky and demanding. In the back of everyone's mind were recent examples of Afghans turning weapons on their British partners. Guardsmen quickly had to work out who was trustworthy. One Patrolman named Farouk seemed friendly. He would come over to the British half of the camp (the two sides were split by a low unwired wall and there was no guard between the Afghans and the British) for a chat and a game of volleyball. On patrol, Trooper Pierce, who had taken a

Pashto course and learned more on the job, would clap along as Farouk sang songs to make hot patrols go a little faster. Gradually the Patrolman's attitude began to change. Instead of chatting, he would make demands of the British soldiers and was always asking for kit. He would be offended when the soldiers didn't give him anything. One day an un-partnered patrol Farouk was on got into a fight. Sergeant McAlpine's gun group rushed to the scene in Jackals. The Guardsmen couldn't identify any firing points, though the police were firing erratically into thin treelines and compounds. McAlpine refused to open fire. Farouk went ballistic.

'Fuck off out of my country – you're no good!' he shouted at the Scotsmen.

It was the sort of incident B Company hoped to avoid.

'Here,' Major Clarke would say, 'arguments flare into weapon systems rather than fists. If we let a split open up between the ANP and us, we're doing the insurgents' job for them.'

Farouk calmed down and apologised to McAlpine two days later. Later in the tour, Farouk stood on the roof of the Afghan compound and pointed his machine gun at the British side of the camp. Then he took it apart and cleaned it, all the while the barrel pointing at Guardsmen. Farouk wasn't the only problem character but, as Clarke would remind his men, the policemen had been and would be fighting for years while B Company had a mere six-month sprint. This enduring exposure to brutality had clearly affected some of the police. Others seemed switched on, especially the Dari speakers from the north who didn't know the area and were clean of any nepotistic links to the local population. These outsiders were kept at the out-skirts of the *Kandak* in favour of Pashtos. While the police from the area were certainly more corrupt, they did have a wealth of local knowledge – something missing from Left

Flank's patch at first. One day they pulled over a suspicious-looking man. He claimed to be a Mullah from a local village.

'I know the village and you're not the Mullah,' replied a Patrolman and detained the man.

'These people are very good,' a police commander told some locals at a *shura* in Ramadan. 'They respect our religion and don't eat or drink in front of us.'

This was one way of minimising the risk of a serious fault growing between the groups. Another was lending kit to the police. After a number of IED strikes and night attacks, Vallon and night-vision equipment were distributed. At first, the Afghans considered possession use but after more casualties and the threat of confiscating the kit, they began to use them. The patrol system also changed. To begin with, Isaf dictated the patrol plan. Many mornings were spent waiting for the Afghans to get out of bed and get ready, by which time it was too hot to go out. A new system began where the police officers would set their own patrol plan. If Patrolmen missed it, then their own discipline system would kick in. Isaf was always available for support, but the aim was to get the Afghans semi-independent by tour's end.

Sitting above all this was Colonel Satir Khan – the king of the 601. A career policeman of 30 years, Satir had come to the road a year earlier. He replaced a commander, he assured everyone, who was highly corrupt. With him he brought his three sons. Satir had been described as 'our crook' by the Americans who handed B Company the Area of Operations. They also said he was firmly anti-British for reasons that never became clear.

'As far as the Afghan Government goes here, Satir's it,' said Major Clarke. Locals with disputes would arrive at Checkpoint Attal and ask to see the Colonel. He would sit them down and offer endless tea and pistachio nuts in his small air-conditioned windowless room. A 12-inch TV played Indian soap operas in the corner. Clarke would often perch in the background, fascinated by Afghan life's eddies – ownership of chickens, land rights, irrigation, feuds. As well as judge, Satir was diplomat. When I interviewed him in his room in August, he reeled off lines on his new British friends – 'They are helping us and we work as brothers' – and why they must stay – 'If they leave, the situation will revert to what it was and many more people will die.' Satir was clear that the area south of Route 601 was a major transit route for drug-runners. He said the nexus between them and the insurgents fuelled violence; the insurgents would fight to keep these lines open, the smugglers would bring ammunition in gratitude. Satir was keen to interdict the drugs trade, though whether to wipe out his own competition, as the Americans suggested, or from a genuine policing instinct was never clear. 'We had to believe he was interested in eradicating the problem. You can dig deeply into any of these things,' said Clarke, 'but you've got to get on with life and protect your own assets, too.'

The way Clarke did this was building an enduring relationship with Satir. Clarke had left the Army in 1995 and ended up spending several years in Afghanistan working for the Halo Trust, a land mine-clearing charity, before re-joining the Scots Guards. Mines he had defused littered his office in Catterick and acted as paperweights and ashtrays. His fluent understanding of Afghan mores allowed him to develop relationships with the Afghan National Police and I watched him saying the right things in *shuras* with locals. Most nights, the Company Commander would go alone and unarmed into the ropey-smelling police building and sit, talk and smoke with Sitar for an hour or so. The Colonel appreciated the attention.

Clarke gradually accrued a bizarre collection of presents from his Afghan friend, including Magic Lantern after-shave and a silk dress for his wife.

More problematic than this king were his princes, who served as Lieutenants in his *Kandak*. The eldest, Mohammed, was travelling in the car targeted by the IED strike that escalated into the wounding of Taj Babi. As on every Friday morning, he was driving back from a night in Lashkar Gah in his prestigious white Toyota. Clearly he had been targeted. When B Company's Second in Command, Captain Jason Alderman, took me to speak to Mohammed that night, the Lieutenant produced five IEDs and an insurgent night letter as a get-out-of-jail card for the wounding. When Alderman suggested going to speak to the people of the girl's village to manage the consequences of the incident, Mohammed took much persuading.

'I was nearly killed,' he told us, 'and the local people knew the insurgents were in the area.'

The 2nd *Kandak* continued to be run on tight nepotistic lines. This was wise of Satir, as the Officer Corps of the Helmand Afghan National Police is a repellent nest of faction and power. Clarke debated the value of challenging the *Kandak* dynamic.

'Do we bring people in from outside? Will that survive when we go?' he asked. 'No, it won't. What will the Afghans revert to when we leave? We don't want them to revert to anything. We want to understand what it is they are of themselves trying to achieve.'

As troublesome as his sons were, Satir was fundamental to Route 601. He was, to misquote the former British Ambassador to Kabul, 'an acceptable dictator'. With Lashkar Gah showing almost no concern for the people of the 601, Satir was the best that they could hope for in 2010.

'I think his interests were for his family and his profile,' said Major Clarke, 'but I think we could say the same about a few people in all organisations.'

★

'Fuck me, that Hellfire was close!' shouted Sergeant Rab Brown.

He was in a ditch outside Popolzai Kalay. The Apache overhead had locked onto some insurgents. The explosion was less than ten metres in front of him. 'That wasn't a Hellfire,' said the fire controller, 'that was an IED.'

Fortunately for Brown, the command wire had been pulled early and the wet bank the bomb was dug into had taken the bulk of the blast. The Apache opens up with 30mm. The patrol extracts, spotting two more IEDs on the way.

With such a huge Area of Operations, B Company had a very tough job. Insurgents knew the ground and set the conditions for fights. As a joint patrol approached a *kalay* the insurgents wanted to defend, they would open up from predetermined firing points and move about to give the illusion of greater numbers. It was difficult to figure out how many or where the insurgents were. Quiet fortnights would be punctuated with a week of insurgent activity. The foot patrols' luck ran out on 2 July, when Lance Sergeant Alexander Bain took a burst through his thigh and wrist. All the time under fire, Guardsman Glen McNally crawled to his Section Commander, treated his wounds, dragged him out of danger and then went back to retrieve the wounded man's rifle. In such situations, the police showed their value.

'When they come under contact, they're basically on a par with us,' said Sergeant McAlpine. 'They're not scared . . . they're absolutely mental.'

The local policemen could also pick out abnormalities. Their naked eyesight was superior to that of some British soldiers with binoculars and they would happily pull IEDs out of the ground and present them to Isaf – 'like a dog with a bone', said Guardsman Gallacher. Always, the Afghans lacked fire control. From their gun positions on top of the Mastiffs, the RDG Troopers would occasionally spot an insurgent through their binoculars. Their orders were always to identify targets before firing.

'I saw one. He had a beard and was very dark and waxy-looking,' said Trooper Pierce. 'He had a chest rig with a medical pouch and this and that. Obviously he'd been looking through the Herricks at how we dress, how we look, so he can improve. You look how they are and how they dress – they're like us.'

Another time Pierce saw two insurgents dragging a wounded comrade away and checked his fire. A policeman stood up and fired an RPG into the group. Pierce put his binos down: 'I didn't want to see. It was pretty weird.'

The insurgents were based roughly two kilometres either side of the 601 but would come into the compound belts nearer the road to aggressively defend their rear areas and the narco hubs. B Company's attitude was that pushing into these areas would be counter-productive. Occasional brushes with the population there would merely open them up to further intimidation. This would make them swing away from the Isaf offer.

'Some people say we don't want you round here because as soon as you leave the insurgents will come round and intimidate us, so don't come near us,' said Lance Sergeant Hay. 'Some places the guys invite you into their houses for dinner and are generally friendly.'

The closer the people were to Isaf bases, the friendlier they were. Life on the road could throw up odd moments. Lance Corporal Robert Duncan, part of a remarkable

family who had four members on Herrick 12, was manning the gun on top of his vehicle one day when a car
pulled up.

'Oi, mate! Down here, mate!' Duncan heard a strong
cockney accent say from the rear window. He looked down
to see an Afghan-looking man in a *shalwar kameez* staring
up.

'Oi, mate? Where you from?'

'Glesga. Where you from?'

'London. I'm over visiting relatives.'

A woman leant over and lifted her *burkha*.

'And I've gotta wear all this fucking clobber!' she said.

The police officer went up to the sleeping police sentry
and fired a round into the sandbag next to him. The
Patrolman slept on until shaken awake. It would have
been funny if 12 policemen hadn't been murdered in their
checkpoints in the past few weeks along the 601. In July in
Checkpoint Gulai, during a particularly dark night, four
Patrolmen had been shot at close range in the head in two
sangars. Another pair were executed in their beds. Six
more police were murdered in a checkpoint in August.
While drug-taking was rife and had an impact on alert-
ness, the premise that both times insurgents managed to
sneak in without any alarm or resistance being raised
seemed far-fetched. There was a strong possibility that
the men knew their killers and that they had come dressed
in Afghan National Police uniform. 'Colonel Satir,' said
Major Clarke, 'my men are going to be jumpy after this.
I'm sorry you've lost your guys but this does lead to the
question: "What is going on with the Afghan National
Police on the 601?" I need to partner with you and I don't
want to throw up barriers between us and start putting up
barbed wire fences.' Satir agreed to look closely at each of
his officers.

Quite who the policemen were and what side or sides they were taking was a murky area. Some sort of nexus between the insurgency and the local police seemed highly likely. Treachery was prudent given the possible outcomes in Helmand.

'Everyone knew people in the Taliban and a lot of the police were ex-Taliban,' Clarke explained to me. 'That doesn't mean they're Taliban, though. Taliban is a religious student fighter. I looked at it like a civil war, with the Taliban as one side, and obviously you've got Al Qaeda and other fundamentalist elements that are affecting it. The police would have some particularly close relationships with elements of the Taliban. Now whether that's for survival or whether that's for their own intelligence . . . but some of these people would be family, would be friends from the past, would be people they have worked with. I'm sure if you look back at the English Civil War and many others, you will see the same in all those cultures, too. Your neighbour could be your enemy or he could be your friend. He might well be Taliban but he might not want to kill you because he's Taliban.'

The motivation for the two checkpoint overruns never became clear. The Patrolmen could have been victims of a brutal attempt by enemies within the police to discredit Satir or internal *Kandak* politics. The events did bolster the argument for renovating the ten checkpoints and the Afghan Development Fund in Lashkar Gah found $850,000 to fully upgrade them.

Whatever the nexus between the insurgents and the police commanders, the ordinary Patrolmen took heavy casualties. In all, 24 died and many were wounded during B Company's time on the 601. These men were unlikely to have trodden on IEDs they knew the insurgents had planted. Despite the loaned Vallons, Patrolmen would take fatalistic risks. On 11 August, the first day of Ramadan, one went to retrieve an insurgent white flag – following a police pattern. He lost both legs and the rest of his body was shredded by an IED. I had watched Captain Gow telling the police not to take this risk with the flags the day before but clearly they had ignored him. Private French saved the policeman by ensuring he boarded the Chinook alive. The price of life remained cheap. One day a joint patrol from Checkpoint Bamba Serai went out. The commander put six of his men on point and then the Vallon men behind. When asked why he was doing this, he replied that his priority was protecting the valuable metal detectors. It was a comment straight out of a Soviet Penal Battalion in 1943. Drug abuse, insanity or burial seemed the only escape for the Patrolmen in 2010.

Gradually though, the Afghans improved. On foot patrols, Isaf commanders wrestled them into formation and in contact could scream them into checking their fire. Map reading classes paid off.

'They're leading patrols,' said Trooper Carter. 'To do that in three months is a great achievement.'

In the mornings, the Patrolmen would be up relatively quickly and usually ready to go on a reactive patrol within 20 minutes of getting word. Some days were still marked with an adolescent frostiness but the Patrolmen had begun to realise the benefit of permanent Isaf partners. They began to sleep on the roof of Checkpoint Attal and shine lights at night, something they never did when B Company arrived. I saw a smartly targeted police-led search operation yield a haul of drugs and weapons in July. Slowly, the partnership between the soldiers and the police began to improve on the back of tangible results.

'We're at that very tricky stage when the police are beginning to take the lead,' Guardsman Scott told me in August.

Major Clarke still worried that the unit was acting like a

militia rather than a police force and, if anything, seemed rather pleased that the locals were scared of them.

'You're meant to be the police, Colonel,' said Clarke one evening. 'You're meant to be looking after the interests of the local population.'

Satir, always keen to thicken his influence in the area, came round to Clarke's idea for a Community Policing Initiative. Each of his Checkpoint Commanders was issued with a list of questions. He was then told to organise a series of *shuras* with the elders around his checkpoint to work out the answers. The hope was that through developing relationships with the people, the police would be keen to protect the population and would feed the Isaf stabilisation effort with accurate requests. Like all the best Counter Insurgency ideas, it seemed remarkable that no one had thought of it before.

★

Stabilisation along Route 601 was tricky. With a vast Area of Operations, there was modesty in what B Company could offer the people. The 'clear, hold, build' mantra was harder to effect in a patch roughly five times larger than Left Flank's and with a fraction of their resources. Like over-ambitious patrols, token stabilisation efforts in areas B Company lacked resources to hold would merely open the population to intimidation. Further from the 601, the population were ceded to the insurgents. A few kilometres from Checkpoint Attal, insurgents ran a weekly drive through court and prison system. Locals reported a curfew and taxation system.

As with other rural areas in Combined Force Lashkar Gah, the Afghan Government refused to seriously engage with the 601. Plans for a clinic were dismissed out of hand, a scheme to turn Checkpoint Attal back into a schoolhouse ground slowly through the Ministry of Education. A dozen wells were sunk. There weren't enough votes for the politicians to get excited about – only one official visited in five months. This further alienated the population from the government offer. The Afghan National Police were empowered by this vacuum, surely storing up problems for Helmand in the future. Along Route 601, B Company's period saw a 23 per cent rise in daytime traffic to 32,000 users a week and a huge 320 per cent increase in night-time use, presumably due to an improved perception of security.

★

Between unpredictable partners and a group of determined insurgents who knew the turf much better than B Company could, a tour on the 601 was a distinctly tough one. The arid landscape sucked heat, the tarmac reflected it back into faces and trucks threw dust into camp. In Checkpoint Attal, tempers often were set to boil and voices frequently rose. People tried to keep things light. A large whiteboard of the Company's mugshots was gradually pasted over with photos ripped from magazines of celebrities who had even a passing resemblance to the soldiers. A special section in the corner marked 'Ballbags' was reserved for men who had screwed up. The Guardsman who didn't return from R&R was put in a separate area marked 'super-mega belter', the Scots Guards equivalent of Dante's ninth circle of hell. Off-duty dress standards were relaxed. Major Clarke would wear a red collared shirt for his evening calls on Colonel Satir and Company Sergeant Major Jason Eadie strutted around camp in tight Union flag briefs and intricately hennaed fingers.

'It's good to have a rank structure who's willing to be

relaxed about it – you can cut about in flip-flops and shorts and I can call this home now,' said Trooper Pierce. 'It's just routine and you get used to it.'

Word of visitors was broadcast through camp and men always changed and shaved to Headquarters standards. B Company's 'old sweats' knew how to stay out of trouble. Improvising furniture and hitting the gym ate time for some. Lance Sergeant Hay raced through Wilbur Smith novels to remind him of Africa, though the Helmand heat melted the glue in paperbacks, infuriatingly robbing books of their final chapter. I found evenings the best times in Attal. As men sat eating Sergeant McAlpine's perfected ten-man ration pack bolognaise, conversation meandered happily. The relative merits of waking up with Cat Deeley or Holy Willoughby on a Saturday morning, the sheer genius of *The Inbetweeners* and an RDG man sticking up loyally for his trade: 'I still think there's a role for Challenger 2 tanks out here, you know.'

Slow weeks were dreadful; the gradual drip of heat and time combined with the little tics of the police ground life out.

'You're very much on your toes here,' said Lance Sergeant Hay. 'It's not so much the combat side of things but the "what if" side. You're sitting there and the stress levels build up quite high, as you don't know what to expect. It's more of a mental challenge.'

There was always risk with the police, something Major Clarke was acutely aware of as the Commander. Short-term efforts to mitigate this risk – beginning to carry pistols in the Afghan compound, for instance – would only feed mistrust and division in the long run.

'I personally could never afford to be unhappy with the risk of partnering,' said Clarke. 'There were times when I was unsettled by it but I could never afford to let that show – the Afghans would notice.'

B Company's mission was to engage in this risk in order to improve security along Route 601 and they did.

*

The officer who handled the incident when a police RPG hit Taj Babi went to see her in the hospital in Bastion. Qadar, her father, approached him. 'I have two people to thank for my daughter's second chance at life,' he said. 'God and Isaf.' The men of the 2nd *Kandak*, Helmand Afghan National Police were notably absent from the old man's assessment.

Hard landing

Guardsman Gary Dykes, 24, had just got back to Bastion from R&R spent with his fiancée in Glasgow. He was getting used to the heat again. The next step to his checkpoint on 23 June is a helicopter to Patrol Base Nahidullah. After that a road move and then three more months of patrols and stag duty beckoned. It would take Dykes seven weeks to make the journey.

The Helicopter Landing Site at Bastion is a stressful place. An hour before the scheduled take-off time, men are dropped off for 'Show Time', a phrase that doesn't conjure up images of Broadway razzmatazz, given the circumstances. They sit and wait in dusty pens marked off with white tape until a Movement Controller comes forward from a small green tent and tells them to get ready. They're up, glasses and gloves on, bergen over one shoulder, weapon over the other. They jog up the short ramp and know they'll be landing somewhere they might rather not be.

In the back of the Merlin transport helicopter with Guardsman Dykes is Sergeant Paxton, also back from R&R, and three new Battlefield Casualty Replacements who struggle with the seatbelts. They're excited about their first-ever helicopter ride. Dykes settles into the front left seat next to the gunner for the 20-minute flight.

It is mid-morning as they come into Nahidullah, and they can see the Hesco-encircled Helicopter Landing Site Delta next to the patrol base out of the 18-inch windows. The dust from Delta kicks up, creating a 'brown out'. Dust pours into the cabin, blinding everyone as the helicopter is engulfed. The pilot pulls up to abort the landing, the power cuts, a wheel

*clips the Hesco. The helicopter flips onto its side and flops
down. The port engine is on fire.*

*Guardsman Dykes is knocked out by the sacks of mail sent
by Left Flank's loved ones. The boot of someone struggling to
get out kicks his face, waking him. It's dark under all the blue
nylon bags and he is on his back, alone. His seatbelt is caught
on the pistol strapped to his chest but his thrashing tells the
gunner that there is someone under the parcels and letters. He
is pulled out, and then collapses as his legs go soft. He sees
Guardsman Sean Kelly's smashed nose. The adrenalin starts
and he's out. Running across Delta he's told to get into camp
and away from the helicopter. The Afghan Company Commander has a rotor blade spin through his tent and is lucky to
be alive. The senior men from the Ops Room sprint out to the
helipad. Surveying the wreckage, the Guardsmen dashing out
of it and the RAF crew in unwieldy helmets and tight
flightsuits, a collective thought went through the onlookers:
'Fuck me, this wasn't on training.' Soldiers rush to the
downed bird to pull the inflammable flare pods out and kill
the engine fire. The insurgents are crowing that they've
brought the Merlin down. Loud-hailers in Nahidullah will
counter-message this locally. In Kabul, HQ Isaf will put out
a press release stating that a 'hard landing' had occurred in
Lashkar Gah District. General McChrystal issues his res-
ignation statement the same day after being shot down by a
hack wearing sunglasses. The two revelations in the* Rolling
Stone *profile – commanders sometimes complain about their
one-up and that guys on the ground aren't wild about
courageous restraint – seem rather benign compared to other
front-line realities.*

*The new boys have had a disastrous introduction to Left
Flank and helicopters. They must have severely reviewed
their career choice. Sergeant Paxton wanders off to see 12
Platoon. Major Kitching looks at £52 million of scrap and
realises Left Flank now own the most expensive helipad in*

Helmand. Guardsman Dykes is sent to the Medical Centre. His back and shoulders are in acute pain. The medics know that getting back on a helicopter will deepen his shock. He is strapped to a stretcher and a sheet is put over his face. The Chinook arrives and he's carted on. The nurses shout, 'Four minutes to landing . . . two minutes to landing . . . one minute to landing' and at this he starts flaying about. 'I was just wanting to get off – it was funny like.' The doctors diagnose him with severe whiplash and his reaction to the flight signposts work for Bastion's Mental Health Team.

Over the next few weeks, psychiatrists get Dykes to talk through the incident under near-hypnosis.

'They get the mind to process it,' he said. 'I didn't realise how powerful it can be, an incident like that.'

He talks to the helicopter pilots and engineers who were on the stricken Merlin. They even walk him through the wreckage of the bird after it is lifted back to Bastion by the US Marines.

Eventually, he's ready to rejoin his unit but knows he'll dread flying for a while.

'I loved flying in a chopper. Fucking brilliant.'

CHAPTER SEVEN

'Horror Ubique'
July and August 2010

Major Rupert Kitching and Second Lieutenant Charlie Pearson are getting the download from an excited Lance Corporal on the morning of 25 July. They're in Camp Bastion, at the Scots Guards Rear Joint Operations Cell (Rear-JOC) and have just returned from a fortnight of R&R. Everything has changed while they have been away. I'm sitting with them. The news from Left Flank's AO has been devastating, so we're listening keenly.

'I used to chew Kabs up for getting me to order up so much milk, but any cheekbone that can take a high-velocity round, well . . .' says Lance Corporal Dan Raisbeck.

The 23-year-old from Durham has been pulled out of 11 Platoon and is heading home to do a Warrior course. Already the reconfiguration back into Armoured Infantry has begun, so there are enough qualified men in 1 SG for the Canadian Prairie in 2011. For now, Raisbeck is mentally still in his outpost and reliving the past fortnight, spattering us with information while we sit nodding.

'Up at Lima 9 X-Ray . . . got myself a white flag . . . aye, he was in bits about Monkey . . . I wouldn't say it hasn't been fun getting the rounds down.'

Company Quartermaster Sergeant Paul Cody walks over. He's Left Flank's Q Bloke and is back in Bastion making sure that everything gets where it needs to go. Left Flank have gone through the Battlegroup's allocation of illumination and ammunition, so having him back in Bastion making sure they're top priority for the kit coming through the logistics hub makes sense. A year ago he was instructing at Sandhurst, shouting at the then Officer Cadet Pearson.

'Do you reckon there's a sharpshooter around Said Abdul, Corporal Raisbeck?' asks Second Lieutenant Pearson, who commands 11 Platoon.

'There is and he's fucking good. The number of head shots . . .' says Raisbeck.

'What are the chances of using 60mm mortar?' asks Pearson.

'That would be fucking good,' the Lance Corporal replies.

'Q Bloke?' asks Pearson.

'They're good, apart from the fact the instructions were in German, which wasn't helpful,' says Colour Sergeant Cody.

'What I want to do is send these fuckers a message,' states Pearson.

'Whatever you want, Napoleon, you crack on. I just send you the ammo,' says Cody.

Pearson notices a crown on Cody's rank slide.

'Have you picked up promotion, Q Bloke?'

'I have, sir. I'm taking over as Company Sergeant Major in charge of Musketry.'

'Oh.'

'You can call me Muskets, sir.'

'Well, that'll look good on your CV.'

'What, when I apply for a job at Tesco?'

The Rear-JOC is a refugee camp for Scots Guardsmen

stuck in Bastion for any reason – internal courses, waiting
for flights in or out of the war, lightly wounded and
recuperating, or even orphans separated from Battalion
at this stage of their career and spammed with extra-
regimental jobs in Helmand. Amongst the vast anonymity
of Bastion, the four-foot-high wooden capstar that the
Pioneer Colour Sergeant has fashioned is a beacon that
shouts 'home'. Driving through the gates, you immediately land in 'Guardsland' and your beret is your passport.
Captain Lawrence Kerr MBE, a Late Entry Officer who
has worked his way up from Guardsman during three
decades in the Regiment, runs things here and is permanently cheery and welcoming. Regimental Quartermaster
Sergeant Neil McClelland is also happy to pause for a
brew with anyone passing through. Of the various cate-
gories of soldier in Bastion, these men and most of their
team belong to the top flight. Experienced infantry soldiers with more ahead of them in their careers if they want
it, they realise that the Army lottery has dealt them the
bum card of six months in Bastion while their Battalion
runs about fighting. They also know that the fighting
comes to a stop without ammunition, water and rations
and the other thousand or so serial number items that
they're asked for every day. They keep current on operations with a daily brief but don't try to get in on the action
with spells of war tourism. They know that the best thing
they can do on Herrick 12 is make sure everything they do
is 'gleaming', rather than poncing about the Cook House
in Bastion wearing combat shirts and bragging about
having 'just come in off the ground' – a favoured occupa-
tion of many *Bastionistas*. They are under no illusions
about their unglamorous job but work hard to get it done.
It's the best welfare they can provide for the young lads
they see coming through camp each day, picking up or
dropping off their mobile phones, passports and morphine

depending on direction of travel. David Beckham dropped in recently, too.

At the moment the tannoy in Bastion is getting too much use. There is a whine and the noise of a man clearing his throat. It sounds like the Call to Prayer in Lashkar Gah but then a British officer's voice comes on: 'Standby for broadcast: Op MINIMISE, I say again, Op MINIMISE. End of broadcast.' The British in Helmand have just taken another serious casualty and all civilian communications are shut until the soldier's next of kin are told.

In some ways it is a call to prayer – let him not be dead, let him not be too badly hurt, let him not be anyone I know, let him not be a Scots Guardsman. The last prayer makes you feel guilty but the Afghans aren't the only ones operating tribally in Helmand. Eyes dart to a screen displaying JChat – a sort of military Facebook wall for Helmand that posts terse updates from headquarters across the province: 'CF NES S – PB Wahid: SALTA: SAF on sangar. 2x rounds assessed as Amber . . . CF Sangin – PB Wishtan: 4 liner . . .' It is gobbledegook to me but I know the code tells of events terrifying and mundane for the men in body armour. If it is a Scots Guards casualty flying back to Bastion, Captain Kerr jumps into a pick-up truck and heads to Helicopter Landing Site Nightingale to greet and assess him so that the man sees his capstar before the medical system takes him. Kerr has been making a lot of trips to Nightingale recently.

In a tent, Second Lieutenant Pearson and Lance Corporal Raisbeck corral a group of battle casualty replacements who have just landed and are beginning their in-theatre training. A few weeks ago, some of them were wearing bearskins and guarding the Queen with F Company in London. Now they are thrown into Left Flank's fight and replacing the men leaving theatre due to death, wounding, sickness or career courses back in the UK.

'It was pretty quiet around Checkpoint Said Abdul and we had a good relationship with the locals. I believe we still do – they're just less willing to inform for us due to intimidation,' says Raisbeck.

'In the first two months of the tour,' adds Pearson, 'we had ten contacts around Said Abdul – which is absolutely nothing. It has totally changed in the past few weeks. There are eight to ten fighters who have moved south of Said Abdul. That doesn't sound like a lot but the amount of firepower they can put down is incredible. You're not going to be bored – that's for sure. Our main effort is Route Trident. Left Flank have got to keep the insurgents away from the Royal Engineers and the Afghan contractors' effort on Trident, which is coming in from the west into our Platoon's Area of Operations.'

'Aye, the Royal Dragoon Guards have come in to help in their Vikings,' says Raisbeck. 'They're good lads, just because they're not from your regiment doesn't mean they're not to be talked to. There's a lot of frustration out there. It will be hard for you at first but the guys there really need you to come in and help them. Mark your kit with your Zap Number in case anything bad happens and tape up your eye-protection so it doesn't fall apart in a contact.'

The young Guardsmen, and some have been flown out here because they have just turned 18, sit trying to take all this in.

'You'll love it. You're fucking lucky. There must be people in F Company wishing they were here. Just don't take it too seriously or you will go mad,' says Pearson lightening the mood, then adds, 'The enemy are nasty; they will hit you.'

'Best thing to do is just laugh the fuckers off,' adds

Raisbeck, 'and just have the confidence to pull that fucking trigger. With regards to the locals, just be nice to them.
They're the ones who, I suppose, we're doing this all for.
It will be a massive learning curve. We're not looking for
VC winners – we're looking for guys who can carry kit and
will muck in in camp. Last thing, I can assure you, just
because you're new, no one out there will leave you out to
dry.'

'Right, guys. Any questions?' asks Pearson.

One of the new soldiers, the perfectly named Guardsman Greenhorn, puts his hand up.

'Aye, sir. What's a Zap Number?' he asks.

'Right,' begins Pearson.

*

At 03:45 the next morning, Major Kitching, Second
Lieutenant Pearson and I head out to the helipad for a
flight to Right Flank at Patrol Base Tapa Paraang. Loy
Adera isn't a popular destination with the helicopter wing
since the Merlin crash, so we will have to get to Tapa and
then drive to Patrol Base Nahidullah. At least the journey
will give Major Kitching a chance to check in on his guys.
The Merlin takes off and sweeps out over the desert. A few
minutes later the Helmand River stretches beneath,
washed by the moon. Looking back, Bastion is a clump
of artificial light amid the vastness of the desert. Below,
spots of light indicate tiny nerve-endings of British foreign
policy where a soldier is huddled in the light of an Ops
Room manning the net. The occasional flare bursts round
to ward off night visitors. The Merlin comes in to land, to
join these thousands of our ambassadors.

In Tapa beds are offered and accepted for a few hours.
Tapa, fairly peaceful after a successful Counter Insurgency campaign, reminds me of a boutique hotel in the

Atlas Mountains – though one with sangars, Warriors and all the rest. At 08:00 Kitching goes up to the Ops Room and talks with Right Flank's new Company Commander, Major Rory Shannon. Right Flank leave Afghanistan in less than two weeks.

'Rory, can you help me out a bit, please? I think we're a tad overextended. If you guys could take Checkpoint South off me then . . .'

'Rups, no bother. We'll make it happen before the Royal Welsh come in to relieve us so you don't have to wrangle with the next guy,' says Shannon.

'Cheers, Rory.'

Captain Iain Monk from the Royal Dragoon Guards walks into the Ops Room. His lean face is covered in dust, save the goggle marks. His trousers are loose fitting and slung gangsta low. Even Kitching, very relaxed by Guards standards, raises an eyebrow at the cavalryman's dash.

'Hi, I'm Monkey – your ride as far east on Mars as we can get you today,' says Monk.

He leads us up to the vehicle park, where three of his Vikings are ticking over. Each of the armoured vehicles consists of two metal boxes articulated together and sitting on tracks. They can go pretty much anywhere – good for outflanking potential IED choke-points – and through anything, though the tracks damage the ground they cover, which is bad for hearts and minds. The RDG are heavy tank boys who now earn their keep driving these mini-tanks and doubling as infantry. The little carbine-length rifles they carry show their cavalry ante-cedents. A Brigade asset, they have been brought in to help keep the Trident upgrade safe but are frequently helping Left Flank out of trouble since conditions on the ground turn towards war.

Mars is shut east of Checkpoint Said Abdul so there are only four kilometres to cover this morning. In the back of the Viking it is ferociously hot as the air conditioning has packed in, and the ride isn't the smoothest heading to Checkpoint North. On arrival Kitching dismounts and finds Platoon Sergeant Major Lilley, who is surprised to see the Company Commander. 'Usual fuck-up with flights,' explains Kitching to Lilley, who nods.

Lilley has sent a bunch of his boys up to Said Abdul.

'Sir, it's just been constant up there – one fucking thing after another. They were getting malleted so we sent Sergeant McCallum up with his .338, two of the Jackals and a Javelin Detachment. If they can positively identify the Firing Points, Dale or the Jav will take care of them,' says Lilley.

'How's Sergeant McCallum getting on?' asks Kitching.

'You know Dale, sir – he's loving it, all over it. He's good pals with Sergeant Gibson, so that helps, and he's a hard man. I've no' had any doubts about him stepping up to anything. If he says: "Get it done," the boys do it.'

'Good. I'm going to try and get him promoted to Acting Sergeant. And things here?'

'It's silly season, sir. You can set your watch by the contacts on the sangars – "Right, it'll be here in ten minutes, lads" – we had one of the new boys shot through the top o' his body armour the other day. He thought he'd been hit and was nearly crying until we pointed out that he was being a big Jessie and to get on with it.'

'Good stuff, Platoon Sergeant Major. Anything else?'

'Aye – I've got seven of Commander Israel's police boys coming in here. Oh and Tam McEwan's up in Said Abdul TRiMing the boys – just so you know.'

'Great – sounds like they could do with all the help they can get. I'll try and get back through once this fucking Bravo Foxtrot 3 thing's sorted out.'

'I'll no hold ma breath, then,' says Lilley.

The Vikings rumble out of the checkpoint, north to the

junction with Mars, then turn east along the part of the route that has been upgraded to Trident. The route has been levelled, had aggregate added and coated with cellular neoprene topping filled and capped with compacted stones. The neoprene netting is meant to be IED-resistant – i.e. it will take someone a long time to dig one in and leave a hugely visible trace (see Chapter Nine). A few sappers are on the road backed up with two Vikings as the local contractors rake aggregate into place and tiptoe towards Checkpoint Inzargul. Each night, an engineer radios Left Flank with an update. Yesterday they managed 90 metres but then ran out of stones and the bulldozer is bust – pretty good going in a war zone. East, in the Gurkhas' Area of Operations, another set of contractors work their way west and eventually the route will meet around Patrol Base Nahidullah. Governor Mangal, along with whichever Brigadier is in charge of Helmand at the time and the Press, will fly in and cut a ribbon. Trident is already months behind schedule. Inside Checkpoint Inzargul, Major Kitching gets a brief from Sergeant Rae.

★

Lance Sergeant MacDougall, now on R&R, has been running the place for much of the time since the successful Mars clearance in early May. He has turned what was an insurgent stronghold into a success story for Isaf in the teeth of serious opposition. Key to success had been a network of informants. Phone calls come into the Checkpoint at all hours, telling of insurgent movements. Locals come in after dark and discuss the latest IED techniques they've spied in the fields and tracks around their compounds. Many families continue to move into the abandoned compounds around Inzargul and even begin building new compounds.

Sergeant Jones's stabilisation work and the rapid processing of compensation claims had also helped win trust in the area. Twenty local stabilisation projects and minor contracts had begun around Checkpoint Inzargul, including six wells, three footbridges and a more substantial bridge. Sometimes the Afghans he had paid let Jones down – bridges would be built in different places to where they were agreed, payment wouldn't go to everyone who had worked on the scheme – but if the local was important to the tactical picture in the area, there was little Jones could do other than express regret. One local was always reliable – the man who had helped clear Mars by dropping the painted stones in May.

'I try to help the intelligence picture but I don't base my projects on it. If someone comes in and gives us a load of intelligence, that doesn't mean that guy is getting all the projects,' said Jones.

However, the informant had projects to suggest and intelligence to offer, so frequently got contracts. One type of project he got a lot of cash from was helping to keep Mars clear. With the route beginning to be reseeded with IEDs, it became apparent that every inch of the road needed to be watched at all times. In June, two Vehicle Checkpoints were put in between Checkpoint Said Abdul and Patrol Base Nahidullah, which each got a million-pound CCTV system to see every blind spot; trees were ripped down and walls destroyed. Rather than sending out sappers to do this and then paying compensation later, Jones went up and down Mars convincing people to cut down their trees for $30 a time.

Jones could settle these claims almost on the spot once satisfied the work was done to his spec. Around Inzargul, 90 per cent of claims had been settled between May and July. Where the claims process was slower, major problems arose (see Chapter Nine). The insurgents noticed the work and in some areas threatened to kill locals who cut down trees for Isaf.

Sergeant Jones's cash obviously helped win support, even if it did sometimes seem that he was constructing a welfare state in Loy Adera on a scale that even his country-man Nye Bevan might have balked at. It was all part of the offer. In contrast, it was simple to tell locals that the insurgents offered nothing. Locals reported a remarkable scheme dreamt up by insurgents whereby if a farmer's livestock struck an IED, not only did he lose the animal but he had to pay for the IED. Others reported taxation of food, water and money. The insurgents also operated through fear. Patrols reported that locals were less and less willing to talk to them, *shuras* were badly attended and, when they were conducted, the checkpoint holding them was inevitably shot at throughout to demonstrate the limits of Isaf's security promises. Beatings picked up but were counter-productive. For instance, the man who had helped clear Mars and continued to feed Inzargul with intelligence had been badly beaten by insurgents in the past and was determined to get his own back now.

Success at Inzargul was based on what Lance Sergeant MacDougall called the 'two-floor war'. On the ground floor informants would come in, taxi drivers would stop, hand over melons and packets of cigarettes and refuse payment. Upstairs in the super-sangar, Guardsmen were taking near-constant accurate fire from multiple firing points. On 1 July, for example, 35 high-velocity single rounds came into the sangar, 80 per cent reportedly within a metre of the men on stag. The three or four insurgents moved around approximately 11 firing points and knew how to avoid surveillance from the air. Over the course of the morning, the Guardsmen could only fire one round back when they saw a muzzle flash and engaged with Grenade Machine Gun. On 9 July, the inevitable happened when Guardsman Jonny McIntyre recoiled after the 14th high-velocity round that had been fired that afternoon hit him. Thinking that the body-armour plate had taken the round, he climbed down the ladder and sat down feeling winded. He then came through the shock and into the pain. When MacDougall eventually got the body armour off, it turned out McIntyre had been shot through the top right corner of his chest. The round stuck just out of his back. A helicopter was summoned. The two-floor war continued that evening when a group of locals came to Inzargul's gates and asked after the injured Guardsman's health.

*

Sergeant Rae takes Major Kitching and me for a wander outside Inzargul. We pass the mosque where Colour Sergeant Cameron and Lance Sergeant Jamieson had their lives changed in April and through the minefield where the counter-IED team found six bombs in May. Rae shows the proposed route for Trident and then points out the white flags a few hundred metres away. They have been put up by the insurgents in competition to the Afghan flags that fly above the checkpoints. Some are marked with messages about Mullah Omar, the Taliban's leader, and many proclaim the Islamic Caliphate of Afghanistan in black writing.

'It's all a political campaign,' as the Commanding Officer is always saying.

Back into the Vikings to trundle the last kilometre to Said Abdul. A few hundred metres down the road the vehicles stop. Detection systems indicate three possible IEDs around us. The RDG troopers dismount and start Valloning. They find a motorbike battery pack hidden in a crisp packet. White flags surround the convoy. There are figures moving about. In the back of the last non-air-conditioned Viking, Second Lieutenant Pearson and I have never been hotter in our lives. We're stripped off, pissing into bottles but can't hydrate quickly enough. I reach the point when I half-expect to see the Cheshire Cat emerge from a ration box and grin:

'We're all mad here. I'm mad. You're mad.'
'How do you know I'm mad?' said Alice.
'You must be,' said the Cat, 'or you wouldn't have come here.'

After three hours, Captain Monk remembers his passengers.

'Oh guys, do open the back door if you're a bit warm,' he says.

Pearson, cheeks like hotplates, swears at the radio and then tries to figure out the door. Then he hears Sergeant Gibson on the net and smiles.

'Two Four Alpha – I've got a call-sign out on the ground moving towards you and from here I can see possible insurgents moving about. One individual dressed as a woman, another in blue. They've stashed a machine gun and are now recceing us unarmed,' he says.

'This is so irritating,' says Monk on the Viking's vehicle net.

'They're fucking good at this,' replies Kitching.

Straight back from R&R and he's having to organise a complex situation from the passenger seat of a Viking. Kitching, Pearson and me dismount the Viking while the troopers begin marking a landing site for a bomb disposal team to fly in and exploit the battery pack.

'What do you reckon, Kitch?' asks Pearson.

'It's got to be an ambush. They know the craic with the counter-IED boys so want us to get them in and maybe have a crack at the helicopter. The battery pack's a come-on,' says Kitching.

'Yep. Reference the white flag 600 metres straight ahead, come a knuckle right and down – you can actually see one of them kneeling down and keeping eyes-on us,' says Pearson.

'Seen. Back into the Viking and we'll mark and avoid the battery pack, I reckon,' says Kitching. A few minutes later, rounds begin rattling the vehicle, whose Commander replies with three warning shots from his GPMG.

'Two Four Alpha – that pair have returned to the machine gun and are having a crawl about,' says Sergeant Gibson.

'Two Zero Alpha – are you seeing that from the sangar or camera?' asks Kitching.

'Two Four Alpha – camera – my mark one eyeball isn't that good.'

'Two Zero Alpha – haven't you got a crystal ball?'

'Two Four Alpha – forgot to put them in today.'

The Viking Commander up top sees more movement so fires off rounds at the gunmen. Gibson spots three more. The helicopter carrying the counter-IED team is stood down.

'Two Zero Bravo – I've just spoken to Blackjack Zero [Headquarters]. We're getting some air in and they're thinking of dropping something on them,' says Captain Hamish Barne.

As Company Second in Command, he's been running Loy Adera for the past fortnight while Kitching has been away. He sounds exhausted. In the back of the Viking, Second Lieutenant Pearson clenches his fist in joy – finally a bomb.

Outside, the foot patrol is engaged. Intelligence reports that the insurgents are moving the weapon with the telescope into position. Five very high-velocity rounds punch the air around the Jackal that is in support. Company Sergeant Major Tam McEwan, sent up from Lashkar Gah to speak with the men in Checkpoint Said Abdul, but then out on a foot patrol due to the lack of commanders, misses getting shot by a inch when a round splits through the bottom of the Jackal he is lying next to. The single round puts the vehicle out of action, though it limps home to Said Abdul. The Guardsman on top-cover responds by bracketing the murder hole with launched grenades, the third of which flies straight into the tiny hole at 150 metres. Pause. The firing continues. The camera can assess that the men are carrying RPGs. The insurgents all filter into a compound and wait and fire. Gibson takes a team out on foot.

'Where the fuck is that air?' asks Pearson in the back of the Viking. 'Zero is probably trying to work out the compensation.'

The ground teams work closer to the insurgent compound to hem them in as the jet comes on station. Approval for the bomb strike is denied. The Jackals pull back to Checkpoint Said Abdul with the exhausted men on foot tabbing in. The Vikings finally get into their destination at 16:30. It has taken almost eight hours – an average run from Edinburgh to London by car – to get four kilometres with two stops on the way. Second Lieutenant Pearson pushes the door of the Viking open. I hope never to have to get in one again. Pearson sees Sergeant Gibson and goes up to him. They go in for the hug but then realise that they're Platoon Commander and Platoon Sergeant and shake hands instead. There's a back slap thrown in to cover up the aborted embrace.

'Fucking good to see you, sir.'

'Fucking good to see you too, Gibby.'

Company Sergeant Major McEwan, the fastest-talking Glaswegian in Battalion, is onto Kitching.

'All right, sir? How's yer R&R? I tell you, I came up here to TRiM the troops – I need to get TRiMed myself now.'

Acting Sergeant Dale McCallum is standing over by the Ops Room, the seat of his trousers ripped in half on something sharp, so he looks suitably warlike. Lance Corporal Izzy Henderson, a medic attached to Left Flank, has made dinner for everyone in camp. 11 Platoon gather around to eat at the large plywood table with their returned Company and Platoon Commanders.

'Right, guys,' says Kitching. 'Tell me about the past few weeks.'

Sergeant Gibson clears his throat and we all listen in.

'Well, sir, as you know on 9 July outside of here . . .'

9–21 July

. . . 'Right, fucking light order and fix bayonets. Back of Mastiff, now!' shouts Gibson, pulling Guardsmen off the wall. The insurgents are in a mosque 200 metres from Checkpoint Said Abdul and using it as a firing point. The contact has been going on for four and a half hours. It started with shots near the sangar, which gradually walked onto their target. An American Cobra gunship had come in but failed to ID the shooters. Second Lieutenant Tulloch's Mastiff arrived and poured .50cal at murder holes but the insurgents kept firing. They moved between compounds, gradually getting closer to Said Abdul. Once they started using the mosque that Gibson usually conducted *shuras* in, he snapped and mounted the assault. This response clearly surprised the insurgents, more used to British soldiers conducting static defences and using firepower to defeat them. By the time Gibson's men stormed into the mosque, the insurgents were gone, leaving plenty of spent cartridges but no blood.

Back in Said Abdul, Second Lieutenant Pearson is waiting for Sergeant Gibson when he gets back.

'All right, Sergeant Gibson?' he asks.

'All right, sir. It just goes against all religion, Jihad or whatever they want to call this war. It just got my blood boiling.'

'Sure. Right, my R&R lift is first thing tomorrow. I've written my mobile number on the whiteboard so give me a call,' says Pearson.

'Yep, I'll call you on your R&R, sir, like in Jellember,' says Gibson. For the next fortnight, he'll be doubling up as sergeant and commander of 11 Platoon. The platoon is split – half in Said Abdul and a large fire team each in the new Vehicle Checkpoints, called Naeem and Mateen, which sit east towards Patrol Base Nahidullah. Gibson is an aggressive and competitive soldier. In Afghanistan his main rival is Sergeant Lee Paxton, who runs 12 Platoon. They've done everything together in the army, so are great friends, but measure their success against one another. He knows Paxton will be keeping a close eye on how he does in the next fortnight.

Second Lieutenant Pearson gets off fine the next day and over the next few days the fire keeps coming onto the sangar for a few hours a day. The agony of trying to identify a shooter either from the ground or with helicopters continues. The white flags creep closer to the checkpoints.

On 12 July, Sergeant Gibson is tasked to standby for the first day of the Trident upgrade along with Second Lieutenant Tulloch from Patrol Base Nahidullah in a Mastiff. The day winds to a close and Tulloch gets called back to Nahidullah.

'Right, Sergeant Gibson, that's us. Same again tomorrow, then?' says Tulloch.

'Absolutely, sir. I'll still be here,' says Gibson.

The Mastiff trundles out through the gates and Gibson goes back to the Ops Room. He turns before going in, stretches his arms out wide and is about to yawn. The explosion is close enough that the sight of a sea of metal and flesh thrown high into the hot afternoon air arrives at Checkpoint Said Abdul at the same time as the vast noise of detonation. Gibson runs to the radio and calls out to Tulloch and the four men in the Mastiff.

'Hello Two Five Alpha, hello Two Five Alpha, hello Two Five Alpha?' he repeats but gets nothing back, so screams to his men, 'Stand to! Mass Casualties. Back of Mastiff right now. Anyone who's dressed goes.'

He powers out of the Ops Room, throws his body armour over his bare torso, grabs helmet and radio, then chucks his rifle and a Vallon into the trailer of his quad bike. As he passes, he pushes the little medic, Lance Corporal Izzy Henderson, into the Mastiff.

'Right, follow me!' he shouts as he kicks the quad into life and zooms out of camp. It is less than 200 metres to the blind spot on Mars where he knows he is going to find dead Guardsmen. He comes round the corner. The Guardsmen are there – alive, untouched. There are dead civilians everywhere and a huge crater.

In the back of Second Lieutenant Tulloch's Mastiff the explosion deafened everyone. The gunner looked back 40 metres and saw wreckage where there had been a minibus stuffed with civilians on their way back from market in Lashkar Gah. A few seconds ago, there were people. Now there were bodies.

'There's casualties, there's casualties – it's the civilians!' he shouts over the Mastiff's intercom.

'Two Five Alpha: contact IED, wait – out,' says Tulloch on the company net. Gibson has been so quick in Said Abdul that he's jumped out the Ops Room before the men in the Mastiff had caught their breath after the near miss.

'Two Five Alpha: the IED has missed our Mastiff. They were aiming for my Mastiff. It's hit a civilian wagon. Mass casualties, wait – out,' sends Tulloch. He scrambles out of the Commander's seat and crawls back through the body of the Mastiff as a Guardsman swings the heavy metal doors open. Their eyes take a second to adjust to the bright sunlight and then focus on the carnage around them.

'Guys, I want everyone looking out for secondary devices and a follow-up shoot,' says Tulloch as he realises he's dealing with a very nasty situation. Between his Mastiff and what's left of the minibus are three mangled bodies blown into a field to the north. The closer the casualties are to the minibus, the better off they seem to be; sitting in a ditch just by it are two old women and a baby, almost unscathed. Mars is strewn with wreckage, so Tulloch puts the Vallon away and walks into the bomb site. One or two of the casualties who are still alive and moving have such horrific injuries that they won't survive. Tulloch starts making decisions.

'Treat him, treat her, don't bother treating him – he's dying – treat her,' he tells his Guardsmen.

Sergeant Gibson tears around the corner in the quad.

'Don't bother trying to Vallon, Sergeant Gibson, there's metal everywhere. We need to sort out a Casevac plan. I'll come to you.'

Gibson looks at his Vallon and tosses it back into the quad trailer. The Said Abdul Mastiff pulls up and the troops dismount and take a knee around Gibson, who directs them out to defensive arcs and then to the casualties. The Counter Narcotics Police stationed in Said Abdul arrive, too.

Lance Corporal Henderson walks through the casualties. The first one she sees is decapitated. The next is a little girl with one foot dangling off; she puts two Guardsmen on her. Tulloch goes into the wreckage of the minibus. Inside, at the centre of the blast, is a two-year-old girl. She is alive. He picks her up and her head lolls back.

'She's the same age as my girl,' says Gibson when he sees Tulloch carrying the child from the wreckage.

Tulloch puts the girl next to Henderson, who gets drawn into her – she is so young and struggling so hard to stay alive. Tulloch needs to snap Gibson away from the girl and onto the Casevac.

'Sergeant Gibson,' he asks, 'what do you reckon for an emergency helicopter landing site in that field to the north?'

'Looks boggy to me, sir, and I'd rather get them back to Said Abdul, treat them in safety and wait out on the helicopters,' says Gibson.

'Yes. Let's do that. We're going to get contacted here in a minute,' says Tulloch.

Gibson pulls the quad forward a metre, does a U-turn and loads the trailer up with the first batch of casualties. He pushes up to Said Abdul and then back down to the wreckage. The gunner on top of Tulloch's Mastiff has seen more casualties blown over a wall to the south.

'How can there be more?' thinks the officer as he jumps up on the Mastiff. Then he sees the bodies and jumps over the wall. Gibson gets Lance Sergeant Tom Morris to punch his Mastiff through the wall and then sends Guardsmen in to rescue the three catastrophically injured men. There is also another body cut in half and another dead civilian up the alleyway into Popolzai Kalay. An intelligence report comes through: the insurgents will detonate another device at the site. As many casualties as possible are loaded into the quad and Gibson takes them up to Said Abdul, with Henderson following him in the Counter Narcotics truck. The Sergeant then goes back down and picks up the walking wounded, leaving Tulloch and his men.

Inside Said Abdul, Lance Sergeant Willie Browning is getting the casualty reports consolidated on the net and throwing them up to Zero, who are onto Brigade, who have already launched a helicopter. The Guardsmen have laid the bodies out in a rough triage and Henderson goes between the casualties re-checking their work. Sergeant Jones, the stabilisation representative, happens to be in camp and is lending a hand with the first aid when a local wanders into the scene and asks him for some money for an old Cash for Works scheme. Jones tells him to piss off.

There are five casualties for the helicopter. Gibson takes more men out to the landing site and provides security as it flies in and picks up the Afghans. As the Chinook flies off, the insurgents try to shoot it down. Gibson goes back into Said Abdul under fire, pours water down his body armour and gives an update on the net. Commander Israel turns up from Checkpoint Yellow 14 and takes the three walking wounded to Lashkar Gah in his truck. Gibson can see the troops who have already been down to the blast site are beginning to process what they've just witnessed so he leaves them. He pulls together another group of Guardsmen who've not been down yet and briefs them on what they're about to see, then gets them into the Mastiff and drives back down for a fourth time.

'What's the procedure with dead Local Nationals do you think, Sergeant Gibson?' asks Second Lieutenant Tulloch.

'No idea, sir,' replies Gibson. He is still retching each time he looks at the sights around him. Word comes down that the bodies should be centralised for easy collection by relatives. Guardsmen go around picking up remains. The intestines of one man spill over Guardsman Delaney, who breaks down. Guardsman Spencer isn't far behind and bursts too. Gibson sits them down in the Mastiff then goes to each body and drapes them in rags. They photograph the scene and send a grid reference at each body to record the incident in full. The Counter Narcotics Police come back down and help. Gibson takes his men to Said Abdul and Tulloch drives east to Patrol Base Nahidullah. A hundred metres down the road they see yet another body blasted from the minibus.

In Said Abdul the first of many relatives begin pouring into the checkpoint demanding news. The casualties were all unconscious when put on the helicopter so there's no way of telling them who went to Bastion. As Sergeant Gibson tries to conduct a *shura* with the traumatised locals, the insurgents open up with a contact on the sangar to intimidate the people into leaving. Down at the wreckage, people are carting the bodies away for hasty burial. There will be no forensics or Afghan police investigation. Guardsman Delaney is flown back to Britain 72 hours later with scars that cannot be seen, along with Guardsman Spencer who also has an injured knee.

Later, a bomb disposal expert tells me how the incident began. An insurgent – later identified as a Pakistani since banned from Helmand by the Taliban after this screw-up – was sitting in a nearby compound on the end of a command wire attached to a massive main charge weighing between 50 and 70 kilograms. The wall in front of him had a 12-foot-long depression along its top that made for a crude aperture. Once the target was framed, he would pull the cord and destroy an Isaf vehicle. Perhaps the heat of the day got to him and he dozed off, and then woke just as the tail end of the Mastiff passed through his marker. He still yanked the cord, though couldn't have seen the minibus from where he was. It collided with the explosion. The men in Vehicle Checkpoint Naeem, 300 metres away, saw him stumble off concussed but unarmed. There was nothing they could do. The charge was big enough to seriously damage a Mastiff. At the least, the gunner would have been sent flying out of his turret. Its effect on an unarmoured vehicle full of civilians was self-evident: eight were killed, five were very seriously injured and three walked away with minor injuries. The young girl pulled from the wreckage was amongst the dead.

*

The following days were spent resolving the incident. Understandably, there was a near-constant stream of family members trying to get more information on what had happened and the counter-IED teams went into Bravo Foxtrot 3 (the name given to the blind spot where the bomb had detonated) to investigate any evidence. The Royal Dragoon Guards Viking Squadron also began to filter into Left Flank's patch.

Second Lieutenant Tulloch had learned from previous incidents that the best way of dealing with events was to get back onto the ground and keep his and his Guardsmen's minds occupied. He was happy then when, on 20 July, he was tasked to take a patrol to the north of Said Abdul and demonstrate presence in the area. The patrol was ambushed from three sides.

'Why are they shooting at us?' asked Guardsman Andre Bekker. 'They don't even know us.'

Sergeant Paxton took a burst. Miraculously, only one round connected with him – splitting his wrist. Others shredded his webbing, day-pack and camera. Major Denis James, the Royal Dragoon Guards Squadron Leader, chose this moment to make his entrance to Loy Adera. He tore up in his Viking, firing his pistol in one direction and his machine gun in the other.

'Gather you could do with a hand?' he said to a startled Second Lieutenant Tulloch.

'You're terribly kind,' replied the subaltern. 'This is like something out of *A Bridge Too Fucking Far*,' he thought as he bundled Paxton into the wagon. With his Platoon Sergeant out of the game and two Section Commanders back in Britain on courses, Lance Sergeant Wood would have to lead 12 Platoon during Tulloch's R&R. The officer hoped it would work.

*

The next day, a Viking struck an IED in almost the same spot (Bravo Foxtrot 3) where the minibus had been smashed. Again, Sergeant Gibson was standing by his Ops Room door looking east when he heard the explosion and again rushed down with a team thinking he would find dead soldiers strewn along Mars. Luckily, the Viking had been only lightly damaged. The men inside had had a communications problem so Gibson brought a pair of mildly injured troopers back up to Checkpoint Said Abdul and then went back down to drag the Viking home. Clearly Mars was shut and a full cordon and search operation would have to go in to investigate and clear the vital route.

*

'Hamish, if I get shot on the day of my R&R, you and me are going to have words,' said Second Lieutenant Tulloch as he left the Ops Room in Patrol Base Nahidullah on the morning of 21 July.

He'd be a small mobile reserve in a Mastiff with a pair of men while a Viking would keep the counter-IED team safe on Mars and Second Lieutenant Cowdry and the Afghan soldiers he advised would be strung out to the north. To the south, in Popolzai Kalay, two fire teams from 11 Platoon would form an outer cordon and block any threat to the men clearing Bravo Foxtrot 3 of any more IEDs. The cordon was in by 10:00.

After foot-patrolling from Said Abdul, Lance Sergeant Tom Morris put his four-man team in a derelict compound facing out to the east and Lance Sergeant McCann placed his men in a nearby compound looking south. With Morris was Lance Corporal Philip Ayers, a 22-year-old mechanic from Oxford who had been stuck west of Bravo Foxtrot 3 by the Viking strike and had volunteered for the cordon. He was pretty excited. As a mechanic his job usually involved recovering and fixing those of Left Flank's vehicles that either blew up or gave up. A foot patrol and cordon would be something different. Also with Morris was Guardsman Glen Murray, a confident 24-year-old from Pretoria who had just returned from R&R in Scotland, and Guardsman James Hobson. The small team took it in turns to keep an eye out and settled down to a long wait in the baking sun. Lance Sergeant McCann's team had a more interesting patrol in. Guardsman Maciu Kabunicaucau from Fiji had found the 30-metre command wire running from a derelict compound towards the site of the IED that had hit the minibus full of civilians.

In Checkpoint Said Abdul, Sergeant Gibson was playing host to the Commanding Officer and his Tac group of three vehicles. The Regimental Sergeant Major was away so Colour Sergeant Denver Nunn was running Tac, and Captain Stuart Rowe had managed to sneak out of his office in Lashkar Gah for a welcome day out. They wanted to get through to Patrol Base Nahidullah for a night but, because of Bravo Foxtrot 3, were stuck in Said Abdul until the clearance was finished. Gibson made his guests as comfortable as possible, gave the Commanding Officer his appreciation of the local situation and then got on with the day's admin. He had to get two men from the Vehicle Checkpoints out for R&R via Patrol Base Nahidullah. This meant getting them to foot-patrol back to Said Abdul to hand in their kit, sending a commander to relieve them, and then driving them to Nahidullah once the bomb disposal team declared Mars open. Lance Sergeant McCann could relieve the two R&R men but he was on the cordon. The solution presented itself: he'd get McCann down to Mars, swap with the men there and they'd go up to the cordon for the rest of the day and then get to Said Abdul, hand in their kit and start the journey home. Such are the working parts a platoon sergeant works with. Colour Sergeant Nunn heard Gibson giving his orders over the radio and offered to drive him down to meet McCann in Tac's Coyote – an open-topped six-wheeled version of a Jackal. The .50cal gunner, Lance Corporal Stephen Monkhouse, 28 years old, from Greenock and a Drummer in the Scot Guards Pipes and Drums, stood up and headed to the Coyote. He'd been chatting to a pal from home, Guardsman Darren Butterworth, who worked in Said Abdul. The two hadn't seen each other for a while. Butterworth mentioned he'd got engaged and Monkhouse immediately agreed to play the drums at his friend's wedding.

'If you hear it going pa-pap-pap-pap-pa,' he said over his shoulder, 'that'll be me getting the rounds down.'

'You'll no get nay rounds down – you're Commanding Officer's Tac and you've done nothing all tour!' teased Butterworth.

Back on the cordon, nothing much had happened. During the first few hours, the local farmers had been pretty active but there hadn't been many people seen after noon. The Afghan National Army had knocked off for the day at around 14:00 and headed back to Patrol Base Nahidullah for lunch. Second Lieutenant Cowdry sat in the back of Tulloch's Mastiff to cool down once the Afghan soldiers left and chatted away. Cowdry ribbed his friend for being the only soldier in Helmand to have received a 'Dear John' letter while not having a girlfriend. The pair had gone through training together where Cowdry had baited Tulloch, insisting that they were 'work colleagues and not friends'. Lance Sergeant McCann got his orders from Sergeant Gibson. He left his three-man fire team behind and went down a safe route to Mars, where Sergeant Gibson and the Coyote were parked. He looked over at the counter-IED team. In six hours of painstaking work they had cleared less than 100 metres. The amount of shrapnel on the road made work almost impossible. McCann got into the Coyote.

Guardsman Kabunicaucau took the third round of the burst square on the cheekbone, spun round and fell to the floor. Guardsman Ritchie Carr was immediately up on the wall and fired off 20 rounds in the likely direction of fire. He got down again and Lance Corporal Berger, a Royal Logistics Corps driver who had also volunteered for the cordon, got onto the wall and began suppressing. Berger's rifle then had a stoppage and he had to cock it each time he fired. Carr went to Kabunicaucau, ripping his med pouch open as he went and grabbing a First Field Dressing. He got onto his radio and began calling for his Lance Sergeant – 'Mo, Mo, Mo!' He sounded heartbroken on the net. Lance Sergeant Morris was already up and running towards the second fire team. His three men ran after him, drawing the fire of a machine gun that spattered rounds at their feet as they dashed over the 70 metres of open ground, firing as they went. As they got into the five-by-five-metre compound where the wounded team were, the pitch changed to single high-velocity rounds zinging above them, their provenance masked with more automatic fire. Lance Corporal Ayers and Guardsman Hobson took cover either side of a doorway. They took turns darting out and loosing off rounds. Hobson suddenly recoiled and looked shocked.

'Are you OK, are you OK?' shouted Ayers.

The Guardsman nodded but his eyes rolled back and he looked like he'd been knocked out. With no sign of blood and more fire coming in, Ayers went back to putting rounds down. Hobson joined him.

Lance Sergeant Morris saw the Fijian slumped on the ground, while Guardsman Carr tried to get the dressing on. Morris thought Kabunicaucau must be dead.

'Two Four Charlie: man down – gunshot wound to face. I need help from any call sign. MIST to follow.'

By now Sergeant Gibson had sprinted up to the position, following the safe route he'd seen Lance Sergeant McCann walk calmly down just a few minutes earlier. He leapt in and saw the situation.

'Right, Mo – win us this fucking firefight while I sort out Kabs.'

He went over to the casualty.

'You're alright, I'm here now, you're going to be alright, I'm going to get you out.'

Gibson tried to pick Kabunicaucau up but even adrenalin won't shift a fully laden six-foot-four Fijian. He dragged him instead. Kabunicaucau comes round and gets up, gets over a wall and slumps next to Gibson, who cradles his head and continues to treat him.

An RDG Viking commanded by Corporal Matthew Stenton smashes uphill and through a narrow walled alley towards the casualty. Stenton is firing into multiple enemy firing points as he commands his vehicle up to Gibson. The back door swings open and Gibson gets Kabunicaucau up and into the safety of the Viking. Gibson closes the

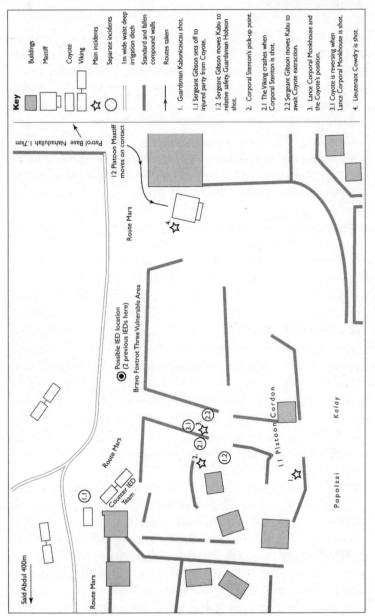

Key

Buildings

Mastiff

Coyote

Viking

Main incidents ☆

Separate incidents ○

1m wide waist deep irrigation ditch

Standard and fallen compound walls

Routes taken →

1. Guardsman Kabunicaucau shot.

1.1 Sergeant Gibson sets off to injured party from Coyote.

1.2 Sergeant Gibson moves Kabu to relative safety, Guardsman Hobson shot.

2. Corporal Stenton's pick-up point.

2.1 The Viking crashes when Corporal Stenton is shot.

2.2 Sergeant Gibson moves Kabu to await Coyote extraction.

3. Lance Corporal Monkhouse and the Coyote's position.

3.1 Coyote is reversing when Lance Corporal Monkhouse is shot.

4. Lieutenant Cowdry is shot.

Patrol Base Nahadullah 1.7km

12 Platoon Mastiff moves on contact

Route Mars

Possible IED location (2 previous IEDs here)

Bravo Foxtrot Three Vulnerable Area

Said Abdul 400m

Route Mars

Route Mars

Counter IED Team

Route Mars

11 Platoon Cordon

Popolzai   Kalay

Events of 21 July 2010

door and in the sudden darkness, the Fijian starts lashing out, screaming and trying to rip his dressing off and disentangle it from his radio and helmet. Gibson tries to calm him down, then gets on the radio.

'We need to fucking move here! Let's get out of here, come on!'

Outside, Lance Sergeant Morris is screaming for air.

'Two Four Charlie – where's this fucking Apache then?'

'Two Zero Bravo – it will be with you in figures two.'

'Two Four Charlie – that's what you said two minutes ago.'

He looks over at the Viking.

'Keep fucking suppressing with that Gimpy!'

He looks out at Popolzai and fires off a few more rounds, then looks back at the Viking as it starts to reverse. Corporal Stenton is no longer visible in the cupola. His gun is silent.

Inside the Viking it had been noise for Sergeant Gibson – Kabunicaucau screaming, the gun up top, the sound of the Viking reversing, a massive bang as it smashed up against a wall, silence when the gun stops, the Viking bouncing forward. Then the door opens, letting in light and noise and Afghanistan.

'The commander's been shot – he's getting extracted. There's a Coyote coming for you up the alleyway,' says Corporal Darrell Winn of the RDG.

The Coyote stops next to the Viking and Lance Corporal Monkhouse on the .50cal puts down a fearsome rate of fire. Colour Sergeant Nunn runs to the back of the Viking and helps Gibson drag the casualty to the back of the Coyote. Gibson jumps in and then drags the Guardsman in next. The Viking reverses and leads off. Gibson sees his men desperately suppressing the area as rounds kick into the walls around them.

'Mo! Start extracting as we go!' he shouts under the din

of the .50cal. The Coyote begins to reverse. The gun
stops. Morris looks round. Monkhouse is lying on his
gun. Gibson tries to drag him down but he is caught on an
ammunition tray. The driver reverses too quickly and
almost tips the six-wheel vehicle, but the narrow alley
walls correct him and he scars them deeply. He regains
control and goes back and then reverses round the corner
onto Mars and back to Said Abdul. Gibson has a hand on
each casualty as they bump along the route. He gets
Monkhouse's helmet off and checks for signs. Kabunicaucau is drifting in and out of consciousness.

Lance Sergeant McCann joined Morris and the two fire
teams began extracting back down the alleyway. One
would put down covering fire as the other moved back
deliberately. They can hear bullets coming over the walls
down into the alleyway from plenty of directions. As they
pass a gap in the alleyway wall, they see Second Lieutenant Tulloch's Mastiff in trouble.

When the firing started, Tulloch had punched his
Mastiff into a field to help suppress firing points, then
to help get casualties out as the cascade of news came over
the net. Once the wagon was parked about 100 metres
short of the casualties, Second Lieutenants Tulloch and
Cowdry jumped out and almost immediately came under
fire. Taking cover behind the Mastiff doors, they took
turns to jump out and empty a magazine into the nearby
compound they were getting shot at from. They could see
the casualties getting pulled out and knew that if they were
getting shot at then the Casevac was getting less attention.
That meant they were achieving something. The .50cal on
top of the Mastiff then stopped working. Cowdry jumped
back into the wagon and pulled out the top-cover's machine gun, rolled out from cover and began firing on
automatic into the compound. Within seconds, he took
a ricochet off the Mastiff and into his face and was stung

into cover. After checking himself, he rolled back out and continued firing. In the Mastiff, Tulloch gave the gunner, Guardsman Mears, his rifle and told him to join Cowdry. He then jumped up to try and fix the vehicle's gun. He would cock it, fire a round, cock it, fire a round and pray that the stoppage would clear as he worked the parts back and forwards. He looked down and saw Cowdry drop his machine gun and move for cover. Tulloch jumped down and went to the back of the wagon, then dragged Cowdry into the Mastiff with Mears and shouted at the driver to get back onto Mars and on to Patrol Base Nahidullah. His friend was clutching a bleeding stomach wound.

In Checkpoint Said Abdul, the Viking had already arrived and Corporal Stenton was laid out being treated by the time the Coyote returned with Lance Corporal Monkhouse and Guardsman Kabunicaucau. Medic Lance Corporal Izzy Henderson had been in the back of Guardsman Butterworth's Mastiff, which had been sent to pick up Guardsman Kabunicaucau. Instead, the Viking and the Coyote had gone up to rescue him so the Mastiff ended up as the last vehicle home. In the Mastiff, she was told there were three casualties – all face. She froze for a moment. Once the doors opened, she snapped out of it and went over to the men. An American Medic was treating Monkhouse with Colour Sergeant Nunn. Guardsman Butterworth sprinted over to his fellow Greenock man to try and help. Men were trying so hard with chest compressions that they would exhaust themselves and then hand over to the next man. Henderson went next to Stenton. She assessed his condition but there was nothing more than the life-saving treatment which was already being administered that could be done. She went to treat Kabunicaucau, who was still talking and trying to slash the dressing off his smashed face. His eyes began to close and he wanted to lie back. Henderson had to force him to keep sitting.

Sergeant Gibson was getting the casualty reports consolidated as the helicopter made its way to Said Abdul. Captain Rowe was motivating Tac to get ready for the helicopter run with the three casualties on stretchers. When news of incoming casualties came in, the Commanding Officer had climbed into the super-sangar – the best place to see and assess the entire incident. At one point he realised the Counter Narcotics Police were spraying fire in the likely direction of what was left of the cordon and screamed them into ceasing. Every one else in camp was on the walls ready to cover the helicopter in. The men left out on the ground, including the counter-IED team, had made it in by now under cover of the Apaches that had arrived and a column of Vikings that raced up from the Trident upgrade to help. They formed a ring of steel for the helicopters to aim for. The Chinook came in and landed on coloured smoke. The Commanding Officer, Sergeant Gibson and Tac sprinted out and handed the three casualties over to the doctors, who were shot at as they flew out. Lance Corporal Henderson sat down with tears in her eyes. The Commanding Officer went over to her.

'I've had to deal with most things. But when it's one of your own, it's different,' she said. They hugged.

Second Lieutenant Tulloch was doing four things at once in the Mastiff. Guardsman Mears was shouting Second Lieutenant Cowdry's vital signs at him, which Tulloch was writing on his leather gloves, the company net was demanding details in one ear, his driver needed guidance through the vehicle net in his other ear and he needed to keep looking for threats. The donkeys on Mars that wouldn't move snapped him, so he drew his pistol and fired a magazine at them. They moved. Eventually the Mastiff swung into Patrol Base Nahidullah, where a team grabbed Cowdry and flung him into the Medical Centre.

Tulloch stayed with his friend as the morphine kicked in but had no idea if the wound was potentially fatal or not. The Chinook from Said Abdul was on its way to Nahidullah, so Tulloch helped load Cowdry onto the stretcher then held his hand across the helipad, screaming at him all the way to stay conscious. On the helicopter, Tulloch saw Kabunicaucau lying down with his face full of blood while Corporal Stenton and Lance Corporal Monkhouse both received CPR. 'Fucking hell!' he thought. It had taken about 45 minutes from the first round to the Chinook taking off from Patrol Base Nahidullah. His R&R began the next day.

In Combined Force Headquarters in Lashkar Gah the ZAP Numbers and reports had been streaming over the radio. Someone had approached Captain Tom Cowdry, the Intelligence Officer.

'Tom, it's about George. He's been shot and is on his way to Bastion. We're not sure how serious it is.'

Captain Cowdry didn't know if his younger brother was dead or alive when he got on the helicopter to Bastion.

A series of incidents like that take some sorting out and assessing. An Apache spotted the machine gun Second Lieutenant Cowdry had dropped when shot and a patrol went out to collect that. The R&R men from the Vehicle Checkpoints still needed to get to Patrol Base Nahidullah, so Lance Sergeant Morris took a Mastiff and set off down Mars. He rather defeated the point of the whole route clearance operation the day had started with when he bounced through Bravo Foxtrot 3 without incident. In Nahidullah, Morris talked the day through with Second Lieutenant Tulloch.

'It sounds like there were eight of them and we may have killed one and injured one. That's great odds for the insurgents, sir,' he said. 'They know where the IEDs are and we don't, so they've got total freedom of movement while we're pinned in on the assumption that the IEDs are everywhere. They had six hours to organise it and get a team together and when they hit us, there were only seven Guardsmen on the cordon. Great odds. And these guys from the RDG and Tac have come up to help us. Off their own backs they'd come up to help us, and unfortunately . . . it felt like the shooter was picking us off one by one in that compound.'

In Said Abdul men got on with kit checks. Guardsman Hobson realised why he had felt knocked out earlier on the cordon when he took off his helmet cover and found a bullet hole in the side of his helmet and another where the round had ricocheted out the top. The suspected sniper had shot four men in the head, another gunman one in the stomach. Guardsmen kept busy cleaning rifles and re-stocking ammunition and medical supplies for the next patrol while a girl from the counter-IED team cooked for the whole camp. It had never been busier or quieter. Sergeant Gibson went into the Guardsmen's tent and packed up Guardsman Kabunicaucau's kit, knowing it would be needed soon. He was devastated that one of his men had been hit, especially as he hadn't been there when it had happened. He was also exhausted from the past days. It had mounted up. He had watched his men go through so much and all he wanted was to make sure they were all right. Senior guys would tell him to stop Vallon-ing – to command. He felt he was leading and could command at the same time. And if he could take some pressure off his guys, occasionally keep them out of harm's way, then that was good too. The problem was that in the past fortnight there was no one to take the pressure off Sergeant Gibson. At least his friend Lance Sergeant McCallum was coming up to Said Abdul in a few days' time and then Second Lieutenant Pearson would be back from R&R. Together they could start fighting back.

A few hours later, the Commanding Officer came over to the dining table in Checkpoint Said Abdul.

'Corporal Stenton and Lance Corporal Monkhouse didn't make it. Guardsman Kabunicaucau and Mr Cowdry are both stable,' he said.

The next day he went to Bastion to see the injured and dead away. In the Intensive Care Unit he went to Guardsman Kabunicaucau's bed. The Fijian couldn't speak as his jaw was half shot off so wrote a note and handed it to his Commanding Officer.

'Sir – I don't want to go back to UK. I want to go back to Said Abdul and 11 Platoon.'

★

It is dark by the time 11 Platoon have told us their story. There is a pall of cigarette smoke over the table in Said Abdul. The men here are all utterly changed from the ones I met in training.

'Right. Well. We'll head up to Nahidullah tomorrow morning. See you all then – I'd better go and listen to the Company Conference,' says Kitching.

26 July–12 August

The next morning, with Mars still shut, Sergeant Gibson takes Major Kitching and me on a foot patrol to Vehicle Checkpoint Naeem, roughly a kilometre to the east. Anxious to avoid paths and not set patterns, we go through streams and thick cornfields where some Guardsmen fixed bayonets. Walking through an alley marked by the Vallon man with yellow spray paint, the patrol took roughly an hour. On the way, Kitching took the patrol south of Mars into some open ground around a derelict compound. Once he'd built the plan up, he'd put a new vehicle checkpoint here to keep an eye on Bravo Foxtrot 3.

Inside Vehicle Checkpoint Naeem, Kitching had a chat with Sergeant Jones, the stabilisation representative. For the first few months of the tour, Jones couldn't understand why the locals had refused his repeated offer to build schools in Loy Adera. The level of violence unleashed in the fighting season had shown why.

'Perhaps the guys through in the winter would be able to establish something,' Jones hoped.

The violence effectively brought an end to much of his job, as he couldn't get out and speak with the people. The increased presence of insurgents in the area meant that many locals were not willing to come and speak to Isaf in their bases. When a well-advertised and free vet clinic took place at Patrol Base Nahidullah, for instance, only two people came in with 41 goats. The days of 50 people attending a Sunday *shura* were also long gone. With patrols getting themselves into firefights and having to concentrate on casualties rather than stabilisation, the 'build' phase of Counter Insurgency became harder to implement. Indeed, the violence had caused a great deal of destruction. Viking tracks had ploughed up fields of crops nearly ready to harvest, bullets and grenades had begun to chip away at compounds. Walls had been destroyed in an effort to clear lines of sight onto Mars. As long as Jones could keep the compensation flowing, he might be able to keep the locals on the side of 'the offer'. Some projects had gone ahead despite the violence but overall Jones was frustrated.

'There's a lot more I wish I could have done, even if it was just wells,' he told me.

Major Kitching headed out of Vehicle Checkpoint Naeem and into a Mastiff. Sergeant Gibson picked up a group of replacements and gave them a terrifying brief on what to do if they got shot at on the way back to Checkpoint Said Abdul and which pocket to put their morphine in. They looked very young. Within minutes of leaving Naeem, they were shot at for the first time in their lives. In Vehicle Checkpoint Mateen, Kitching got a brief from the commander and looked around the primitive compound and then up at the sangar.

'Ah, I should go and have a word with Guardsman Plant, ' he said and climbed the rough wooden ladder to the sangar. Michael Plant was an older Guardsman who had never made it up to Lance Corporal. Some senior Guardsmen are revered – everyone respects that they're happiest without official responsibility but welcomes the experience they bring; often they act as an older sibling to the 18-year-old 'crows' that come into a platoon. Plant was not that type. The problem was, he just never helped himself and kept screwing up. With no muckers to talk to in a tiny outpost, Plant began to crack under the mental pressure of six months in Helmand. There were also unfortunate dramas back in his hometown. He began to suspect that his fiancée was seeing another man; something had felt wrong on the phone since R&R. Plant hatched a plan to win her back. One night he gave the interpreter the Satellite Phone and got him to phone the girl and tell her that Plant had been blown up in an IED but was fine and only needed treatment in Bastion. The fiancée, distraught, phoned up the Scots Guards Families Officer in Catterick. He, obviously, had heard nothing of the IED incident. Clearly the communication chain had broken down – an unforgivable error. He phoned the Adjutant in Lashkar Gah and gave him an earful. The Adjutant phoned Captain Barne in Nahidullah and did the same. Barne explained that there had been no IED, and, as far as he knew, Guardsman Plant was still intact and probably on stag in a checkpoint as they were speaking.

The episode reflected badly on everyone. While it was miraculous there weren't more instances like it, the saga had shown that isolation and separation were additional enemies Guardsmen had to contend with on tour. After a long chat with Plant, Kitching got back into his Mastiff and moved off to his headquarters.

Patrol Base Nahidullah had continued its transformation from basic Hesco polygon to a major operational hub. The RDG Squadron Headquarters was parked in the middle of the camp, the helipad had been upgraded after the Merlin crash, there was a new CCTV system and all manner of other attachments. Perhaps most important, a shipping container was plugged into a generator and functioning as a fridge. It was stuffed with cold water, the most desired commodity in Helmand for those who lack it. Kitching opened the stiff metal doors and pulled out a litre and a half of Kinley water. (Processed and bottled by the Coca-Cola Corporation abroad, delivered to Bastion by civilian contractor and then moved to Nahidullah by the Royal Logistics Corps.) He walked towards his Ops Room. Hanging by the door was Left Flank's blue company flag decorated with silver wings, thunderbolts and the company's motto: '*Horror Ubique*' ('Striking Fear Everywhere').

★

The people in Brigade who counted the bullets and bombs had declared Loy Adera the most violent place in Helmand. Major Kitching considered this a failure on his part rather than something to bask in. The years of boasting about 'punchy' tours of Afghanistan and 'giving the insurgents a bloody nose' were gone – as far as the Scots Guards were concerned. In 2010, success was measured by how safe a company made an area rather than how many people they'd killed. It's still an evolving attitude but hopefully the shift will be made soon. I'll know the campaign in Helmand is nearly won when the first thing a recently returned soldier in a pub tells me about is how many schools he's built, not how 'fucking cheeky/punchy/kinetic' his tour was.

The upside of this failure was the vast resources now thrown at Left Flank to win back Loy Adera. At times the Company had as many as 450 soldiers on its books, from dog-handlers to electronic warfare technicians. Assets held at Brigade level – the Brigade Reconnaissance Force and a taskforce of specially mentored Afghan commandos – had also begun thinking about mounting operations in Major Kitching's sector. The risk in these plans was that a group who came in, kicked in doors and then left could create havoc for the troops permanently in Loy Adera who had tried to build relationships with the local people. By now, though, the situation had become so grave that any and all help would have to be accepted. In the longer term, shiny plans about government outreach offices, community centres, seed distribution programmes and police precincts could come to fruition. First, Left Flank would have to regroup and pacify the area.

Key to sustaining the soldiers through their experiences was keeping them mentally stable. The Army's Trauma Risk Management (TRiM) process was vital to this, especially as men began to develop signs of battle shock. TRiMing involved trained members of Left Flank, battle-field counsellors so to speak, getting to soldiers who had witnessed horrific events. After 48 but within 72 hours, they would encourage them to talk through what happened in a non-judgmental environment. The assessor would look for elements of self-blame along with physical symptoms such as changes in sleep patterns. Everyone is taught to recognise symptoms and refer their friends to the right person if they think they're beginning to suffer. Three months after the incident, a second session would revisit the incident. Company Sergeant Major Lawrie coordinated the TRiMing in Left Flank. Initially, he'd noticed the troops had considered it 'a big fluffy group hug thing', but it isn't. He was astounded at the amount of men the four TRiMers talked to and how it seemed to be the same men over and again. Those who had drawn a bad base at the start of the tour went through trauma after trauma. July in Checkpoint Said Abdul in particular had been endless and inescapable – each day Guardsmen patrolled past the places where they'd seen horrendous events. By the end of the tour, Lawrie's four-man team had conducted around 100 sessions, TRiMing many soldiers three times. Two sessions had resulted in sending soldiers home immediately; two spent time in Bastion while the others were not assessed as immediate risks. How many would have developed problems later in the tour and become casualties without the TRiM process is impossible to say.

'Some of the younger boys who've dealt with casualties . . .,' said Lawrie, '. . . hats off to them. In my younger days, I never seen any of that but these boys are pretty much expected to now.'

Lawrie also noticed the mental pressure placed on commanders. They make life or death decisions about the men under them, and their priorities were always their men's welfare and not their own.

*

To pacify Loy Adera, Left Flank had to get the message across to the people that the insurgents were to blame for the violence, though clearly there was a counter-message that if the infidels were gone, there would be no need for an insurgency. The minibus tragedy had presented a twisted opportunity to Left Flank to push their message. This read that the indiscriminate insurgents needed to be kicked out through a combination of Isaf and Afghan muscle and communities standing up to them. 'I thought we were onto a winner,' said Sergeant Gibson. 'I thought we were going to get loads of information and the people would help us out. But it was just another event for the locals round here.'

One local questioned why he should try to stand up to the insurgents.

'How many nations are there in your coalition, 42? And you have the Afghan forces, too. And still you cannot defeat these insurgents. How am I supposed to?'

It was a very strong argument. The ruthlessness of the insurgents – take them trying to shoot down a helicopter they knew to be full of local civilian casualties – was documented and intimidating. Major Kitching maintained that he wasn't asking the locals to stand up as individuals but as a community: 'everyone locking their compounds to insurgents, everyone standing up together and providing information that can help us'. The risk of intimidation to locals was real but, for Second Lieutenant Tulloch, group action seemed bound to succeed.

'These guys are utter bastards and the local population have been slightly wet in not doing more about standing up to them . . . they all give us the "we're scared" excuse but we generally think that's bollocks. It's very easy: the insurgents aren't going to start massacring whole communities. I would be scared of them individually but I do think that these communities can get up and just tell the insurgents that it's not going on.'

Could it have been that, in fact, the people of Loy Adera were more in favour of the insurgents, and, though willing to take cash from Isaf, their interest in 'the offer' was scant and their failure to stand up to the insurgents a form of passive resistance to foreign occupiers? Bahadur Khan, the Counter Narcotics Police Commander in Loy Adera, denied this when I asked him.

'The people here are impartial at the moment. The insurgents force them to give information and use their compounds as firing points.'

According to his own informants, the insurgents were also foreign to Loy Adera, many hailing from North Waziristan in Pakistan. His own men were 85 per cent Tajik, so with both armed factions in Loy Adera 'out of area fighters', these farmers really were the prize. It just seemed ridiculous that so many of their limbs and lives were lost in the battle for their hearts and minds.

⋆

In 12 Platoon, Lance Sergeant Steve Wood was getting used to being a platoon commander. In some ways the differences between Second Lieutenant Tulloch, now away on R&R, and him were slight: they were the same age, from Lothian and natural soldiers. Wood had been in Iraq while Tulloch had been at university and the degree meant Tulloch could jump a few ranks. For the next fortnight, though, a Lance Sergeant would command 12 Platoon. Despite losing much of its command element to career courses, bullets and now R&R, 12 Platoon retained a strong ethos. The non-commissioned officers were mostly C Company men who had known each other for years and the youngsters had gone through training together. It was also a very Scottish platoon, from Tulloch down, and this kept them even tighter.

They were still recovering from losing Sergeant Paxton, though his wound had been light enough that he had stayed in Camp Bastion and would return after six weeks of physiotherapy and properly cooked food. More permanent was the loss of Guardsman Watson. On the day of the incident, much of Watson's kit had been left in the stream, as the absolute priority had been getting him out. Once back in Nahidullah a patrol was stood up to go out and recover it but due to bad weather grounding helicopters, it was decided to delay the mission until the next morning. Everyone in 12 Platoon was glad not to have to go back to the site that evening but dreaded going the next day. Major Kitching decided to spare the junior men and asked for volunteers from the senior men in headquarters to go on the patrol in the morning; a move that earned them the platoon's gratitude and perhaps respect. In two of the Vehicle Checkpoints, those who had been on patrol when Watson was hit were seen staring from sangar positions at the site of the explosion, reliving it during their time on guard. They were quickly rotated out. Guardsman Wannuwat, who had gone down with battleshock during the event, came back from Bastion after three weeks. Any illusions he might have had of being over the incident were dispelled on the day Sergeant Paxton was shot. An RPG had gone off and the noise had sent him back to that stream in Chah Bagh and induced a panic attack. He'd got back to Vehicle Checkpoint Naeem on his legs but had then collapsed. From then on he was mostly confined to Patrol Base Nahidullah, though his skill with a Vallon got him sent out in the Mastiff occasionally to check out likely IED positions on Mars. In camp, 12 Platoon were understanding and tried to help talk him through the experiences, especially when a loud bang set him back. Wannuwat decided to pull his weight in camp and cooked Thai spicy noodles for the 12 Platoon multiple in Nahidullah most nights. He'd also get teas and coffees for the guys without having to be asked. The horror of his experience in May had turned the feted Vallon Ninja into a dogsbody. Everyone agreed, Wannuwat included, that what was vital for him was staying with the Platoon and finishing the tour. For some of the Platoon, the incident with Guardsman Watson had led them to question the need for fighting patrols through ground that wasn't going to be held subsequently.

'What's the point of patrolling out and sending triple amputees home if you can't hold the ground?' asked one non-commissioned officer in August. 'You'll no be changing the area by doing that. Unless you put a checkpoint in, it's going to stay the same.'

Life in the Vehicle Checkpoints had improved marginally. The replacements coming into the platoon had boosted numbers to about seven Guardsmen in each garrison, meaning the men had six hours' sleep at night rather than four, bookended with stags. The platoon's policy was to throw the new boys into the little bases immediately to get them used to a stripped-down lifestyle. Here, they'd be forced to make friends quickly at close quarters and would soon get combat experience during the almost daily shoots on the sangars. Unlike at Inzargul and Said Abdul, the gunmen around the Vehicle Checkpoints seemed to be less experienced, though bursts of automatic fire would still pass disconcertingly close to the man on stag. At night, the shoots were even wilder and for the men in the Vehicle Checkpoints, they were – and there is no way round this – extremely good fun. With limited numbers to fight off a concerted attack, even the smallest engagement had to be robustly fought in order to show insurgents the firepower in the small fortresses and deter anything more organised. Also, if the Vehicle Checkpoints began to take casualties during an attack, especially at night, things could become untenable quickly. This meant firing off a lot of ammunition at muzzle flashes during night attacks. Attacks would generally come in around

20:00 after both sides had eaten and the air had cooled down. I was sitting in Vehicle Checkpoint Rabiullah one night when stories and cigarettes were interrupted by the crackle of rounds in the distance as another outpost in Loy Adera was hit. The man listening to the net relayed: 'Contact Nahidullah.' The Vehicle Checkpoint Commander, a young Lance Corporal, knew what was coming.

'Every fucker, stand to – we're next,' he said and was drowned out as rounds splashed through the air above. A long burst of fire from the sangar followed in reply. The insurgents, rather than hitting one position in strength, sometimes preferred to hit every Isaf base at once to show off their range and coordination to the locals. From the walls, I could see tracer rounds pouring out along Mars, bursting amber sunsets as flares sacrificed themselves 1,000 metres in the sky and mortar rounds arced above. It was terribly beautiful. The sangar gunner, calmer after his first reflexive shoot, shouted out compound numbers to tell the others where the gunmen were and we waited for the next flash of incoming. The Afghans were on the walls by now and someone else had dashed out to the Mastiff and got the Grenade Machine Gun ready. When the next burst came, it was dovetailed with an enormous explosion at the base of the sangar. Everyone ducks, screaming, 'RPG!' A Counter Narcotics man comes round the corner reloading his RPG and we realise it was outgoing and curse the crazy bastard for not saying he was about to fire the thing.

The Afghans want more, so keep firing into the treelines and compounds. 'Check fire, you maniacs!' says the checkpoint commander. 'I admire your fucking spirit but calm the beans, yeah?'

Another bang.

'Was that incoming?'

'Incoming!'

'No – outgoing! Outgoing. Fucking idiot. He curled it right in the air into Compound 22. Fuck it, mate, it's their country; if they want to do that, then let them.'

Tins of ammunition are opened and men restock in case there's another attack.

'That was awesome,' says the commander.

'Superb,' I truly agree.

'That compound's wasted.'

'Fuck 'em.'

'I've been wanting to waste that compound the whole tour. We'll probably need to do an assessment on it tomorrow.'

Another RPG goes out.

'Fucking maniacs!'

'I've got to change me underpants – they need a fucking change after that.'

There's a pause of a few minutes, then another burst on the sangar.

'Right – get some rounds down.'

Tight, controlled bursts drill the area of the muzzle flash for 30 seconds.

'Check fire! Two Six Bravo – contact, wait out. Everybody all right? Do not fire that missile – it won't be accurate from here and we'll just waste it.'

The Afghan Commander wanders over with the interpreter.

'You should shoot anyone you see out there tonight – they will be insurgents. If your men don't want to shoot them, wake me up and I'll do it. Goodnight.'

'The whole Company was just engulfed in fucking violence there – that was fucking outstanding! Conference will be a good one tonight.'

Two other Afghans wander over, clearly stoned and offering rice to the men on the walls. '*Tashakor*,' say the Guardsmen and start laughing.

'I enjoy every one [contact]. When it gets unenjoyable is when they're landing round you – that's when your heart starts going, when you see the dust coming up – or when you get hit. Touch wood I haven't been hit. It's great. Beats any big dipper.'

Intelligence suggests that's it for now but they'll hit again at 02:00. That turns out to be a ruse to get everyone out of bed unnecessarily. What a game!

*

Five days later, on 1 August, Acting Sergeant Dale McCallum was shot and killed instantly in the super-sangar at Checkpoint Said Abdul. During a daylight shoot on the sangar, McCallum grabbed his .338 sniper rifle and stormed up the ladder to help identify where the men shooting at his Guardsmen in the sangar were hiding. As usual, the single accurate rounds were masked with bursts of automatic fire around the sangar. McCallum and his sniper rifle had been sent specifically from the Checkpoint North to Checkpoint Said Abdul to defeat this gunman, who could well have been the man who wounded Guardsman Kabunicaucau and killed Corporal Stenton and Lance Corporal Monkhouse on 21 July. McCallum was one of the best snipers in Battalion. He would have exposed only a few inches of his profile above the parapet and most of this would have been under the cover of a helmet. He was a genuinely brilliant soldier and much loved Scots Guardsman. The sense of loss throughout Left Flank and the whole of Battalion was profound and reinforced by knowing McCallum left a fiancée and his son Kevin. In Said Abdul, Sergeant Gibson mourned a good friend, carved a simple wooden cross in memorial and lit a candle each night. His men paraded smartly in their berets when the Padre came to conduct a memorial service. Those familiar lines from Ecclesiastes flashed out of the King James Bible:

> To every thing there is a season, and a time to every purpose under the heaven: A time to be born, and a time to die; a time to plant, and a time to pluck up that which is planted; A time to kill, and a time to heal; a time to break down, and a time to build up.

In amongst the grief and paid respects was the knowledge that an insurgent sniper had shot his opposite number and was still up north.

★

For Major Kitching, the priority had to remain keeping Mars clear as the Trident upgrade crawled east. Since his return from R&R, another IED had been dug into the route, precipitating yet another cordon and search operation on 29 July, which was engaged throughout with accuracy. Another Vehicle Checkpoint was needed, this time with views right onto Bravo Foxtrot 3. The plan was to get the new outpost established on the same day as a cordon and search of Bravo Foxtrot 3. This double operation would be supported by every asset Kitching could lay his hands on.

On 5 August as the sky began to scar blue and the call to prayer rose, three Warriors from Right Flank arrived in Checkpoint Said Abdul to support the operation. Fire Support Group Jackals pushed feints to random spots on the map to confuse the insurgents. The Royal Dragoon Guards Vikings then moved into cordon positions to the south of Bravo Foxtrot 3, while a mixed Isaf/Afghan cordon was established to the north alongside the Warriors. Major Kitching then drove into the new checkpoint location to run the operation from there. The last part of the cordon were Guardsmen from 11 Platoon who were going back to the site of the civilian massacre and the shootings of 21 July once again, this time in Vikings. They took me with them. As the armoured vehicles powered into Popolzai Kalay, Second Lieutenant Pearson called out the compound numbers and gave the men a countdown to the doors swinging open. Everyone fully expected to get contacted immediately. I joined the nervous smoking. The Viking halted in the middle of a field and the Guardsmen jumped out. A farmer came over and asked about compensation, as the Viking had just ripped up his crops. The patrol fixed bayonets, Valloned into Popolzai, sat down in the same place where they had seen comrades shot and killed a fortnight before and waited for a response. Nothing happened, apart from the temperature rising. It is hot and boring work for the Guardsmen who lie down and stare through their sights for their shift of sentry duty. In the alleyway, the scars from the Coyote as it reversed out of danger are still dug into the walls. Lance Sergeant Browning looks down at the wreckage of the minibus still strewn along Bravo Foxtrot 3, thinks 'you can still smell the death here', then goes over to half-dozing Guardsmen and screams, 'Do your job!' in their ear. After a few hours, I opened a sachet of tomato and basil soup – heated to perfection in my thigh pocket. Lying back, drinking soup and looking up, I could see and then imagine the war in the sky: wee hand-launched drones checking what was round the corner; larger Reaper drones scanning a wider area; the Attack Helicopters, support and casualty evacuation helicopters; the Spectre Gunships looping lazily like the first fly of spring and pregnant with death; Electronic Warfare planes intercepting and jamming insurgent communications; A-10 tank busters; the French, American, British and other jets, providing another set of eyes and ready with bombs if you were in a really tight spot; American Awacs but no longer Nimrods; the B-1 Bombers; the U-2 spy planes out of the UAE, scanning the ground for IEDs from 70,000 feet; above all the satellites – a link with home via the phones men had half an hour with a week. A firmament of support.

Browning looks at one of his Guardsmen.

'Young Ritchie Carr, 18-year-old from Durham and you've already done an Afghan. What are you going to do with the rest of your life, then?'

'Guess I'll just keep coming back here,' said Carr.

The operation succeeded. The feints seemed to draw the insurgents away from the cordon, allowing the counter-IED team to confirm Bravo Foxtrot 3 clear. Occasional rounds were traded to the north, Afghan soldiers responding with an RPG, but once an Apache got up, the insurgents hid. The Vikings went through Popolzai flattening the walls of abandoned compounds with their bulk to give better lines of sight from Said Abdul onto Bravo Foxtrot 3. As they pulled back, they were engaged and returned fire. As soon as the fighting stopped, little boys rushed out of compounds to harvest the brass bullet casings for scrap metal, shouting, 'Taliban, fuck you!' at weary Guardsmen. We were back in Said Abdul by 16:00. As soon as it was dark, I lay on a cot bed, intending to read for a bit and then go for a wash, but I woke up, fully clothed and drenched in sweat at 03:00. Quite how the Guardsmen do this for six months is beyond me.

The insurgents fought back the next day with an ambush on a Counter Narcotics Police convoy along Mars. One of the Afghans was shot in the head. There was confusion about whether the man was alive or dead and the Afghans accused the Isaf troops escorting them of not responding quickly enough. The Afghans raised their weapons and formed a roadblock. The main threat was a second ambush. Some quick talking and the promise of a helicopter calmed the situation down. In Said Abdul, the wounded man stumbled out of a Mastiff – some synaptic impulse keeping him going. Once he lay down, he died in front of the Padre and me.

★

The battle against the IED cells was endless. Each time Isaf brought a new tactic into play, the insurgents would find a way around it. With remarkable skill, they seemed to know exactly where the Guardsmen could and could not see at all times, negating the time spent tearing down trees and walls to clear eye lines. The owners of these trees and compounds would then turn up and demand compensation from Sergeant Jones. He had to seek proof of ownership – especially when more than one person turned up making a claim for a particular piece of destruction. By August, Jones had spent $70,000 on compensation and Cash for Works in Loy Adera – $10 for every metre of the seven kilometres of Mars Left Flank held. This did not count the money paid out in Lashkar Gah or from White-hall for really large claims. Keeping compensation flowing was a major irritant related back to the overarching issue of land rights, ownership and the Afghan Government's desire to engage in rural areas.

The new surveillance cameras were clearly another threat to the IED teams. To get round them, they used distraction shoots onto the camera and the sangars around it to draw the eye of the operator to an immediate threat. Even without shoots the insurgents managed to get IEDs into blind spots through a superlative use of cover. For instance on 14 August, they got an IED onto Mars a mere 400 metres west of Patrol Base Nahidullah, under the nose of the CCTV system, which then watched a Mastiff drive over and detonate the bomb. Fortunately, the Mastiff withstood the blast and we all laughed at the footage. On 15 August, the IED teams succeeded in getting another device onto Mars on Bravo Foxtrot 3 – despite the new base put in on 5 August, the camera system at Said Abdul and the eye lines cleared by ripping down walls and trees. Yet another cordon and search was launched. As well as their lethality, IEDs were a pure nuisance. Over the course of the tour, Left Flank encountered 76 of them: 13 functioning, six resulting in casualties. But each of the 63 bombs that were reported by local people or detected before they blew up took up valuable time from the main mission of engaging with the people. Thus, a well-supplied IED cell ties up a rifle company. The devices on Mars had to be cleared because of the freedom-of-movement mission, but each time a clearance operation went in, a juicy, near-static target went in with it. Knowing the reaction to an IED found on Mars, the insurgents expected this target and within a few hours were ready to pick a fight with the cordon, sometimes with lethal results, as on 21 July. Perhaps the Afghan National Army sergeant who shocked Lance Sergeant John Thorpe at the start of the tour by detonating a bomb with a tossed brick had the right idea: destroy them quickly and move on with your mission.

*

Sergeant Gibson could see the enemy streaming towards him. He picked a group that had bunched themselves up nicely, selected which of them would die first and pulled the trigger. The figure fell. He kills the rest of them, then sits back and has a sip of juice.

'Anyone else want a go?' he asks, offering the PlayStation controller to the Guardsmen.

Call of Duty, the hyper-realistic war game partially set amongst today's wars, was a favourite in the checkpoints. War films were also popular. For the Guardsmen, one of the downsides of deploying over the summer of 2010 was missing *Pacific* on Sky TV.

'I've heard it's nae as good as *Band of Brothers* but I'm still getting it sent out on DVD,' one of them said to me.

Football was another focus. Operation World Cup was meant to get televisions and dishes into every base in Helmand in time for the opening match in South Africa. Given the way England played in the Rainbow Nation it was probably a good thing that some garrisons missed out – tensions between English and Scots could have totally boiled over. When the recently elected Prime Minister was visiting Lashkar Gah, he asked one Scot his greatest fear in Helmand.

'England winning the World Cup, sir,' replied Lance Corporal Jean-Paul Barnes.

Most bases had something by the end of the tour, even if it was just a bit of British Forces Broadcasting Service television. The network serves soldiers everywhere, leading to a unique weather forecast that takes in Alberta, Ascension Island, Helmand and Brunei. There's even a Nepali channel for the Gurkhas. The choice of films is eclectic, though watching *Midnight Cowboy*, a film about a young man wearing odd clothes and trying to figure out who he is in a bizarre new environment, made a strange sense to me, surrounded by soldiers in Helmand. Forces Radio was a constant: in between keeping boys on top of the latest tunes, the DJs read out moving tributes written by soldiers who had lost friends.

Before anyone could take Gibson up on his offer, real bullets began flying around the super-sangar and he sprinted off to kill the man who shot Sergeant McCallum.

For two hours, bullets whined off the super-sangar, missing Guardsmen by inches. One round ripped through a sandbag, kicking grit into Gibson's eye as he scanned the walls for the man who had shot his friend. The Sergeant radioed down to Second Lieutenant Pearson whenever he identified a firing point. Pearson managed to get an Apache overhead. It fired into a treeline but couldn't engage the two buildings where more rounds were coming from. One was identified as a mosque and the other one could have been stuffed with civilians as well as insurgents for all the pilot knew. It was wildly frustrating for the men in Said Abdul as they continued to take shots through the sangar; it boils over and Pearson screams at the radio while punching the wall. There was no escape – both on patrol and on stag they had seen men shot and killed but the rules of Counter Insurgency demanded restraint. Gibson keeps putting rounds through a murder hole and is convinced he makes the insurgent sniper safe. The firing died away. The Commanding Officer drove into Said Abdul with Tac and saw Pearson in his standard order of dress in camp: tight black running shorts, flip-flops, Marlboro Light.

'Charlie?'

'Oh, hello, sir,' said Pearson, leaping up from his chair and putting aside a month-old copy of *Nuts*.

'I brought you these,' said the Lieutenant Colonel.

He handed over some rank slides with a second star sown on, denoting Pearson's promotion to Lieutenant.

'Thank you very much, sir,' said Pearson.

'Well, congratulations. I'd pin them on you but wouldn't know where. See you later,' he says. Pearson looked at the slides. Receiving them meant it had been a year since he left Sandhurst.

*

Battalion had squared Sergeant Gibson away. Knowing how close he was to Sergeant McCallum, they had rearranged Gibson's R&R so he could get back to London in time for the funeral. The Sergeant had endured a tough couple of months in Checkpoint Said Abdul and getting him home a few weeks early was a good call. Before he went, he would conduct a few final patrols deep into Loy Adera to guide a group of specially mentored Afghan commandos to some compounds that interested the intelligence experts. It was the sort of operation Left Flank couldn't conduct alone while manning all their checkpoints, so Major Kitching was glad of the commandos' assistance. Night patrolling with them was exceptionally taxing – crossing ditches on ladders while robbed of depth perception by night-vision goggles was particularly hard. Trying to keep an eye out for the disturbed earth that could indicate an IED was almost impossible at night. On the morning of 12 August, the second day of Ramadan, the commandos proved the intelligence correct and found an IED factory and drugs cache. The drugs were blown and the IED components brought back for forensic analysis. Five suspects were also detained. On the way out, the patrol was engaged from a treeline and compound. The British fire controller attached to the Afghans called in an A-10 tank buster, which made two passes over the firing points, strafing all the way. The firing stopped. Everyone got back to Patrol Base Nahidullah elated with the morning's work and Sergeant Gibson headed to Checkpoint Said Abdul to pack his kit and hand over to the Lance Sergeant who would look after things while he was away.

The bodies were brought into Said Abdul. Five died on the spot; two made it to hospital. Three of the dead were children; one of the wounded was pregnant. The best medical care in Loy Adera was at Nahidullah, closer to where the A-10's 30mm guns had ripped the civilians' lives apart, but Said Abdul had dealt with so much horror that month, the locals just assumed the medics there would know best.

There are various things to say. The first is that the loss of human life was inexcusable. Second, that the Scots Guards were furious that this had happened in their patch – though not at their behest or by their hand. Third, the investigation cleared the British officer who ordered the gun run and the American pilots of any wrongdoing. Fourth, the civilians who died inside the compound were related to one of the two gunmen who had been on the roof accurately engaging the Afghan patrol. Lastly, the gunmen got away.

Sergeant Gibson went to Lashkar Gah the next day before flying out for Britain. Headquarters was buzzing with 'Consequence Management' plans for the incident. Officers watched the gun tape from the A-10 and monitored the media for any mention of the incident. (There were none.) Coincidentally, the Deputy Provincial Governor was due to fly to Patrol Base Nahidullah to conduct a *shura* on governance with the local people the next day. The focus of the discussion would clearly be different now. Facts were needed from the ground, so Sergeant Gibson marched in front of the Commanding Officer's desk to give him the full debrief on what had happened that day. He finished his narrative – he'd be home in 48 hours. 'Very good, Sergeant Gibson. And get your sideburns up, will you,' said the Commanding Officer.

Mission rehearsal exercise

This is not a realistic picture of Afghanistan. It is February in England, minus 11 centigrade and it is snowing.

Copehill Down Village on top of Salisbury Plain is home to the Scots Guards for the Brigade Mission Rehearsal Exercise. Modelled on a typical East German village from the 1960s, it was built to prepare troops for when the Cold War went hot and they might have made it four miles into East Germany before tactical nuclear weapons turned them to radioactive dust. It has a church, streets of semis and no running water.

Headquartered with the Scots Guards are elements you know you'll never see in theatre: a company of Gurkhas giggling away in an agricultural shed, RAF bomb disposal teams, the Battalion's chefs (where did they all end up?).

Outside the gates, disgruntled Fusiliers, who are playing the enemy, wear shalwar kameez, *play touch rugby and get ready to up the ante and attack the base. Afghan refugees supplied by a civilian contractor walk around the town in 20-minute cycles playing Helmandis. Ex-Gurkhas pretend to be surly Afghan patrolmen and refuse to put two hands on their weapon. Experienced soldiers like Sergeant Fyffe, the Battalion Police Sergeant, have their exercise boxes ready to go – old ammunition tins stuffed with essentials.*

'And this is the most important piece of kit,' he says, brandishing a folding shovel, 'because everyone needs a shitter.'

Three genuine Afghan National Army officers turn up, no one knows from where (Helmand, presumably) and we don't really know what to do with them. It's tea and 'Tell me about your country' from polite young Guards officers who'll turn anything into an approximation of a social occasion.

Everything has changed, of course. Driving down to Wilt-shire phone calls came through stating that the Scots Guards would now be ground-holding and not the ANSF Develop-ment Headquarters, so the entire exercise will be redundant. Officers root around in the back of their cars for lever arch files marked 'Battlegroup Operations' that haven't been opened since Canada. The Chief of the General Staff visits. The Duke of Kent visits. The Army's Chief Imam visits. Gordon Brown (Army codename Haggis – superb) doesn't actually turn up but the press does, en masse, and gets treated to a demonstration shura *and Casevac.*

The open-air lectures on IEDs don't really work below freezing, especially when a blizzard is blowing into the conducting officer's gob. The contents of the portaloos freeze each night.

Spam or porridge for breakfast; noodles, beans and rice for lunch and supper. After a few days, noses lead men round the back of a Bedford truck where the Q Bloke and Guardsman Murray are making a mint selling burgers to the young and frikadellen to those who pine for Germany days. The Com-manding Officer serves the Battalion breakfast each morning with an enthusiastic:

'Good morning, Rank and Name. Beans, tomatoes or both?'

He's conducting an influence crusade and I haven't even shaved.

Cigarettes and tea. Tea and cigarettes. The Padre and I latch onto each other. No one is much interested in being interviewed in this weather, and anyone having a spiritual crisis is keeping it to themselves, so we shuffle about from nicotine high to sugar low.

On which Herrick was Lashkar Gah Main Operating Base mortared every 20 minutes for three days? Why are we all wearing our helmets? Why is a Guardsman telling me that watching shemale porn is half as gay as watching straight porn, 'because you get twice as many tits with a tranny involved'?

In the Ops Room, the Adjutant is trying to control things.

'Can everyone put their paper in the correct bin, please? I've just found something marked 'SECRET' in the non-burns bag.'

In a mud-spattered Portakabin the planning cycle grinds on. Every few hours, the Commanding Officer walks in: 'Right, question four.' Enormous colour printers chuck out maps of Wiltshire re-christened 'Bolan Desert – North'. There's a fire drill at some stage and an inconceivable number of soldiers stream from every nook of the house. It looks like the end of Record Breakers *attempt to see how many people can work and sleep in a two-storey detached house.*

Captain Chris Jaunay, on exchange from the Australian Army, is chained to a laptop and radio for the week. In Lashkar Gah he'll be Operations Bravo Officer. His job is to keep tabs on what everyone, everywhere is doing and he appears to be able to do this job without the aid of sleep. When a spot of research yields a great-grandfather who served with the Scots Guards in the First World War, Jaunay is embraced by all ranks and his Australian uniform overlooked. Late Entry Officers, men who've worked their passage from Guardsman to Captain in 22 years, work round the clock as Battle Captains. They conduct a sly influence campaign each time they pick up the phone, answering 'Scots Guards Battlegroup, Captain McLaughlan speaking' to try and get Brigade to let them have the Regiment's identity front and centre when the new Battlegroup name is issued. Fragmentary orders torrent down from Brigade, while exercise follows exercise in an effort to test the Ops Room to breaking point.

Bunking with the signallers is Captain Malcolm Dalzel-Job. Son of a Scots Guards Company Commander at

Tumbledown and grandson of one of Ian Fleming's many models for James Bond, he is the sort of officer who would have escaped from Colditz. This tour he's been tasked as Unit Press Officer, Brigade Liaison Officer and is doing a bit of influence work as well. His life is the preparation of a vortex of slides. He sleeps about three hours a night and seems to see even this as an unwarranted luxury.

Observer Controllers swarm about taking notes. One old Para has done his beret into a flat cap that wouldn't look out of place on Last of the Summer Wine *and scowls permanently, while an American from Delta Force smiles out from behind wraparound shades, despite there being not a chink of sunshine all week and very little to smile about.*

'At least it's not Poland,' say the old sweats, recalling a memorably horrendous exercise on the wasteland north of Krakow in mid-winter. On cue, a platoon of Poles arrives to join the fun for the last 48 hours of the exercise. It's decided to make them play Afghan soldiers, which they do rather too convincingly, getting utterly lost after a helicopter insertion and charging round the Plain without GPS. Eventually, the Adjutant sends a helicopter to search for them. They turn up to their target six hours late proudly announcing, 'Hello Blackjack – Dragon 43 is at the objective' as everyone else is breaking out the fags and celebrating taking the plywood compound/mosque/IED factory in the face of some very annoying tests.

The exercise is over, for the Scots Guards. To the west, another Battlegroup are making a meal of their last parts of the exercise, so it's tidy time for the Guardsmen.

'Every vehicle will be scrubbed down. I will not have my Monday morning ruined by a phone call from a General who happened to be on the M1 to see a filthy Bedford with an Ever Open Eye on it's back bumper,' says Captain McLaughlan.

A staff officer looks around and sums up the exercise and much of the training.

'*I sometimes wonder if it would have been better if we'd just been told: "Right, this is where you're going. You have six months to prepare. In your own time, go on.*"'

The Poles leave, handing out PR pamphlets about their Armed Forces from which we glean that their entire navy consists of busty girls in tight T-shirts. They give the Commanding Officer a paperweight.

'*Poor guys, that was their MRX [Mission Rehearsal Exercise] too. They deploy next month,*' *he says, waving them off.*

I leave the village and realise I've not drunk a glass of water all week – just tea. And then the purpose of the exercise becomes clear: that even when you're in the worst possible situation in Helmand, you'll thank God that you're not in a blizzard on Salisbury Plain.

The debrief takes place in a converted truck. The Observer Controllers are released from their vows of silence and a stream of banal criticism flows out. Then the Brigadier comes in.

'*I know you are ready. You know you are ready. You are ready. Oh, and sorry about your new name – Combined Force Lashkar Gah,*' *he says.*

We flee home by any means available.

CHAPTER EIGHT

'The fight for intelligence always starts in your own headquarters'

April–October 2010

On arrival in theatre, Scots Guards Headquarters were still only half sure of where they'd headquarter. As they filtered through Bastion and on to Lashkar Gah, roles appeared and disappeared. Much of this was due to the 20,000 US Marines surging into Helmand. They would take control of the Province in a newly designated Divisional Headquarters: Regional Command Southwest (RC SW) in July. Whole districts swung to their lead. 1st Battalion, The Mercian Regiment was disenfranchised of their role in Musa Qalah and split to the winds. Their Battlegroup Headquarters was after a job. The Scots Guards pointed them towards Police Mentoring Headquarters and gladly divested themselves of the task. Then Colonel Klink, US Marine Corps, arrived one April morning to announce that he was taking over the mentoring of Helmand's senior policemen. Free of these provincial level roles, 1 SG turned into a proper ground-holding Battlegroup: Combined Force Lashkar Gah (CF LKG). Assiduous flattery of outgoing members of 11 Light

Brigade's Headquarters then brought Right Flank into 1 SG's Area of Operations.

'It's the gold-plated solution,' Captain Kerr told me when I landed in Bastion in May.

'Some very good people made some very good decisions,' the Commanding Officer said, counting his blessings.

He had got his whole Battalion under him in the role envisaged a year earlier (see Chapter One). The constant changes had weakened Headquarters, though. Key men had flown to random tasks – Company Sergeant Major Brown ended up closing down Britain's involvement around the Kajaki Dam, for instance.

This lean Headquarters ran roughly 770 British troops in four sub-units alongside around 2,000 Afghan partners. Their role would be to extend security, then enable the Afghan Government to do something with this improved situation. Local people would then see the benefit of their offer and choose it over that of the insurgents. Despite theirs being Helmand's most populous district, the Scots Guards went into relatively 'new' space for Isaf, taking over from one rifle company and an itinerant American team along Highway 601. This seemed remarkable to me given the people-focused approach the British Army in Helmand had supposedly been following since 2006. It was also the largest Area of Operations in Helmand, though CF LKG was the smallest in terms of manpower. Quickly realising how local the campaign was, almost all their troops were thrown into hastily constructed checkpoints. This sacrificed a manoeuvrable reserve but the Commanding Officer would assure people that, 'in Counter Insurgency, the real manoeuvre space is between the ears of every Afghan'.

Having so small a Headquarters, though taxing on the men there, was not necessarily as much of an issue as it would have been in a traditional Battlegroup. Companies fight the campaign in Helmand locally and the Head-quarters mostly guides and facilitates. It has access to Brigade, who holds assets – Casevac helicopters, spare parts, fire support – which the companies need. The companies also run their planned operations past Head-quarters. A smart staff officer, and there were several in CF LKG, could then put a spin on the plans to ensure that Brigade gave the operation the assets it needed. The Headquarters also shielded the companies from the deluge of emails flung down from Brigade, allowing them to get on with their actual job. When a 90-page document came through on changes to detention rules, Headquarters had to ensure that only the relevant chunks made it to com-panies who lacked the IT luxuries of Brigade. The Chief of Staff, Major Martin French, described his role as 'the clutch plate' between Brigade and the sub-units.

Along with access to fire support, only Battlegroup Headquarters could grant changes in the Rules of En-gagement. The Commanding Officer had retained this prerogative and made his thoughts on the escalation of violence well known to commanders before the tour. They therefore knew what he would allow and in turn kept their men on a leash in terms of firing heavy weapons or expecting changes in RoE. Over the course of the tour no bombs were dropped in the District. Only one round of artillery was fired in the whole of CF LKG – a 105mm smoke round fired for effect in the Queen's Royal Lancers' patch. The shell casing made its way into the Command-ing Officer's hands. He paraded it round Headquarters like a Mohican chief wielding a totemic scalp, much to the dismay of the gunners, who looked set to cry at this meagre haul. It was a remarkable record. CF LKG were blessed during the fighting season to get a US Marine fire co-ordination team from Regional Command (South West) whose accents unlocked previously undreamt of assets. They were efficient and had names like Captain Chad Bonecutter. Their arrival was set against the wider context of President Obama's 'surge' and the US Marines' 20,000-strong flood into Helmand. Quite why this backwoods province – Somerset, if you like – swallowed quite such a high proportion of Isaf forces is beyond my ken.

The Commanding Officer's zeal for courageous restraint may have lost him popularity at Guardsman level but the A-10 tank buster gun runs that killed five civilians in Loy Adera horribly illustrated the point he made. Responsibility for those deaths was firmly not with Scots Guardsmen, though as the Commanding Officer wrote to the Brigadier after the incident, 'I have been devastated that these children died on my watch. I take no comfort from the fact that another Task Force were the troops on the ground. On every level it is a disaster.'

Amongst the war fighting and intelligence gathering, the routine lives of Scots Guardsmen had to be looked after. I was pleasantly amazed that such 'normal business' continued in a war zone. The Education Officer, Lieutenant Katie Nelson, toured the District. The arrival of an attractive, blonde and sympathetic officer in a remote garrison took the sting out of maths lessons conducted under a sunshade between patrols. Captain Stuart Rowe, Careers Management Officer, ensured that six months in Helmand didn't disturb the rhythm of men's progress in the Army. The Commanding Officer wrote over 100 annual career reports on Scots Guards officers and non-commissioned officers, alongside citations for gallantry and valuable service by soldiers of every capbadge in Combined Force Lashkar Gah. The Adjutant, Captain Guy Anderson, led the personnel side of things – who the Combined Force had, what they were doing and what needed to happen to them next. Aside from managing the casualty process from incident to inquest, the Adjutant's roles included arranging compassionate leave after a death in the family and sorting out disciplinary issues.

There was a certain theatre to Commanding Officer's Orders, the judicial side of life in Helmand. A soldier charged with an offence such as accidentally firing his weapon would be flown or driven to Lashkar Gah. He would have at least 24 hours from being served with his papers to going before the Commanding Officer. He would meet an officer appointed Accused's Adviser and then get a haircut. Orders were in the evening, allowing the accused to build up a sense of anticipatory dread while sipping juice by the volleyball court all day. At the appointed hour, he was marched in front of the Commanding Officer's desk flanked by his Accused Adviser and the Drill Sergeant shouting out the movements. They would turn left, stamp their feet down and be kept at attention. The Regimental Sergeant Major glared in the corner of the room and the door was slammed shut behind the accused. The Commanding Officer – judge and jury – would then finish looking over the case notes, eyeball the accused and ask for a plea and any mitigation. The more interesting charges usually related to drunken misdemeanours back in Britain and the dramas soldiers could get into were remarkable. Charges from Afghanistan were more predictable but sometimes acutely life-threatening. Mitigating factors – sleep deprivation, involvement in stressful incidents – were taken into account. Generally, though, men who fell asleep on guard lost their next 21 days' pay. This appears harsh but men sleep well in Helmand only because they trust that the man on stag is doing his duty. Sentence passed, the guilty, or occasionally innocent, man would then be drilled out of the office and go for a smoke, where they'd usually be joined by the Commanding Officer. The Victorian performance is designed to deter and discourage but it also makes the accused aware that those involved are playing a part too. CF LKG held over 20 hearings in six months.

CF LKG shared digs with Brigade in the Lashkar Gah Main Operating Base (MOB). This was a blessing or a curse depending on whom you asked. The food was exceptional: contracted out to KBR, Inc. (who else?) every night seemed to be steak night. The British division of the company formerly known as Kellogg, Brown & Root, that colossus of construction and engineering, has cornered the market in war zone services in Helmand. British managers command little platoons of South Asian cooks and *dhobi wallahs*. The British Army has plenty of both but they must sit at home – the government puts a cap on the number of British troops in Helmand, so anything that can be outsourced is. I wasn't convinced this represented great value to the taxpayer. My hunch is that as the 'nudge' of troop drawdowns increases in the future, the British Army will outsource all sorts of roles (postmen, firemen, movement controllers, CCTV operators, lead Vallon men?) rather than lose Battlegroups. I would be interested to know what the Treasury makes of this. The upshot in 2010 was outstanding food in the Main Operating Base – all hail the private sector! Only the sound of staff officers from Brigade complaining that their *filet mignon* was underdone left a bad taste in the mouths of those lucky enough to sample the cooking in 'Lash Vegas'. A shop selling cold drinks, ample Internet access and a volleyball court were other bonuses. For the two multiples of Guardsmen left in the Main Operating Base on standby and local patrolling tasks, the 3:1 ratio of officers to other ranks was an inversion of Army life; the insistence that sleeves were rolled down after 18:00 a reminder that their Regiment dated from the same century Jesuits first brought Quinine to Europe. Being based with Brigade had advantages for the Commanding Officer. While some said he lacked the bluff charm of some of his predecessors, the Commanding Officer was a tireless operator on behalf of his men and getting amongst the Brigade staff helped him fight his Guardsmen's cause each day. While other Combined Force commanders in faraway districts of Helmand were represented in Brigade Headquarters by captain Liaison Officers, Combined Force Lashkar Gah had a Lieutenant Colonel with 'MC' on his signature block. He took the view that 'influence never takes a day off' and sat in Brigade meetings like Banquo's Ghost. Knowing what made Brigade tick meant he could present his men's efforts and needs in a way that would be noticed. It also kept him up to the minute on the wider situation in Helmand, to the dismay of his own staff officers, who would stand up to brief him and be told, 'That's not what I've heard.'

Headquarters was the best place to get a feel for what was happening across Helmand. The companies filtered intelligence updates down to the checkpoints but, realistically, everyone was so caught up in their own little campaigns to pay any attention to anything other than the most headline stories. Ships in Nelson's navy have been described as 'wooden worlds'. In the little Hesco worlds of Helmand, the battle is so local that what is going on in the next company's area is often reduced to a pithy one-line assessment and, for the junior ranks, the next Combined Force's efforts are hardly known. In Lashkar Gah there was more of a sense of how it was all fitting together. 4 Brigade had sensibly eschewed a large Brigade operation that would suck in resources from across the Province. Instead, Herrick 12 was about the long slog of local Counter Insurgency set within the context of Operation Moshtarak's legacy. The summer's two big headlines were the US Marines' arrival in earnest and the British swap out of Sangin. Much was made of this in Britain, possibly in an effort to make Helmand follow the narrative of the Basra withdrawal. My own sense was that the British were happy to let the US Marines take that dreadful place. Subsequent events have shown that some of the criticisms levelled at the British campaign in Sangin were false and the Americans seem to be having as hard a time of it as the Rifles, Royal Marines and others endured.

Also in the Main Operating Base were the Foreign Office and Department for International Development-led Provincial Reconstruction Team (PRT), along with a slew of assorted men with sideburns. Apart from providing eye-candy for the Guardsmen – there were many female Crown and Civil Servants in designer sunglasses – the PRT's presence had little impact on most of Combined Force Lashkar Gah.

'It would be wrong to say we have a bad relationship with the PRT,' said one officer, 'because we don't have a relationship with the PRT.'

The Commanding Officer sought to build bridges with the thematic heads of the Mission – health, education, law and order – but didn't get very far. 'Sadly, we found that we could have been in Sangin for all the additional influence being co-located with the PRT had,' he said.

Whenever visitors came through Lashkar Gah, which was often, the Commanding Officer would try to give them a Combined Force briefing. The headline of this was the proud announcement that, 'this Combined Force works to the Stabilisation Adviser', at which point a civilian from the PRT who was now working with the Army was introduced. In a unique take on the job title, four Stabilisation Advisers passed through Headquarters Combined Force Lashkar Gah during Herrick 12 and, at times, there was none.

★

Having gladly shed the mantle of Commanding Officer ANSF Development HQ, and knowing that Counter Insurgency was a company campaign, the Commanding Officer found himself an additional role in Lashkar Gah City. His primary job was partnering Colonel Kamullidin, the Deputy Chief of Police in Helmand and the capital's top cop. Together they put together a District Stabilisation Plan for Lashkar Gah and its hinterland. Each Sunday they met at the Lashkar Gah Security *shura*, along with the various branch heads from the Afghan forces. This was a good opportunity for the Commanding Officer to put his 'ask an Afghan' mantra to work and gain as much information about how the Afghan forces and Lashkar Gah worked. Despite being the capital of the province that has been one of Britain's main foreign policy priorities in recent years, there seemed to be a remarkable lack of knowledge about the city. UN Habitat, the World Bank, the IMF and elements of the PRT had been involved there for years, but 'the fight for intelligence always starts in your own headquarters', the Commanding Officer wearily concluded, 'and this stuff was known to someone with a British taxpayer's pound in their pocket somewhere'. Inside the uniformed Afghan forces and across the provincial government lay a myriad of factions and allegiances. Some harked back to the days of Sher Mohammed Akhundzada, a former governor of Helmand sent to Kabul at Britain's behest. He retained influence and ambition in his home province. Others were placemen of Governor Mangal. The provincial power-plays were beyond the scope of Combined Force Lashkar Gah, though keeping a close eye on them was wise. At the district level, the new Mayor of Lashkar Gah, Mohammed Daoud, would have a greater impact on the success or failure of Herrick 12. In the city there was little in terms of manpower that Combined Force Lashkar Gah could add.

They had at best 22 Guardsmen in the Main Operating Base split between patrol and reserve duties. Technically, there had been no formal transition to Afghan-led security in Lashkar Gah, so Kamullidin and the Commanding Officer would formulate plans together. In reality, the Afghans had greater resources and a far better understanding of how the place functioned. The British didn't even appear to have a consolidated grasp of Lashkar Gah's population – the Army's figure of 45,000 seemed way off and the Commanding Officer believed he was working in a city of around 120,000, with a further 70,000 in the rural areas of the district. The overriding British assessment of Lashkar Gah was: 'It works; it goes bang from time to time, but it works.' Using this pithy analysis as a starting point and keen to show people in Britain that this was the case, the Commanding Officer began walking around a market in the west of the city without his body armour and helmet. This became something of a party piece during the tour, as 18 embedded journalists and sundry academics were driven out to the Bolan Market and then walked through chatting to shopkeepers. His heavily armed Tac Group were always lurking nearby under the watchful eye of the Regimental Sergeant Major. The walkabout's message was effective visually and spread. The Commanding Officer began to get sharp emails from his wife.

'I don't know who you think you're trying to impress doing this. You could get yourself killed so easily.'

The point he wanted to make was that the improved security rested on the new, improved policemen coming out of the training academy. He was also the first to concede: 'The risk I take is nothing, nothing compared to a day at the office in Checkpoint Said Abdul.'

Life in the city, by Afghan standards, was good. Uniformed Afghans were legion and kept things under a semblance of control, though bombs hit the Kabul Bank and a school during the summer. Salaried employment was stable. Electricity was available, as were basic medical and education facilities. These people were the 'haves' of Helmand. A few kilometres outside the city the 'have-nots' were abundant. The Afghan Government remained unwilling to engage in a meaningful way in the rural areas of Lashkar Gah District.

'We find it much easier to sell your government in areas where you're doing things for the people,' the Commanding Officer suggested to the Provincial Governor early in the tour.

Mangal agreed and set up a Rural Development Commission the next day. This produced no results. Six months later at a farewell feast for the Scots Guards, the Commanding Officer made the same point to Mangal, who again set up a development commission, this time led by the police rather than the Mayor. Perhaps future Herricks will see its successes for the people who live away from the city. On Herrick 12, space was being made for the Afghan Government to engage with the people in these areas at risk and cost to British soldiers. That the Afghan Government had to be dragged kicking and chuntering into this space was hugely frustrating.

17–18 September

From the start of the tour, the whiteboard in the Operations Cell in Headquarters had '18 September: Parliamentary Elections' written on it. The elections, it was hoped, would be the most visible sign of progress in security and governance in Helmand for Operation Herrick 12 and planning for them began in April.

'Lincoln, you forget we did one of these last year and it

was fine. It will be fine again,' Colonel Kamullidin told the Commanding Officer at a joint planning meeting in late April. That assessment of 2009's presidential elections was questionable.

Helmand has eight seats in the *Wolesi Jirga* (lower parliamentary house) in Kabul. Two of these were reserved for female candidates in 2010. The 53 candidates had all demonstrated to the electoral authorities that they were not criminals or members of armed groups. There were no parties as such, though some candidates came from factions unpalatable to Governor Mangal. The son of Abdul Rahman Jan, a former Provincial Chief of Police with known links to the insurgent/narco nexus, was standing. Through Sher Mohammed Akhundzada, the former governor, he also had links to the Karzai family. Several other candidates were known associates of Akhundzada, though of course this did not prevent their standing for election. Other candidates included a young engineer standing on an education platform and various tribal leaders. Nine of Helmand's districts would vote in 143 locations. Three districts were considered too dangerous and the people there were disenfranchised. Theoretically, the election worked on the one man, one vote precept. The first eight candidates past the post would win a seat in Kabul, with the rider that two of them were women. The entire electorate, from Sangin to Marjah, had to re-register to vote in Lashkar Gah, only a year after registering for the presidential elections.

'I'm hopeful,' said a member of the PRT. 'It won't be an overwhelming endorsement of the principles of democracy, but it should be better than 2009.' By August, Lashkar Gah was strewn with posters.

In the months leading up to the election, patrols across CF LKG were tasked with asking Afghans about the election. In rural areas, many were unaware of the need to re-register. Most seemed unsure or unwilling to reveal voting intentions and 90 per cent of people polled on Highway 601 on 13 August were unsure of who they would vote for. Most of those hoping to take part indicated they would vote along tribal lines in rural areas or for local candidates in the city. In rural areas, the elections were poorly advertised and campaigning was minimal. Blackjack 15, the patrols multiple from the Main Operating Base, spent a week driving around the district finding and then assessing the 20 Polling Centres the Independent Election Commission (IEC) had designated in Lashkar Gah District. There were very few in rural areas. 'UK Plc. had been burned in the past for raising election expectations and then it turned out they weren't very credible,' said one British Commander. There was severely limited British media coverage from Helmand. Embeds had all but stopped, partly on the grounds that the air-bridge needed every seat for the arrival of 16 Air Assault Brigade. I'd made my way home via Kabul. Election Day was spent hitting 'refresh' on the MoD website.

*

On 17 September, Lieutenant Dalrymple-Hamilton's Blackjack 15 multiple and an American dog handler left the headquarters to sweep the 20 Polling Centres around Lashkar Gah District for explosives. In each of the 20 schools and mosques (which were not searched by the dog) the men found a small team from the Afghan Security Services acting as the inner security for the voting process, with concentric rings of Afghan policemen and soldiers spread out from the Polling Centres. Apart from the dog search, readying an emergency reserve and aerial monitoring, Isaf were directed to stay away from the process. US Marine Major-General Mills had put out a directive,

warning of punitive measures for any Isaf soldier photo-
graphed near a Polling Centre by a journalist on Election
Day. The Afghan face would be front and centre. Lashkar
Gah was locked down that evening and flooded with
Afghan forces manning checkpoints to try and minimise
the risk of suicide bombers getting through to Polling
Centres.

The sweep done, Blackjack 15 headed to bed. Less than
an hour later, Lieutenant Dalrymple-Hamilton was woken
and told to go the Ops Room. Major Martin French, the
Combined Force Chief of Staff, had got the report at 23:00
– ballot boxes that had arrived in Marjah with IEC
officials had shown signs of explosive handling.

'Fuck!' he thought. 'Can we re-search them all by
06:00? Is that even the right thing to do? Some of the
IEC lot weren't too happy about the first search. Are the
police aware of this? Has Mangal been briefed? Better
issue a warning order, stand up the sub-units and write a
plan.'

French had hardly slept in the past 24 hours and
wouldn't sleep that night. He had the middle-of-the-night
taste in his mouth familiar to anyone who has used caffeine
and tobacco to get through a pile of work. French knew
that the British position on the elections was to be stood
off. He also knew that if a ballot box blew up, the British
Army would take the rap on the world's front pages. At
00:30 he issued the final orders and pulled the trigger.
'Hello, Eddie,' he said when the sleepy Lieutenant walked
into the Ops Room. 'Great news. You've got to go out and
check these Polling Centres. In the next five hours,
ideally. Other multiples will do the city, the Bolan and
Basharan.'

Twelve men and a dog were crashed out of bed and
began speeding through the city. For the first time in
nearly six months, the men felt cold in their open-top

Jackals. They picked up a group of policemen from their headquarters and told them that they would explain to the IEC and guards at each Polling Centre what had happened. They'd then lead the dog handler in. Dalrymple-Hamilton felt awkward going back to stations he'd searched just a few hours previously. He was embarrassed, feeling that the Afghans would think Isaf didn't trust them. All the Polling Centres, bar one mosque, were cleared in time, and by 06:00 people were queuing to vote.

As with every morning of the tour, Captain Chris Jaunay was in the Ops Cell when the Commanding Officer walked in. Jaunay was suited to his role as Operations Officer Bravo in the headquarters. The job relies on someone who is able to play the mental game of keeping up to the second on everything that is happening across the battle space. He then has to inform the Commanding Officer and Brigade about what the sub-units need. As an exchange officer from the Royal Australian Regiment, Jaunay didn't have a career to build in the British Army or in the Scots Guards. He could afford to be refreshingly blunt with those below and above him. Equally direct was his Operations Warrant Officer, Company Sergeant Major Tam McEwan. Both were infanteers who knew the realities of battle. They accepted that Herrick 12 would be a thankless tour for them, as they slaved away in the Ops Cell. The presence of the Battalion colours in their office was acknowledgment that they were the control centre of the daily battle. Jaunay briefed the night's developments to the Commanding Officer, who then set off with Tac for the Helmand's Police Headquarters with the Operations Officer, Major James Leask. While Jaunay's role was to keep current, Leask had coordinated the Combined Force's future operations from his laptop for six months. The son of a Scots Guards General, he had left the Army after eight years and ambled into the City just as it detonated in 2007. He realised Army life was a safer bet and returned to the certainties of the Officers' Mess. Along with Major French and the Adjutant, he formed the overworked centre of the staff. Long hours were mandatory but there was always time for the trio to sneak out of the long, brown semi-circular tent that housed the Headquarters. They'd sit on a concrete sewage sump, indulge in a cup of tea and a cigarette and figure out what needed to happen next.

In the rural areas, the insurgents had performed an exceptionally effective influence campaign in the lead-up to 18 September. Everyone knew that if you went to vote and were found with an ink-stained forefinger, the insurgents would chop it off. The people drew their own conclusions: 'Why should we risk our fingers if the government never lifts a finger to help us?' The insurgents' groundwork was backed up with theatre on Election Day. Near Kunjak, in Loy Adera, an insurgent checkpoint was set up. Next to it, a bloodied machete stood in a stump of wood. No fingers were cut off – none needed to be. The intimidation was clear and the insurgents could later say that they hadn't killed anyone and that the people had chosen not to vote. The general air of intimidation was reinforced by shoots on Isaf checkpoints, though not generally on Polling Centres, and fights with Afghan forces. Combined Force Lashkar Gah responded with disruption patrols in depth to try and intimidate the intimidators.

Inside the Ops Cell an unprecedented number of reports were coming in. Sub-units would radio in on the Battlegroup net. Guardsman Alex Lochrie was one of the two signallers getting into their 12-hour shift as things began to pick up after 08:00. Messages thick with call signs and jargon would come into his left ear as he scrawled them down in shorthand in the logbook. He would relay the message up to the watch keeper, who would then either give him a quick answer to send back down to the sub-unit or pass it up to Company Sergeant Major McEwan. Much would then go onto JChat – the Brigade-wide instant-messaging wall. Serious incidents – a casualty, for instance – would call for Jaunay's input and he would phone Brigade if he had time and let them know the outline. As the day went on, this nicety was dropped as the Ops Cell began to stretch under the weight of events. Head-quarters' actions would then go back down to the sub-units via the signaller.

'You don't think, you just do,' said Lochrie of the autopilot the signallers get into as they guide the passage of information up and down the system.

There were multiple skirmishes in B Company's area, including RPG attacks on Checkpoint Bamba Serai. Left Flank was hit constantly along Route Mars. Each incident had to be opened, assessed and dealt with, assets requested if necessary and everyone in the chain told what was happening. 'We're in a relatively safe area and someone a few miles down the road is getting shot at,' said Guards-man Lochrie. 'It is one of those strange situations – the contrast.'

With the Commanding Officer out with Tac, the radio would occasionally crackle, 'Blackjack Zero Alpha: Send update. Over.' Captain Jaunay would then pull together everything that was happening and what the Ops Cell were doing about it. He would give an update within 30 seconds of hearing his master's voice. At any time, the Ops Cell were dealing with around seven separate events on Election Day, the incidents reaching a pitch of two to three a minute at one stage. Company Sergeant Major McEwan didn't have time to write one up for Brigade before the next came in.

'Blackjack Zero – all call signs. Everyone needs to stop

and take a calm-down moment here,' he said on the net. 'We're dealing with multiple incidents, so just think about what else is happening before you come on the net with anything else. Out.'

Captain Rowe came into the Ops Room to try and ease the pressure but the system remained maxed out. Brigade was phoning for information, companies needed assets in the air to help troops in contact, emails were flooding in, JChat had to be kept up to speed. Getting clarity on any situation was almost impossible with so much happening concurrently. The need to feel the battle, assess and prioritise continued. Everything else stopped when the call came in from Fondouk Squadron, Queen's Royal Lancers.

'Mustang Zero Bravo – Contact IED, casualties. Wait, out.'

1st Troop's reassurance patrols deep in the south of their patch had gone well. Six of them – half the Troop – plus an interpreter had gone out in the morning. They'd been out for six hours and were about to make their way back to Checkpoint Dre Dawal in two Jackals. Insurgents had massively increased the number of IED markings in the area by putting rows of stones and twigs across tracks. The assessment was that dummy minefields had been placed to intimidate locals against travelling to Polling Centres, hence the patrols to prove safe routes for potential voters. The atmosphere still seemed good and some people were telling the patrol they were going to vote. Lieutenant Clayton turned his Jackals around and crossed Route Mouse, a small track that Isaf had hardly used since Operation Moshtarak seven months earlier. They reached a deep five-metre-wide ditch. The Vallon man jumped out. Clayton commanded him from the vehicle. The Vallon operator cleared the vulnerable area along two tyre tracks then remounted the vehicle, which drove through to the other side. The second Jackal followed, struck the IED just as it crested the home bank and flipped back on itself. Trooper Andrew Howarth was fatally injured, Sergeant Andy Jones, Trooper Aaron Hobbs and the interpreter were thrown clear. The three uninjured men – Lieutenant Clayton, Lance Corporal Bowers and Trooper Wilkes – rushed back to the stricken vehicle. It was clear they could do nothing for Trooper Howarth. Clayton got on the net. They were very far from help. Trooper Hobbs was sitting silently when they got to him, his left knee ripped open and multiple lacerations across his body.

'Help the others, I'm fine', he said calmly.

Sergeant Jones took morphine. Lieutenant Clayton went to clear a space for a helicopter to land. It took 25 minutes for the nearest patrol to get to them.

Back in the Ops Cell, the all-too-practised Casevac system got going as soon as broken reports of the injuries came over the net. A helicopter was detailed within minutes. Without badgering the QRL, facts needed to come through and the situation assessed. Major French walked in and sat in the corner to make sure the right questions were being asked. The Commanding Officer correctly headed to Fondouk Squadron's Headquarters to offer support. Cutting equipment was needed for the Jackal, perhaps even a recovery vehicle, and the extent of the injuries on the ground also needed clarifying. Reserves were stood up to escort these assets to the scene with a counter-IED team. The rest of the Battlegroup cut away from the net to give space to the major incident. The signallers calmly told the QRL what was on its way and how long it would take.

5th Troop arrived on the scene and relieved the three men from dealing with the incident. They had given all the first aid they could with the kit they carried and had done everything else right. By now they were in a bad way and had stopped making sense. They were put in the back of a wagon and driven back to Checkpoint Dre Dwahl. Inside they met up with the rest of 1st Troop, less Sergeant Chappell, who was on R&R and would return to a shattered unit. That evening, Fondouk Squadron's new Officer Commanding, Major Ben Cossens, arrived at Dre Dwahl.

'Jonny,' he said to Clayton, 'I've got to go over there and tell those guys something but I've got to tell you first. Andy Jones died in the air.'

The Major went over to the men, broke the news, then said a prayer and read a poem.

'That was quite huge, actually; it meant a lot to them,' said Clayton. 'The mood in the Troop – it just straight out didn't get back to normal. I don't know whether the mood in the Squadron ever got back to normal after that. We ploughed on and it was business as usual and you do your job and some things make you laugh and some things make you pissed off.'

In Lashkar Gah reports from the 55 incidents the Ops Cell had managed that day were typed up. Guardsman Lochrie peeled his headset off after 12 hours on duty. He handed the noise over to the next signaller and headed to the gym to get the day out of his head. It had been the busiest of the tour. Across the Brigade on 18 September, there had been around 120 incidents, so the insurgent focus had clearly been to disrupt Helmand's capital. The two deaths had been only tangentially linked to the election. The IED was assessed as a legacy device from before Operation Moshtarak and would not have been placed to target the patrol as Route Mouse was so rarely used by Isaf on Herrick 12. However, the reason 1st Troop was there was to provide reassurance to the people of Bolan South on Election Day. Elsewhere the attacks had been aimed at the elections though no one else had been killed in Lashkar Gah District that day by insurgent activity.

'It certainly wasn't the Armageddon that some had been anticipating,' said the Chief of Staff, Major French, 'but retrospectively it was pretty clear that the aim was just to intimidate primarily and that intimidation, by all accounts, was effective. It stopped some of the population voting. Although it could be argued that most of the population weren't that interested in voting in the first place.'

*

In a province whose population is estimated to be between 800,000 to 1.5 million, 36,162 votes were cast on 18 September 2010, of which 2,485 were disqualified, according to IEC figures. The eight MPs elected won with a spread of between 3,042 and 574 votes. Approximately 40 per cent of votes cast were for the eight candidates elected from a field of 53. The Electoral Complaints Commission disqualified one candidate, Haji Mahlem. Between the allegations of fraud that leaked into the international media and the palpably low turnout created by apathy and intimidation, the 2010 Parliamentary Elections, in Helmand at least, were not a victory for the Afghan Government.

Visitors

'*Influence,*' *as the Commanding Officer pointed out, '*never takes a day off.*' Headquartered with Brigade, CF Lashkar Gah sucked in a huge amount of visitors. Ministers, high-ranking officers, medium-ranking officers, journalists and academics all came through. In retrospect, the flow of visitors on Salisbury Plain had been prophetic. General McChrystal's emissary, Command Sergeant Major Hall, came through in late May and described himself as a '*recovering kinetic*' to Guardsmen, who may have missed the Alcoholics Anonymous reference. He looked me (another visitor) up and down.*

'*One day I'm going to write a book about reporters,*' *he said.*

*Maybe he already knew about the rolling storm coming to engulf his doomed master; maybe his generation are lining up another '*blame the press*' campaign if the war follows Vietnam's trajectory.*

Many soldiers like getting visits. It makes them feel appreciated. Lance Corporal Mick Little recalled a cancelled visit during Right Flank's second Sayedebad mission back in February.

'*The boys were a bit pissed off that the Brigade Commander couldn't make it out. [11 Brigade's James Cowan had wanted to visit but the amount of fire coming in made this impossible.] It's always good for the boys to see a high-ranking officer come out of his office and come out on the ground and be with the boys. If you're the Company Sergeant Major, you're probably flapping because he thinks he's got to show this and all that but, realistically, these guys probably want to see the truth. They want to see how the boys are and for the boys obviously, if he turns up they'll be like: "At least he's bothering to come out and see us." '*

Visitors also brought news of the outside world to the checkpoint bubble: the BP spill in the Gulf of Mexico – 'Is that still happening?' – and the Chilean miners – 'Is that still happening?'

The volume of visits could be overbearing. The QRL were victims of both the perception of their success in Bolan South and proximity to Lashkar Gah. The internal PR machine thought they demonstrated current success and possibly a signpost for Britain's future in Afghanistan. They ran a largely pacified area and partnered with half-decent Afghans, so streams of visitors came to see Counter Insurgency in action, the subtleties of which could be lost in the fight Left Flank were enduring. B Company also got a fair share of VIPs.

Like a breeze turning to a gale, rumours of a VVIP visit spread through the Main Operating Base. He is referred to as 'The Visitor' for security reasons by those in the know – which is everyone. Briefings and Fragmentary Orders cascade from Whitehall to Permanent Joint Headquarters to Brigade to Combined Force to Company to the Guardsman told to get his sideburns up. The night before The Visitor arrives, a man from Special Branch arrives at the rural Checkpoint armed with a submachine gun and gossip. The day of the visit starts with a thorough search of the base, in case a suicide bomber has hidden in a shipping container for this moment. Shirts come off hangers, berets out of bergens. The Diarrhoea & Vomiting (D&V) tent is re-tasked as a shura hall and the Afghan Commander is told to be there at 10:45. He is not told why. The volleyball court becomes an IED lane and gleaming weapons are laid out. Men read their lines to take in prep for the journalists accompanying The Visitor. The

Commanding Officer arrives an hour before showtime and does a dry run. The Regimental Sergeant Major throws a man off a stand as he's lost his beret and is wearing a sun hat.

At 10:55 the Commanding Officer walks out to the open helipad without body armour or helmet. It's a good psychological trick: the men getting off the helicopter that lands at 11:00 might stratospherically outrank him but they're in body armour. His nakedness cuts them immediately down to size, establishes Alpha credentials and marks territory. Clever chap.

The Visitor has a comet's trail. Close Protection teams, a 3-star officer, the Brigadier and his team, advisors, special secretaries and a man from the BBC with a cameraman. They sit on borrowed carpets in the D&V tent on top of the ground a Guardsman was moaning over 24 hours earlier. The Visitor begins his shura. *The Afghan Commander, a hardened PR pro, is slightly taken aback by the 'reveal' of The Visitor's identity but plays a beautiful flush of lines to take. Security, governance, the excellence of relations with Isaf all trip off. The BBC man stands back and doesn't listen in.*

'To be honest, once you've seen one Patrol Base, you've seen them all,' he says as he tries to work out who exactly I am.

The Visitor heads over to the weapons stands. He is suitably impressed with a Lance Sergeant's account of killing a running insurgent at 1,400 metres with his sniper rifle. He knows how to play the game and engages well with the Guardsmen in their tents. He seems to know his stuff. He's also wearing the right kit – dark shirt of a shade that won't show sweat patches, light trousers, sensible shoes. Two US Marines who've arrived at the checkpoint that morning bluff through their introduction to The Visitor with winning smiles.

'We won't get much from this,' says the man from the BBC. 'I have to edit and file from the next base.'

The hour has gone quickly. Purple smoke is popped out on the helipad and the Chinook is heard. It is impossible to look good in body armour unless in uniform but The Visitor does fairly well with a pair of designer shades that draw the eye away from the bulk. The civilians stroll out slower than they came in – the visit has put them at ease and thus succeeded. The Chinook, though, has already been on the ground a little too long when what looks like a violent disagreement breaks out on its ramp. The man from the BBC is shouting pointlessly against the rotors. He is waving his right hand up and down in the air and pointing at it with his left then opening his fist and closing it. Then he points back at the Checkpoint. A soldier's mouth opens and shuts. He shakes his head and pushes the man into the helicopter. It finally gets airborne.

'That was excellent,' says the Commanding Officer, then he jumps back into his wagon and darts back to Lashkar Gah.

'In all the years I've known the Commanding Officer, that's the first time I've heard him use that word,' says an officer with wistful pride as he heads into the Ops Room. Men strip back into T-shirts and shorts.

'Blackjack Two Zero – Blackjack Zero: your man from the BBC left his laptop at your location,' says a voice on the net from Combined Force Headquarters in Lashkar Gah.

'Blackjack Zero – Blackjack Two Zero: roger,' says the signaller, writing the message in his log. 'What a belter.'

There was a second type of visit – those that crop up regularly at the nightmare Checkpoint. After each serious incident, TRiM coordinators will turn up to ask men to go over incidents again; after each fatality, the Serious Incidents Branch of the Royal Military Police arrive and interview everyone about what happened. New pieces of kit are sent to try and win the local battle; the Combat Camera Team pitches up to take war photos but journalists rarely get in.

Eventually, a Lieutenant Colonel from the Field Mental Health Team arrives and talks to everyone about 'moving furniture around the room that is the mind'. This is the sort of checkpoint you want to avoid. This is the sort of place Checkpoint Said Abdul had become by mid-August.

CHAPTER NINE

'Like it never even happened'
August–October 2010

The accurate fire on Checkpoint Said Abdul continued through August. The addition of a large CCTV mast allowed Lieutenant Pearson to zoom in on likely firing points. On 10 August, after receiving ten rounds onto the sangar, a Javelin strike was authorised. The missile flew straight into the identified firing point. This calmed the situation down for about a week. The bottomless talent pool the insurgents drew on then resumed the fight. The sniper known to locals as 'the hunter' was also still at large.

The mental strain the Guardsmen on stag were under was considerable and visible to me. Voices were dappled with emotion during interviews. This was especially the case after the death of Acting Sergeant McCallum, though Sergeant Gibson was sure he had killed the sniper who had shot his friend. The R&R plot meant less sleep and more time in the sangar for the Guardsmen. Sleeping through the night in their ten-man tents was a rarity. If they were lucky, the tent itself was noisy. If it was creaking, then there was a breeze and that meant it was cool enough to sleep through without drenching your roll mat in sweat. Every two hours someone was shaken awake for stag and from the non-commissioned officer's area, someone else was woken to watch the radio. To a fitful sleeper in the heat like me, it seemed there was a constant procession of men with rubber soles kicking about all night. There's also the constant shuffling of young men trying to make themselves comfortable as they shift their bodies under imitation Gore-tex bivouac bags. A new boy used to air conditioning in Bastion coughs through the night. A Guardsman having a recurring dream about being in the sangar mumbles, 'Fuck, fucking hell!' as imaginary rounds pass through his sub-conscious. Before too long the man with the last stag comes through and shakes everyone's mosquito nets: 'Reveille, reveille!' And another day in Said Abdul starts.

'The relation of officers and men, and of senior and junior officers, had been very different in the excitement of battle. There had been no insubordination, but a greater freedom of speech, as though we were all drunk together.' Robert Graves wrote that about life in Flanders' trenches with the Royal Welch Fusiliers. The same freedoms were present in Said Abdul in 2010. Living conditions were shared and manageably austere. The equality of deprivation and risk bred familiarity. Contempt only surfaced if mistakes were made. Everyone ate together each night, Lance Corporal Henderson emerging as the star with the ten-man ration pack, though Rose, the interpreter, made decent flatbread. The men washed together at the well most nights, sluicing the day away with cool water and adding to the quilt of in-jokes they had made to stave off their surroundings. With six months as the only officer in a small base, Lieutenant Pearson opened up to his section commanders. By the end of the tour, they knew his family and girlfriend well – a sign of the trust Pearson could put in his capable sergeants. Only the British would require the chance of death in the morning to completely break down the barriers of class, wealth and education that separate a Lieutenant and a

Lance Sergeant who are the same age, listen to the same music and drink the same beer. Pearson's name remained 'Sir' to his face. A rumour, possibly begun by him, that his Guardsmen knew him as 'War Horse' gained traction throughout the Scots Guards.

24 August

'We were struggling for a bit,' Major Kitching told me later. 'The guys in Said Abdul were under considerable pressure and there were, and I know we're not supposed to use the word, but there were definitely snipers operating against us in that area. It was having a massive effect on morale and on our own ability to operate and engage with the local people.'

Warrior Sergeant Major Brettle's Intelligence Cell put together a detailed picture of how the insurgents worked from various sources. With this knowledge, Kitching planned a Company patrol through the Firing Points north of Said Abdul and beyond. This would disrupt the sniping network in depth. He wanted to hit where they slept, where they kept their supplies and their command structure. This would hopefully have a long-term effect on the area rather than what could be achieved by picking off the shooters individually.

The operation illustrated the complexity of operating in Loy Adera. While Lance Corporal Henderson treated sick young children in one compound and chatted with their mothers, Lieutenant Pearson and Lance Sergeant McLeod led bayonets-fixed, grenades-thrown assaults into a neighbouring compound 50 metres away. The patrol was surrounded; machine gunners ran out of ammunition; a young replacement Guardsman shot an insurgent dead less than 20 metres from his position just days after arriving in Loy Adera. The weather became so bad that helicopters were grounded, robbing Left Flank of on-the-spot fire support and the ability to get casualties to Bastion quickly. Once again, Kitching used his discretion as a commander and pressed his men on. A recently abandoned IED factory was discovered – possibly explaining the dogged counter-attacks on the patrol.

When the patrol was over, the men were elated. The cocktail of heavy contact and close calls pushed endorphins high. Cigarettes and water were broken out. It was stunning that they'd taken no casualties.

'That was nothing short of a miracle,' said Lance Corporal Ramsay.

'Sheer luck,' agreed Lance Sergeant Wood.

'Wasnae like the majority of contacts – none of yer shoot 'n' scoot there,' Ramsay said.

'Not a bad morning's work, guys,' said Major Kitching.

It had all, finally, been like the training on that wet Friday afternoon in Otterburn – a full company advance to, through and then from contact. Many had waited for it since they decided on the Army.

'It was the closest to war fighting we'll ever get and the boys loved it. They absolutely loved it,' said Lance Sergeant Wood. It was almost a relief from the complex counter-insurgency operations they'd been stuck into – a proper toe-to-toe fight with a determined enemy in numbers.

'Your search operations and all that stuff – dealing with the local nationals – is quite difficult. That day was hardcore, but it was right down to your bread and butter. It's what everyone knows how to do: "You give fire support, we're going to extract and then we'll swap." Everybody knows it. It's easy in a certain sense. It was a good day,' concluded Lance Corporal Ramsay.

Taking his men off the leash had yielded results for

Major Kitching – the IEDs destroyed, a great deal of intelligence gathered and the usual firing points heavily disrupted by various means. The shoots on Checkpoint Said Abdul tapered off for some time. However, Left Flank had been in Loy Adera long enough to know that the insurgents would be back – in their own time and on their own terms. An operation like that of 24 August was tactically valid but would never defeat the local insurgents.

★

'Was that a petrol bomb?' asked the CCTV operator in Checkpoint Said Abdul.

'Hang on – rewind and freeze it,' said Lieutenant Pearson.

The Lance Corporal paused the live feed and went back to the frame where a cloud of grainy flame leapt onto the passing Viking.

'Little fuckers – it is. What do I put up on the net?' asked Pearson.

'Contact Petrol Bomb?' suggested the Lance Corporal.

'Yeah, cheers. Blackjack Two Three Alpha: Contact Petrol Bomb on the Viking Call Sign heading to my location. Seen on the camera, looks like it came from Compound Number, um, wait one . . .'

News of the petrol bomb flew up the chain of command in Helmand. The Brigadier expressed interest at that evening's conference. While a petrol bomb was something new, it fitted with an emerging pattern. Quite a few of the Brigadier's men had got lucky – relatively – recently and trodden on IEDs that had failed to fully detonate. The theory went that the insurgents were running out of bomb-making materials and possibly bomb-making expertise. The supply issue may have had its roots in the

Pacific. La Niña had cooled the ocean a little more than usual, causing the clouds that triggered the floods over Pakistan. This disrupted supply routes. As for the bomb makers, men with nicknames and sideburns had hunted them to the verge of extinction, many thought. So the petrol bomb became another bit of information feeding the consensus up at Brigade. The truth in Loy Adera may have been slightly different.

To expedite the Trident upgrade and to clear their eye lines, Left Flank did a lot of necessary damage to Loy Adera. In consultation with the locals, walls were toppled and trees ripped down. The claims clinic that Left Flank's stabilisation representative, Sergeant Jones, organised was overrun with farmers demanding compensation. Small claims could be settled on the spot. Larger claims would have to be settled in Lashkar Gah. Still larger claims would go to London for sign-off. In one case, a large orchard had to be flattened to make way for Route Trident. Compensation, which affected 50 local families, took months to come through.

'I have huge frustrations here about bureaucracy and the red tape about what could be very, very quick wins for us – compensation and claims,' said Major Kitching.

For locals told to settle compensation with the Afghan Government, the journey to Lashkar Gah was clearly a hazardous one. A round trip by minibus was also expensive by local standards at Afs 120. On arrival, they would be asked for ID and documentation proving land ownership. Sometimes, if a piece of documentation was missing, an arrangement could be made with an official – but would the cost of the arrangement be larger than the claim? As in other parts of Combined Force Lashkar Gah, insurgents had been peddling their information operations line: the corrupt Afghan Government was after farmers' land and those without the right documents would forfeit. To

subsistence farmers bottoming out on poverty, the calcu-
lations added up. They examined the offer again. Perhaps
one of them decided to throw that petrol bomb.

September

Some came to believe that the issue of who owned land
went right to the core of what could be achieved in Loy
Adera and indeed across Combined Force Lashkar Gah.
Land rights were a trump card for the Afghan Government. Once they'd officially parcelled out the land, their
leverage over their people decreased. Retaining land ideo-
logically references the Soviet style of state that elements
of the Afghan Government were trained in. Others, such
as one British Commander, wanted 'the Afghan Government to divest itself of the security blanket that is land
ownership'. Once people own their land and have a stake
in the state, the argument runs, an effective taxation
system can begin to fund state provision of services. This
would then push the people away from the insurgency.
This argument could be seen as advocating a 21st-century
version of the Ryotwari land tenure system created by the
East India Company in parts of 19th-century British
India. Picking a way through this issue is something that
has to happen at a national level. The process will be a
reminder that it's not just IEDs that make up the minefields of Afghanistan. In the meantime, it is the farmers of
places like Loy Adera who are caught between opposing
groups armed with arguments as well as weapons.

Compounding the issue of land rights was the vacuum
of governance in Loy Adera. The area's representative on
the Provincial Council visited once in six months. Mayor
Daoud of Lashkar Gah District also visited just once. It
was no wonder that the people were referred to as 'the

forgotten'. Without a visible link to the Afghan Government, the people of Loy Adera were unlikely to go with the offer it claimed to bring to their lives.

'Any British politician would want to extend his hinterland,' the Commanding Officer noted. 'These guys were very keen not to extend – essentially, there's not a lot there for them.'

Getting the political class in Lashkar Gah to recognise their ownership of the area was tricky. The Rural Development Commission (see Chapter Eight) stalled. The Mayor seemed permanently unavailable when offers were made to escort him to the rural areas of his district. The Provincial Reconstruction Team seemed unenthusiastic about projects in rural areas – though this could have been driven by their knowledge of what the Afghan Line Ministries (health, education) would stomach. One sign of progress was a $20,000 Government Outreach Office delivered to Patrol Base Nahidullah in August. The plan was for this converted shipping container to be staffed by a member of the mayor's office. This civil servant would process ID cards and land registration documents and give some sort of pulse to governance in the area. As at Left Flank's departure, the office was not manned. In order to force the Mayor to engage in rural areas, Isaf created a tripwire in the stabilisation cycle that directly brought him into the process. The plan was that he could deny no project in the District unless he went and explained to the people why he had turned it down. Whether the Mayor will simply sit on projects he doesn't like rather than go out to the rural areas he seems so loath to visit remains to be seen. What was clear was that lives were given in a fight for an area that the Afghan Government seemed quite unwilling to engage in during the summer of 2010.

The issues of tardy compensation process, concerns over land rights and lack of governance undermined the tactical progress made in Loy Adera. Worryingly, in some parts of the area the locals stopped cooperating in Isaf's efforts to clear lines of fire. Perhaps this was due to insurgents threatening to harm anyone who helped Isaf. Perhaps the locals were now on the other side of the offer. Either way, Guardsmen had to go out and do the job themselves.

The dangers of this were very horrifically shown on 2 September, when Guardsman James Murphy was shot in the head outside VCP Rabiullah while clearing shrubs. He had just turned 18 when he was flown out to Helmand as a Battle Casualty Replacement. When Sergeant Paxton, on his first day back from his recuperation in Camp Bastion, saw Murphy, he was convinced the boy was dead. He came round in the back of Lance Sergeant Wood's Mastiff and somehow survived. At the time of writing, he is making good progress.

*

On 4 September, Guardsman David Duff was shot in the lower left leg while helping clear an IED on Route Trident, which had claimed its latest casualty. As the area's main effort, everything had been focused around turning Route Mars into Route Trident. All Isaf's bases were strung along the route and the RDG Squadron was specifically there as intimate security for the upgrade. It was sold as a key part of 'the offer' to the people of Loy Adera. It was also vital to sustaining Isaf in the field. The road was a key battleground for the insurgents, who shot at the contractors and emplaced IEDs whenever they could. There were, however, some significant concerns surrounding Route Trident.

The most fundamental issue with the Trident build was that it was an enormous replication of effort. Only a few kilometres to the north lay a $9m Department for International Development-led project: Route Morpheus. Morpheus will connect Marjah to Gereshk via Nad-e-Ali, with a branch route to Lashkar Gah. As with Trident, the build will be carried out by local contractors. Unlike Trident, British soldiers will not provide advice, security or a counter-IED capability, as these functions are also contracted out. Morpheus will be tarmacked in full, unlike the neo-cell (cellular neoprene), stone and sand 'IED Resistant' Trident.

'We need to mention that the neo-cell is manufactured in Israel – so it's essentially a Jewish road going straight through a Muslim country and I love that,' said one Royal Engineer.

While the local nature of the campaign is obvious, it seems strange that two multimillion-dollar main routes were needed for the people of Central Helmand.

'It gives options and it is all about Freedom of Movement,' explained Major Kitching. 'It is funny, though – we hark on about this comprehensive approach and we're still getting there . . . but we're being asked to do x, y and z up here and people are losing their lives doing that, sadly. And it is all for a very good reason, but when things aren't tied up across the board it can be frustrating.'

Route Trident was also a supply route for the Central Helmand Patrol Base line. This was laid out by previous Brigades and does not marry with the main route between the population centres – Route Morpheus. Their intent was to conduct the 'clear, hold, build' dogma deep into insurgent-held areas, rather than along existing routes from where they could then bubble security outwards. Trident is now necessary, as the IED resistance it purports to bring allows supplies to get to the garrisons at a reduced risk. With more heavy-lift helicopters, the IED risk for supply runs would be completely avoided but that's another story. In the end, the British taxpayer has now funded the Department for International Development to build Central Helmand's equivalent of the M1 and the British Army to build its A1. I was slightly confused as to how this is an excellent use of stretched resources.

The centrepiece of Trident was the 'Stabilisation Bridge' built over the canal on the boundary between Left Flank and Right Flank. Despite the language barrier between the Royal Engineers and the local contractors – there was a shortage of interpreters – the causeway built either side of the bridge was completed on time to a one-inch margin of error. A 50-metre bridge was then laid between the banks of the causeway. On his first and last trip beyond the city limits of Lashkar Gah during Herrick 12, Mayor Daoud opened it on 14 August. It replaced a concrete bridge built by the Russians in the 1980s.

Whatever the replication of efforts between Morpheus and Trident says about the campaign in Helmand, the Patrol Base line was where it was in 2010. For Left Flank, the additional protection promised by Route Trident couldn't come quickly enough.

*

'Blackjack Two Zero – Blackjack Seven Zero Alpha: just confirm those Zap Numbers?' barked Platoon Sergeant Major Lilley over the net.

A few moments later a set of letters totally different to those sent minutes earlier came over.

'Seven Zero Alpha – I'm not having that. That's a different set of Zap Numbers to the ones I've just heard.'

Then Lance Sergeant McDougall came over the net and gave the correct number: LI7042. The Platoon Sergeant Major leant back in his chair. He now knew for certain that his son John had been caught in the IED blast he'd heard minutes ago. The next half-hour was definitely the worst of his life. There was no point badgering on the net and he just had to wait to hear what state his son was in. Word came over: 'Category B'. Not life-threatening. Relief. 'Back injury.' That could be quite punchy. Guardsmen Baleiono Rabukawaqa and Craig Bentham were also injured but not as badly as John Lilley junior. A Chinook lifted them from Patrol Base Nahidullah.

The Platoon Sergeant Major was packed off to Lashkar Gah in a Mastiff. Ever since his son had moved to Checkpoint Said Abdul, Lilley had worried. Hours were spent next to the radio, waiting on news. The death of Acting Sergeant McCallum had hit his men terribly. Knowing his son was heading to the place where one of Battalion's finest had died made things even harder for the Platoon Sergeant Major.

'He's a good Guardsman, he can handle himself,' he had to think. 'Afghanistan's one of those places where it doesn't matter how safe a place you're in. If you're going to get shot, it doesn't matter if you're in Bastion or wherever – it will happen,' Lilley thought. 'I know he's surrounded by a load of really experienced soldiers and if he can be protected from anything, those guys will protect him.'

It seemed, though, that no one could be safe at Bravo Foxtrot 3.

The Platoon Sergeant Major phoned his wife, Elizabeth. She was at a Sergeants' Mess wives' barbecue in Catterick.

'Right, I don't want you to panic. John's been involved in an IED incident, but he's all right – he's got all his limbs. He's just got a few broken bones in his back. He'll be fine,' he said.

Having not seen his boy yet, he wasn't sure who he was

trying to convince more – himself or his wife. It was a very difficult phone call.

After a flight to Bastion, he saw his boy briefly before the RAF took him home. He was lying in a pair of shorts covered in blood from tiny cuts along his arms. He was on a drip, sedated. He wasn't a soldier any more – he was just his father's wee boy.

'Fucking hell! I need to hold it together here,' thought Lilley. He spied a pack of cigarettes. 'Whose fucking fags are they then, son? I thought I told you not to smoke!'

The next morning, Platoon Sergeant Major Lilley was back in Loy Adera on a Company Operation, getting shot at. He fired at a man wearing blue shooting at him. The figure went to ground. A while later an Afghan came up to Lilley.

'You've shot my son,' the Afghan said.

'No, I shot a gunman. I seen his weapon.'

'No, no. You shot my son in the nose – here, see,' the man said and beckoned over a younger man missing the front of his nose.

'You tell him he's lucky I've not check-zeroed my weapon, otherwise he'd have a fucking round in his head,' said Lilley. Then he noticed the spotless white *shalwar kameez* the wounded man was wearing.

'He's been changed.'

'No, he hasn't,' said the older man.

'That nose must have been pishing blood. There's no way he has been shot in the nose wearing that. He was the man in blue with the weapon,' said Lilley.

'When's this thing ever going to end?' he thought.

★

Guardsman Lilley and the two others injured in the blast of 5 September were lucky they were travelling by Mastiff.

Luckier still was Lance Sergeant McLeod's team, who had travelled through Bravo Foxtrot 3 minutes earlier in open-topped Jackals, which could have been flipped by the blast. Despite Vehicle Checkpoint McCallum and the CCTV system looking onto the blind spot, insurgents had once again got a device in. They were a truly patient and cunning enemy.

Four days later, Bravo Foxtrot 3 was checked by Vallon teams and declared clear. Before the men had walked back to their checkpoints, a Mastiff drove through the blind spot and was hit by a massive device. It had been hastily laid in a culvert under the road. Lance Sergeant James Thorpe and Guardsman Ryan Gowans were both injured in the blast. Again, they were lucky in their choice of vehicle.

The men of 11 Platoon had tried everything to disrupt the skilled IED cell troubling Bravo Foxtrot 3. Routines were changed daily, as patterns couldn't afford to be set. Vehicles would stop short, men would dismount and Vallon through. This put them at risk from accurate small arms of the type that hit Guardsman Duff. Random foot patrols went through the area. More walls and undergrowth were ripped out to deny cover from the CCTV system. Mastiffs were parked in sentry positions. Devices still got into the blind spot.

'The guerrilla warfare that they're using is generations-taught and we just had to learn it,' concluded Sergeant Gibson, now back from R&R.

Eventually, night patrols were used. Despite the Brigadier's directive to 'own the night' on Herrick 12, night patrolling had been used sparingly in Loy Adera. It offended local sensibilities (and who would want a dozen soldiers crashing into their home at all hours?) and reduced to almost nil the ability to detect signs of IEDs with the eye. The situation on Bravo Foxtrot 3, and the importance of keeping Route Mars/Trident open to Isaf and civilian traffic, meant night patrols had to go out. The increasing availability and range of night-vision equipment and surveillance cameras also meant that patrolling in the dark was less hazardous than it had been at the start of the tour. At first the locals were angry about the increased night patrols. The interpreters and Afghan partners proved their use and explained to the population why it was a necessity. The patrols, using an insurgent tactic, dropped off night letters. Along with information about the upcoming parliamentary elections, they stated that joint patrols would be going through Loy Adera each night. The local population informed the insurgents. For a while the IED cell appeared to move north rather than contend with Left Flank in the dark. This was a superb example of getting the people to spread an Isaf message for the soldiers and thereby intimidating the insurgents into dropping their activity. It didn't come easily, as the Guardsman who fell down a well one dark night can testify.

★

Left Flank was held to have the worst standards in the Combined Force. Much of this reputation rested on the length of their sideburns. This, held the traditionalists, showed a creep towards the attitudes of the 'chippies', which was abhorrent to the Guards. Other symptoms included the wearing of baseball caps rather than sunhats and calling platoon commanders 'boss'. The fear was that this attitude would lead to truly important details being neglected: batteries would not be charged before patrol, protective gloves and glasses would not be worn. When this begins to happen, the traditionalist has a field day. This in turn damages morale by driving a wedge through a unit.

The root of the argument was the us-and-them divide between front-line soldiers and those supporting them in the near and not-so-near rear. It must be as old as warfare. There were probably hoplites at Marathon who dismissed Pheidippides as 'that belter from Signals Platoon' or similar. Today's subaltern responds to an attack on his base by jumping onto his garrison walls wearing only flip-flops and running shorts. It is impossible that he wears combats for six months but vital that he responds to events at once. In his dress, he is certainly tipping his helmet, perhaps subconsciously, to the 8th Army 'Sandman' who went into battle in a yellow shirt and suede boots in 1942. Over a six-month tour, a degree of insouciance is some-times required to keep everyone sane. As one non-commissioned officer put it, 'The boys can wander round the base wearing a dress if it helps them get through the day. So long as they do their job on patrol.' None could accuse Left Flank of not doing that.

Standards became an overblown issue in the discourse of Herrick 12. Perhaps it was a reflection on the tour going fairly well that people were purging about sideburns rather than about running out of ammunition or having their lives put at unnecessary risk by poor officers. Whatever the rights and wrongs of the standards debate – and it struck me as an odd one to be going on about in a warzone – the fact remains that the Commanding Officer had said to the Officers' and Sergeants' Messes before the tour that high standards were something he wanted maintained regardless of circumstance.

The best response to the standards debate came from Sergeant Chappell, Queen's Royal Lancers. A close read-ing of *Queen's Regulations* shows that no soldier may cut another's hair. Chappell used this to get his men into Lashkar Gah for a haircut by 'Zohan', the permed Afghan barber in the Main Operating Base. Once this piece of vital business was concluded, the Troopers would spend time on Facebook, grab a decent meal and stock up on pop.

★

Every Herrick has its touchstone stories – the ones that everyone from the mechanic in Bastion to the lead Vallon man in Sangin knows about within a few hours of the event. Some are dark and play on everyone's worst fears. The night of 13 July, when Talib Hussein, an Afghan National Army soldier, fired an RPG into a Gurkha Ops Room, killing three, was tragic. Hussein's 'WANTED' poster was in every base in Helmand in days. The story about the Royal Engineer in Sangin shot through an inches-wide gap in his sangar's ballistic glass had some muttering about Chechens armed with Dragunov sniper rifles. The other category of story was the fuck-up. In an organisation as competitive as the Army, it's no surprise the fuck-up is everyone's favourite type of story – so long as it's another capbadge's. The only Herrick 12 story to have its own Facebook fan page is the one about the Gurkha who decapitated a dead insurgent. One version of the story was that he'd been counter-attacked, remembered the importance of biometrically enrolling dead insurgents, so removed the head in a unique take on evidence gathering. He was sent home sharpish to face an inquiry. The Brigade Reconnaissance Force's missile lesson was my favourite. Concluding his class on how to fire the light missile, the instructor aimed the dummy tube at a parked engineer tank and pulled the trigger. Both he and his pupils, caught in the back blast, then realised that it wasn't a dummy missile. The fact that no one was killed turned the story into an instant classic for everyone apart from the man's parent unit. The consistent rumour about a shipping container of Light Machine Guns going missing in Bastion was another good one. The story went that a team of Royal Military Police spent all day, every day, going around the vast camp opening shipping containers in the hope that one day they'd find the rogue arsenal.

Hearing about a fuck-up always brightened a day but they raised a couple of problems. First, it reflected a cultural tendency to highlight worst rather than best practice while in theatre. The stretched Lessons Learned Cell at Brigade churned out dispassionate accounts of errors – 'The Mastiff should have preceded the Warrior through the known Vulnerable Point' – rather than stories about what was working elsewhere in Helmand. The other problem with the fuck-up was that over six months, inevitably, your own capbadge would make one.

'You're the guys who missed with a Javelin, aren't you? Classic.' Quite a few Scots Guardsmen heard that on their way through Bastion as they peeled out of theatre. The Lance Corporal responsible may never live it down. In mitigation, he was being shot and shouted at a lot. When he pulled the fire trigger and the missile went where he'd locked it onto – which wasn't the target – he must have known the scale of the error instantly. The two things everyone who hasn't trained on Javelin knows about it are that each costs the same as a Lamborghini and it never misses. It just had. 'Javelin team – Platoon Sergeant. You'd better have your gumshield on when you come back here,' said Sergeant Gibson on the net. He was furious that a chance to hit a shooter who'd harassed his boys for so long had gone awry. The story flew out of Said Abdul, was giftwrapped in sarcasm by Left Flank and delivered to Brigade:

'Aye, I heard he only meant to fire a warning shot – a £60,000 one, but a warning shot.'

'He was denying the enemy a tactically vital watermelon field.'

'He was being shot at – it's Courageous Restraint.'

Sergeant Gibson was right to be angry at the wasted opportunity. The insurgents were a canny enemy loath to show themselves.

'It was a case of waiting. We learnt about how they were doing it and that had to come from local sources,' Gibson said. 'It was then a case of locating where the single round was coming from and then firing.'

On 1 September it all fell into place.

A patrol went out to cordon the Route Trident upgrade, by now approaching Checkpoint Said Abdul. The RDG in their Vikings were coming under accurate fire. A round hit one turret's ballistic shield heavily enough to crack it. This indicated the presence of a sniper. A dust cloud had shown up on the CCTV system monitor just before the RDG radioed that he'd taken a high-velocity round to the shield. Sergeant Gibson asked the Viking to put rounds in the general direction of the incoming fire. The insurgent gunman then gave his position away to the surveillance system by firing another round in self-defence. His location was confirmed by a drone that Combined Force Headquarters had got to the scene. He was seen pouring water in front of his barrel to minimise the kick-up of dust when he next fired. A Royal Artillery missile was teed up but then cancelled. An Apache with its missiles was called forward instead. The men in Said Abdul were told to prepare to mount an instant assessment of the missile strike. Gibson got his men into the back of the Vikings parked in the checkpoint and they headed 200 metres out from Said Abdul. The Hellfire missile was fired from 4,200 metres away. Inside the Vikings there is a massive bang as the missile hits the firing point with precision. The Viking smashes over the ground. The doors swing open; the Guardsmen dismount. They Vallon into the scene of a massive explosion. 'He was, literally, in bits,' Gibson said of the gunman.

The stock and bent barrel of a marksman's rifle were found along with a medium machine gun with tins of ammunition. A flip-flop and the man's foot were removed for DNA purposes.

The episode is currently taught back in Britain as a model for co-ordinating surveillance, air and ground assets within Counter Insurgency's rules of engagement. Left Flank had more than atoned for the Javelin miss.

★

One of the handicaps Left Flank had contended with in Loy Adera was the lack of local knowledge that their Afghan partners held. Mostly Dari speakers from Kabul, they were almost as much outsiders as the Jocks. The advantage of this was that they weren't dragged into local feuding and behaved with something approaching impartiality. In other words, they weren't the Afghan National Police. From Major Kitching's relationship with Major Kamal down, Left Flank had learned to embrace and respect Afghan soldiers. In 11 Platoon's Vehicle Checkpoints, 'There were a couple of raised voices now and again but you never felt scared,' according to Lance Sergeant Browning. At Eid, Afghan and British soldiers sat, ate and chatted together. Despite their chronic logistical chain, the Afghans shared their food with the Guardsmen. Lance Sergeant Thorpe, one of the Advisors to the Afghan National Army, summed up what he hoped Left Flank had achieved in partnering in their tour.

'You're not going to turn these guys into British soldiers in six months. So everybody just does their little bit of partnering. Come to the end of six months and the next lot who come in take on the next little set of tasks [to improve the Afghan soldiers].'

Thorpe felt the Afghans had developed their teamwork

– there were no more fights – tactical awareness, and their fire control in contact. What was remarkable about the Afghan National Army Company was that they didn't suffer a single fatality or serious injury during Herrick 12. Despite wandering outside of the IED-cleared lane to pick watermelons, and many going without helmets or body armour, none were picked off. The Afghans seemed to amble along a knife-edge of risk. They will continue to do so long after the last British soldier has left the Helmand Valley.

Only one group of uniformed men really knew Loy Adera – the Afghan National Police. The problem was, the local population hated them. They had operated as an Isaf-funded militia from around 2001 until 2007. As so often in Helmand, this group had ended up losing consent for the Afghan Government. There were allegations of rape and corruption against them. Isaf cut off funding. The militia fled west. In Basharan, Commander Mira Hamza and Lieutenant Israel both looked over the Stabilisation Bridge and wanted back into Loy Adera. Israel wasn't alleged to have been a bad boy in the old days, but his tribal links to those who ran the militia meant he had fled his village.

Major Kitching had been 'crying out' for local police. He was fully aware of the reputation they had in Loy Adera. He hoped the men coming through Lashkar Gah's new police training academy would seek to cut rather than commit crime.

'They would bring more to the party by being there than by not,' he concluded. He was therefore delighted when it was announced the new 175-strong Babaji Police Precinct would be headquartered at Patrol Base Nahidullah. Despite their lobbying, Mira Hamza and Israel would remain west of the Stabilisation Bridge to fight over control of Basharan. Colonel Mazallum, another local

man tribally linked to Israel, would command. Less encouraging was news that Commander Ahmadi Gul would
be Second in Command of the Precinct. He had commanded the old Loy Adera Militia. Left Flank also knew
the local police would have significant links with local
insurgents.

When the Afghan National Police arrived in Patrol Base
Nahidullah in early September, the welcome they received
from the Afghan National Army didn't bode well for pan-
Afghan relations. In a message that puts British regimental rivalries into context, the police were told: 'If you come
into our camp, we'll fucking kill you.' A sentry was put on
the gate to ensure that the newcomers, who the Afghan
soldiers regarded as Taliban, didn't sneak in at night. The
police also arrived without the equivalent of a Lance
Sergeant Thorpe, so there was no conduit to pass concerns
through. This new, hostile intra-partner relationship was
yet another issue for Left Flank to contend with.

On joint patrols, locals would approach Guardsmen
when the Patrolmen were out of earshot.

'That policeman is no good,' the farmer would say.

'How do you know? They've only just got here.'

'No, these were the same ones who were here before.'

Out of camp, the police carried no spare ammunition or
water and wore flip-flops. Many were stoned. This hardly
mattered – they were never shot at. Police commanders
would tell British commanders, 'I couldn't guarantee Isaf
safety in this kalay. I can guarantee that all the police will
come back from a patrol down there, though.'

There was always one Patrolman at the back of the line
chatting into his mobile phone. Intelligence would then
come through: 'They're going to go past the mosque in a
bit.' A glance at a map would tell the Isaf commander that
his planned route was taking him past a mosque. Once,
near Vehicle Checkpoint Naeem, a Patrolman walked

away from the line and pulled two IEDs directly from the ground. One Afghan soldier went ballistic.

'How does he know they were there? We weren't even going over there and he just walked up to them. He's fucking Taliban, for sure.'

The policeman claimed he had been an insurgent IED emplacer in his time. This was an interesting example of both the fruits and frictions that can arise from Isaf efforts to 'reintegrate' former insurgents. The police element of the patrol then went into a compound. Shortly afterwards the Afghan and British soldiers were shot at.

Knowing the Afghan National Police would compromise any patrol plan had to be turned into an advantage. Major Kitching would tell Commander Ahmadi Gul where he wanted to patrol. Gul would reply, 'No problem, three of my guys are from there.' The patrol would walk calmly in the next day. That they could do this in previous no-go areas meant the insurgents had clearly been tipped off that a joint patrol was coming in. They clearly preferred to scarper for the morning rather than shoot at the police. This allowed Isaf to get amongst the locals and bring smart Counter Insurgency to them. One example was female engagement patrols that, using female medics, reached out to the half of the population that were truly 'the forgotten' of Loy Adera. Left Flank had used the police to get around the insurgents and to the people – the essence of their mission. Some pretty unsavoury people were used to facilitate this, people that many in Loy Adera seemingly hate. The fact that the policemen have links with the very insurgency that sprung up partly as a rejection of the militia's old ways is further proof of the complexity of the situation Left Flank was asked to guide for six months.

★

Company Sergeant Major Lawrie walked over to the shower block and paused briefly when he saw the large wooden wings with the words 'Air Assault Engineers' written underneath them. He ripped the sign down and chucked it in the bin. The 16 Air Assault Brigade Engineers who had moved into Nahidullah weren't making themselves popular, unlike all the other engineers Left Flank had worked with. The signs were an irritant. Eventually Major Kitching told them to please wait until the Scots Guards had left, after which they could do as they pleased. More annoying was their refusal to provide sappers for sangar duty. They argued it was an infantry task. Their reluctance to help protect the camp that housed and secured them was at odds with their attitude when a few rounds were fired at the Patrol Base one night. To a man, they were on the wall firing away. Lawrie and some other Guards Warrant Officers ran round pulling them from firing steps.

'Have you lot never heard of Courageous Restraint? Can you identify a Firing Point? Have you even seen a muzzle flash?' one of the senior men asked.

'What a hat!' muttered one of the young sappers, using the Para term of abuse for non-Paras.

'Eh, fuck-nuts, what did you just call me? Are you even in the Parachute Regiment?' shouted a Guards Warrant Officer.

Hand over/take over was always going to be fraught. Left Flank had transformed an area the Royal Welsh had only had limited time and resources to work on. Now they were passing it on. Obviously everyone wanted to get home but a degree of possession was felt about 'our area'. Consent and intelligence had been earned from the local people at great cost. Left Flank certainly felt they knew better than the fresh-faced men filtering into Loy Adera from Salisbury Plain.

Inevitably, Bravo Foxtrot 3 claimed Left Flank's final casualty. Guardsman Andrew Hanratty was Valloning through that ulcerous place on 19 September. He was hit by fragmentation from a Command Wire IED in his right thigh. Gunfire came in from prepared position as he crawled into a ditch alongside Guardsman Carr, who was also blown back by the blast. Sergeant Gibson performed his usual commute down from Checkpoint Said Abdul and scooped up his Guardsmen.

There was horror at the idea of taking any further casualties as the tour wound down. Rolling shoots continued onto the checkpoints right to the final hours of the tour. If anything, there was a final nasty spike as the men from C Company, 2 SCOTS came into Loy Adera. The insurgents were keen on giving them a warm welcome. Lance Sergeant Morris had one night to hand over his base to the incoming commander. He knew the men coming in were a capable lot but couldn't help notice some fresh, bewildered faces. But then Left Flank had been the same in April.

Commanders were pulled off the ground to help run Camp Bastion's training package for the incoming Brigade; some pleaded not to be separated from their men at this late stage of the tour. Incoming units hungry to top up on the latest realities beyond the wire emptied the veterans' minds. Each time they heard the dreaded 'Op Minimise' on the loud hailer, they rushed to hear if the news was coming from Loy Adera.

In Checkpoint North, Platoon Sergeant Major Lilley's men were preparing to go on patrol. The sangars had been hit three times since the new boys had come in. A signaller leant out of the Ops Room.

'Yep, there's helicopters coming in. Get your kit ready to get on – you're offski to Bastion.'

'And there you are,' thought Lilley, 'Gone. "Fucking

hell!'' And it was just finished. Just one minute you're fighting like fuck and the next minute – boom. Nothing.'

★

In Bastion, the readjustment process began. How long it takes is up to each man. Men used to reacting to sudden events realised they could utterly switch off. They happily queued in the cookhouse wearing berets and tans and smiles. They went through decompression as a Company. After an early-hours flight from Kandahar, they landed back in Cyprus at dawn. It was much cooler than Afghanistan. It began to rain. The men rushed down to the beach, mucked about in the surf all day and knew they were really going home. Some of the Company's wounded came out to the island to meet them. Lilley and Lilley were reunited. In the evening they got changed. Most into strange-feeling civilian clothing, 11 Platoon into Afghan dress. They listened to a comedy show and got stuck into the beers.

Late on Saturday, 16 October – the concept of days of the week returned when they landed in Teesside Airport – Left Flank returned to Catterick. They marched out of the darkness, along the parade square and into their families' arms, then went inside for cake and squash. Sergeant Gibson looked out over the hall and saw for the last time the Left Flank of Herrick 12 assembled in one place.

'By Monday morning, it'll be like it never even happened,' he said.

Looking out at the expressions on the men's faces, a tear formed in his eye. By Monday, he knew, the men would be back in UK uniform. They'd then disperse to career courses, cushy recruitment jobs, different companies. The talk would be of getting the guys trained up to go to Canada to jump out of Warriors so that they could then forget that in time for the next dismounted tour of Helmand in 2012.

After a speech by Major Kitching, the men scattered and drove off with their loved ones. Outside the camp gates, police cars stalked soldiers who 48 hours earlier had been in Afghanistan. They waited to pull them up for drink-driving or speeding back to Glasgow for 36 hours before they had to be back at work. It was an eloquent welcome home from the society they'd been fighting for.

CONCLUSION

'A necessary job'

August 2010–April 2011

'Come on, let's get your guys off the track. Tracks are for IEDs, fields are for soldiers. Commander?' said Lieutenant Pete Foster to the Afghan National Army officer. The Major couldn't even read a map. Foster's team had perhaps the least enviable task in the Combined Force. Designated Advisors, they had sweated round the District with a Company of Afghan soldiers. On 9 August, we were up at 02:00 to be in position for a dawn clearance operation through the Bolan Desert. Hundreds of Afghan police, paramilitaries and soldiers are sweeping the area with limited numbers of Isaf troops guiding them. Of course, Warriors are blocking to the north and the drones are in the sky, but the Afghans are leading. Lurking in fire support is Lieutenant Dalrymple-Hamilton's Blackjack 15 multiple. Lance Corporal Sample has been on a few of these clearance operations before.

'Big pheasant shoots – it's the simplest plan in the world. They're effective, though, and the Afghans are leading their own show. We just sit at the back and it's actually pretty rewarding to see them doing their own thing. They just need us to point them in the right direction. We still have doubts about them.'

It is a long morning's work. By the time we collapse into

Checkpoint Spina Kota we have covered six kilometres – a jog in Britain but a vast distance when operating in Helmand. Rorke's Drift Company, Royal Welsh has taken over from Right Flank, who are already home. I clamber onto a Warrior and take an abandoned Scots Guards pennant from an aerial as a keepsake. The Commanding Officer meets up with Colonel Kamullidin at Checkpoint Two Flags. Afghans of various stripes are milling about. Invited local media film this show of cooperation between Army and Police. The footage is important – yesterday a fight broke out in Gereshk between the Afghan soldiers and policemen and four of them ended up dead. A female police officer approaches Colonel Kamullidin and gives him some news. He relays it to us. His men have busted an IED cell. Minutes later, two pick-up trucks arrive laden with bombs and detainees. The six suspects are made to wear yellow palm oil containers as dunce's hats and pushed about quite roughly.

'Colonel, who found the devices?' asks the Commanding Officer.

Kamullidin turns round expansively.

'I found them, you found them, we all found them!'

Everyone smiles for the cameras.

This, roughly, is what success looks like in Afghanistan. It isn't perfect – in fact, it's downright messy – and there's still plenty of support from foreigners. But the Afghans are leading the fight against the insurgency and making some headway. Most importantly, no one – civilian, soldier, policeman or insurgent – has died today.

★

On Hyde Park Corner, a few hundred yards from where Company Sergeant Major Lawrie now wears a bearskin and changes the Queen's Guard on the Forecourt of

Buckingham Palace, sits a memorial to the First World War's Machine Gun Corps. The inscription is from the First Book of Samuel: 'Saul hath slain his thousands, and David his ten thousands.' For too long, this mentality dominated British thinking in Afghanistan. It still has its adherents. There was a depressing story about a senior officer from another Combined Force walking into an update in Lashkar Gah on Herrick 12.

'My lads have killed x insurgents in the past week – of which I've personally killed y,' he said.

Now Counter Insurgency is a local game, so maybe that was the right approach to take in his area. However, the idea that the British Army will kill their way to success in Helmand is deeply flawed on whatever level you pick. Many understand this but it takes a while for the message to filter through. The men are trained for, and possibly want, a war – these troops are paid to be the most aggressive members of our society. The most Damascene conversion to population-focused Counter Insurgency I saw was from certain members of the Scots Guards Reconnaissance Platoon. Getting into the Recce takes a lot. Only the most committed and fittest need apply. The men Captain Charlie Turner took to Helmand were itching to fight and trained to kill. Instead, they spent their time rolling around the area east of the River Helmand in their wagons. They visited isolated police checkpoints, held snap *shuras* and organised stabilisation projects. The work grated at first – endless tasks and rarely a firefight worth mentioning. Bragging rights back in Catterick would be almost nil. However, as the tour wound on, some began to realise the value of what they were doing.

'It was a boring job but it was a necessary job,' said Lance Corporal Sample. 'We may not have brassed anything to bits but the locals are on side with Isaf now and that has coincided with Commander Isaf's Directive.'

Spot on. Unfortunately, they don't give out medals for this sort of work.

★

There is an explosive document published by the British Army. It is an excellently written campaign critique stuffed with useful tactical and strategic insights.

'Permanent vehicle checkpoints rapidly became targets for attacks . . . no permanent vehicle checkpoint had ever detained terrorist suspects or captured any terrorist arms or equipment.'

'One further policy . . . took a long time to resolve. The value of the Army and the police using the same boundaries was obvious, and well known to the Army from previous campaigns.'

'Information Operations were probably the most disappointing aspect of the campaign.'

'The policy would be discontinued and then "rediscovered" again a few years later.'

'Tendency of individuals at various levels to seek short-term tactical results through positive action where a more measured approach was probably required.'

'Absence of a single campaign authority.'

'It was a campaign without a campaign plan.'

This document is the British Army's post-mortem of operations in Northern Ireland. It was published in 2006 – that year of original sin in Helmand that troops still pay for today. Each of the above points holds in Afghanistan as it did in Armagh. A British Officer once reminded me about Mark Twain's maxim that history doesn't repeat itself, it rhymes. I started out with the objective of examining how my generation soldiers. They do it well but perhaps, like the youth of many ages before us, we haven't paid due heed to the lessons our elders learned the hard way.

Military history, of course, is one giant After Action Review that only a few choose to read. This isn't to argue that the Afghan mission is in any way doomed due to previous form in the region; too much noise is given to a view of Afghan history that takes *Flashman* and *Rambo III* as its starting points. On the evidence of what I saw, success is possible and the British Army can get there.

While I don't identify with the arrogance of some that lost the British face in Iraq, this sort of campaign remains in this Army's genes. Linguistically, Jock and Tommy never left Asia. Today he arrives in Kandahar Airfield and stays in a colonial sounding *cantonment*. Next, it's Camp Bastion, where he'll do some *dhobi*. He'll then make his way to a base, inherit tons of *buckshee* rounds and spend six months on *sangar* duty. Success in today's campaign might now be in his grasp. Adequately resourced, finally, and well trained, he could prosper in Helmand if he thinks more like Lance Corporal Sample and the rest of Combined Force Lashkar Gah and less like that senior officer bragging about his kills elsewhere in Helmand. The larger question is what success will achieve.

★

Having begun by saying I would avoid the whys and wherefores, I cautiously offer a few observations. Having seen the blood sacrifice made by the Afghans and the British, it is hard not to want to find some meaning in the campaign.

Once foreign troops leave, Kabul will almost certainly collapse whatever projects have been put in place in the rural areas of Lashkar Gah District – if not flee Helmand outright. They recognise they are fighting a civil war, even if we don't. The people around Lashkar Gah will revert back to the complete control of men like Colonel Satir,

Commander Israel and Mira Hamza, who will squabble for decades over who controls what. This is fair: it is their country and with the limited resources Kabul will enjoy when the pipeline from Washington dries, the government would be wise to concentrate on areas they can hold and win. Whether it is just that the ordinary people fall into yet another cycle of violence is another question, but *ferengis* should learn the difference between intervention and interference. However, while explicable when viewed strategically, the Afghan Government's refusal to tactically engage in areas cleared and held at great cost caused enormous frustration to Scots Guardsmen. It also made their job a great deal more dangerous.

Until the pull-out, well-resourced, trained and led men such as those of Combined Force Lashkar Gah in the summer of 2010 will continue to make progress in Helmand. The insurgency will be pushed about. Wells will be dug, schools built. If the British Army continues to act in the manner I saw them behave, then tactically the campaign in Helmand should succeed. It will only do so if the campaign's existential threat – political will and public support drowning back home – doesn't come to pass. President Obama's announcement in June 2011 that his 2009 surge would be more of a spike, a move perhaps precipitated by the audacious raid on Abbottabad that led to the death of Osama bin Laden, or perhaps by the US election cycle, surely means that 2010 represented high noon in Helmand. We can only hope that the strides the Scots Guards and many others made that year will not be lost in any rush for the exit.

Some pretty serious work remains to be done at all levels in Afghanistan. Ten years in and it's hard to know where to begin. Justice and land rights jump out as two areas that need more thought but everyone has their own hobbyhorses and magic bullets. Britain needs to figure out how to work coherently across departments, as there will surely be another one of these adventures some time soon. I'll never forget listening to a brief on an insurgent-run drive-by court and detention centre.

'Thanks for that,' a senior officer said to the briefing officer. 'In five minutes you've given me more information on what the insurgents are doing in law and order than I've been able to find out on the Afghan Government's efforts in five months sitting 30 yards from the Provincial Reconstruction Team.'

This failure to communicate between departments could stem from the deepest malaise surrounding Britain's Afghan mission: no one has set out why we are there and how we will succeed. The 'narrative' appears to change every so often: counter terrorism, counter narcotics, counter Taliban, nation building and security forces training, Counter Insurgency, getting ready to leave. The Scots Guards hit the cycle when the British Army were determined on Counter Insurgency. They did this very well. Yes, plenty of ammunition was fired but all in the cause of fulfilling their commanders' intent: to hold the ground they had been assigned and then make a credible offer to the local people alongside the partners who they would bring along during their tour. The soldiers had been tossed this doctrinal bone and gripped it very hard. It was vastly different to the conventional warfare they are designed to execute – degree rather than GCSE-level soldiering, as one officer put it. The problem was that other cogs in the system were operating at different settings and tempos. The local Afghan government had little or no intention of developing support in the rural areas; the Provincial Reconstruction Team were concentrating on other objectives; the British and American political classes were marching to a different timescale altogether. That other parts of the structure were redefining the mission as it went should not detract from the superb work the soldiers did. It is surely the case, though, that until there is true strategic direction from the Western capitals and Kabul that links all lines of development together we, the public, will continue to concentrate on the one absolute in this conflict: casualties. A realistic picture of mission success needs to be presented to the British people, otherwise they simply will not stomach the Chinese water torture of announcements on the *News at Ten*. I would argue that we are probably less squeamish about *realpolitik* than some suppose. If, strategically, we are serious about Afghanistan, someone needs to get an atlas out and tell people why it is important to engage there. The point should also be made that, having seen the West's financial system individually and collectively fail towards the end of the last decade, the world will take a view if our military system is seen to individually and collectively fail in the first part of this decade.

Away from the statements to Parliament, the briefings and the policy papers, the soldiers in the checkpoints will remain as long as they are asked. On top of battling a tenacious insurgency, they will stave off sandflies, boils and disease. They'll be doing this in close proximity to Afghan partners whose personal conduct often challenges every instinct in a British soldier's background and training. They will continue to fight primarily for each other, to maximise the chances of as many of them as possible getting back to Britain in one piece. That is a fitting and just way of conducting yourself in a war-zone that your government has sent you to without really telling you why.

★

Operation Herrick 12 ended – in the physical sense. A battalion is a fragile thing. After a tour it shatters into its

550 constituent parts and is never the same again. Every-one dispersed on leave and forgot themselves. A month later, queues formed outside Company Sergeant Majors' offices. Men who could be relied on to beat insurgents were hauled in for drink-driving, assault and a litany of other abuses. Not all heroes can be angels too.

'Heart breakers and risk takers,' said the Commanding Officer about his men.

I like to think they broke his heart as they filed into his office in Catterick. The civilian system could be unforgiving. Lieutenant Tulloch, in court yet again to defend one of his Guardsmen, stood up to give his character reference. 'Before you begin, Mr Tulloch,' said the Magistrate, 'if you tell the court that this soldier is an excellent GPMG gunner, I will rule it inadmissible.'

The officer glanced down at what he'd written and made something else up on the spot.

Single men found solace in suddenly available drink and sex. The young officers deservedly detonated over south-west London. They would be six-month celebrities until the next bunch of Helmand-thinned young veterans returned to slay the Fulham dinner party circuit. The captains were invited to London and were asked to stay in the Army over champagne with the Major General followed by an impromptu piss-up in St James's Palace. I could tell the lifers sitting round the table: the ones who'd bounced straight off tour into Staff College or tough selection courses. The ones for whom the music had stopped sat isolated amongst the splendour, perhaps knowing that no matter what they went on to achieve, a coin and ribbon in a box in a drawer might say more about who they were than they'd ever care to admit.

Guardsman Stafford returned to the cadet force where he'd first glimpsed soldiering to give a talk to eager children keen on becoming tomorrow's veterans. For all ranks, home meant family. Tour's end triggered marriages and divorces as relationships were secured or broken by the pressures shovelled on by separation.

Reminders of what happened flashed up. A photo of Captain Murly-Gotto with the Prime Minister and Arnold Schwarzenegger, Guy Fawkes Night, the rash of men with issue kitbags catching the evening's first off-peak train from London to barracks as leave ended. Some missed it – I did. Dreadfully, stupidly and self-indulgently missed it. One sergeant was very clear and didn't apologise for quoting *Apocalypse Now* to describe his condition a few months after returning:

'When I'm there I want to be here and when I'm here I want to be there.'

As another put it after a contact in Helmand, 'Taking the kids on Pepsi Max in Blackpool will be a bit of an anticlimax after this.' Weaned on *Band of Brothers* and *Platoon*, then shown 9/11 and Ross Kemp, this generation is hyper-conditioned and the youngest can hardly remember a time without a war. When they return, laptop full of photos and videos and eventually, yes, books are written about them, it's surely no surprise that some half-miss it. Guardsman to Brigadier, you are definitely somebody in Helmand, which isn't always the case in Catterick and beyond. But Helmand isn't Alton Towers with IEDs. Others had endured enough for a while. Some of the bravest men I know were glad of two-year postings to training establishments – they'd miss the next tour. But what will the place look like by 2012?

Back in camp, the next cohort was already coming through. School leavers and university kids who thought they'd give Sandhurst a go were grilled over pints in the Officers' and Sergeants' Mess. New nominal rolls were full of names I'd never seen before. Reunited with broadband, videos of the Guardsmen's exploits made it onto

YouTube. In teenage bedrooms, youngsters watched and posted comments under videos – 'scot guards number 1 job choice in jan!!!!' They were partly recruited by the reflected glamour of watching a war in real time. The videos didn't show guys on stag or just sitting around a checkpoint, smoking and hoping that by some miracle simply staring would make the countdown calendar go quicker.

Finally home, the dead could be mourned and the wounded considered fully. Helmand is not Stalingrad, and even within the province other units had far higher tolls exacted on them on Herrick 12. The kit, the training, the Casevac process and the treatment help keep fatalities down. This comparatively low death rate almost makes it worse when there is one. A platoon lives together for a year. The training makes them close, fighting bonds them and the counterfeit domesticity of life in a checkpoint turns them to kin. Occasionally they bicker, like all families, but they always look out for one another. The relationship is more intense because they all know it lasts for just the tour and then they'll be scattered. They know they live in dangerous times but the odds are they'll all make it home alive. When one of them doesn't, the effect on the rest is vast. All the Battlegroup's dead had shown by their actions that they were exactly the sorts of men you wanted with you in demanding situations.

Many of the Battlegroup's 36 non-fatal battle casualties and 36 non-battle casualties will live with visible scars of their time in Afghanistan for the rest of their days. The impact in terms of mental health is too early to assess, but there have already been several cases of men (and there were no boys after that tour) who are struggling with issues. As one very brave man said to me, 'I'd swap any medal for a decent night's sleep.' Veterans of Vietnam are said to have a 1,000-yard stare. Those from Afghanistan will be limited to a five and 20-metre scan, as they constantly check their immediate surroundings for anything that looks like it might want your legs, anything that is out of place. It will be up to the British public in years to come to ensure that our veterans never think they are the ones who are out of place in this society.

The tour's epilogue was the Operational Honours and Awards list. I examined it with disbelief. Apart from Lance Corporal Monkhouse's hugely deserved posthumous Military Cross, not a single Scots Guardsman had earned a post-nominal decoration. There were some Mentions in Dispatches and a few more Queen's Commendation for Valuable Service but that was it. Corporal Stenton, Royal Dragoon Guards, had also picked up a posthumous MC and Lance Corporal Henderson an MBE for her life-saving work at Said Abdul – both thoroughly earned. Overall the Combined Force had done poorly, though they'd never say so themselves. Perhaps the tally was a reflection of that admirable reticence I always found amongst the Guardsmen – always happier giving rather than taking credit. Perhaps I may be permitted to make their claim for them: in the summer of 2010, Combined Force Lashkar Gah, to go back to this book's original question, 'got it' at every level. Their success was built on the efforts of Isaf and Afghan forces right across Helmand. Many of those units were operating in areas where the type of campaign Fondouk Squadron, for instance, enacted was impossible. The Battlegroup was pointed in the right direction in training and was a coherent Counter Insurgency beast that focused whenever possible on the population rather than the enemy. Junior commanders led the way at the tactical level and the Guardsmen grafted hardest, as always. At headquarters level, the decision not to start dropping bombs saved lives. By the time the tour was over, most realised this. Simply put, more bombs would have meant more dead Afghans. That would have meant *more* insurgents, *not fewer*. This would have meant more dead Guardsmen. That's no way to win the campaign but, sadly, being 'punchy' and dropping bombs is still the way to win a medal.

In March 2011, President Karzai announced that Lashkar Gah would transition to Afghan National Security Forces control. It is the only place in Helmand where this has been possible. Much of the credit for this must go to the men and women who served on Herrick 12 – the first tour to establish a Battlegroup Headquarters in the city. At the start of the tour, Governor Mangal had expressed concern that Lashkar Gah was surrounded by insurgents. By tour's end, the insurgency had been pushed back and local consent had increased in many areas. The Afghan forces had improved, gradually, though it is in this area that I retain significant reservations. These successes were due to the right resources and plans coming together. Significant risks were taken across the Combined Force.

'What I have seen in Combined Force Lashkar Gah,' said Command Sergeant Major Hall, General McChrystal's envoy in May, 'is the Counter Insurgency paradox of having to take risk in order to be safer, executed like I have never seen before in all Afghanistan. And the Afghan Forces and the people feel more confident as a result.'

*

'We thought the tour was over,' said the Commanding Officer down the line.

Colour Sergeant Alan Cameron had been found dead that morning. Fifty weeks after taking the brunt of an IED to his head on Route Mars, his injuries had overtaken him on an anonymous March night. He had been making stunning progress, thanks to his determination to conquer an injury that took nearly half his skull and much of his brain. His condition had stabilised, thanks in no small part to his loved ones, who had enveloped him with support from the day he had been flown home. He was feeling positive about his future. Weeks earlier, he had been presented to the Princess Royal at the Calcutta Cup and watched a final game of the sport he loved so much. Days before he died, he was told he would be medically discharged from the Army but he passed away before the papers came through. This meant he died as he had lived – a Scots Guardsman. 'What a team is waiting for him,' the Commanding Officer told a packed church. 'Davey Walker with the quickfire banter; Guardsman Paul McGee, the model Scots Guardsman who died standing up for his mother; Guardsman Andrew Gibson, a young blade who will bring life to the party; Lieutenant Peter Rous, who, as the Platoon Commander, will happily sit there presiding over the high jinks; Acting Sergeant Dale Alonzo McCallum standing at the side of the dance floor shaking his head as Davey struts his stuff, and Lance Corporal Stephen Monkhouse pointing out to anyone who'll listen that his son is the proud owner of a Military Cross. And there he is. Cammy. Father to all. Looking across at all of them with that knowing smile, proud of his team but also worried for us, left out of the party.'

*

In the summer of 2010, the Scots Guards showed what a crack infantry battalion could achieve in six months. How many more Herricks are needed to accomplish campaign objectives is unclear. Probably more than political timelines will allow. The schedule is set for an end to combat operations in 2014. After that date, one thing is surely certain: Afghanistan is a knife that will continue to fall long after the people of Royal Wootton Bassett are no longer disturbed by corteges. Those of us who were there will continue to meet in pubs and have a laugh about the whole thing, but basically we'll move on. One day when there is peace, I would like to drive down the 601 into Lashkar Gah, out across the Bolan, then north to remember life, and death, on Mars. For the Scots Guards, though, there's another tour to get ready for.

The last line goes to Guardsman Murray on a hot night in Helmand. 'What we're doing out here, well, it's the closest our generation will have to the Second World War. When I get home, I'm going to wear my campaign medal every day. People in South Africa, they might not know what it means, but I will and my family will. I'm going to wear it every day.'

You fight the war you're given by the mistakes the generation above you makes. You gave them Afghanistan. They took it.

POSTSCRIPT

St Andrew's Day 2010

'Morning, Ballbag' said Company Sergeant Major Tam McEwan. Of all the ways to be woken as a Guardsman, still pissed from the night before with McEwan inches from your face is possibly the worst. The Guardsman's eyes rolled back and to the side, focused and snapped open.

'Have a drink,' ordered McEwan, pushing a mug of gunfire – tea and whisky – into the young man's hand. 'Happy St Andrew's Day, wee man. Muster at 08:00, Church Parade for 10:00, then medals.'

Across the Scots Guards lines before first light, officers, warrant officers and bagpipers were going door to door rousing their men.

The snow had been falling for nearly a week. There had been talk of doing the medal parade in the gym. The Commanding Officer had vetoed this. Before muster, Warriors were doing circuits through a blizzard on the parade square, furiously ploughing the snow.

In the Officers' Mess, Captain Jimmy Murly-Gotto hobbled down to breakfast. His right leg was still entombed in a plaster and metal frame nearly a year after a dark night in Helmand. He had driven up from London the day before in the specially adapted automatic car the MoD had bought him. He had arrived after dark and found no trace of his former existence in this place that had once been home. His pigeonhole was gone; a new

Subaltern he had never met occupied his room. But then, it never is your pigeonhole, your room or your platoon. It is the Army's and you merely look after it for a set period of time. Perhaps the only thing that truly is yours is the Regiment you joined and fought with. Like everyone else, Murly-Gotto was back in desert boots and multi-cam for the parade. The Master Tailor had stitched two right legs together so that Murly-Gotto's leg would fit into a pair of combats, a dress he hadn't worn since February and never would again.

By 10:00, the Battalion was in the gym ready for the church parade to begin. Joining them was Davey Walker's extended family. At 10:30 the Battalion stood to attention as the colours were marched in by two Subalterns and an escort found by two Sergeants. Lance Sergeant Jamieson struggled out of his wheelchair, and then stood unaided. We sang 'Thine Be the Glory'. The Padre spoke his sermon: 'These colours before you tell a story which all of you have added to this year.' The Commanding Officer stood at the lectern and read out the names of the Scots Guardsmen who had died under him. Each name stuck in his throat. The Pipes and Drums played a tune they had written. It began with a deep beat from the bass drum which sounded like distantly heard IED detonations. When the pipes kicked in, it seemed the chairs in the gym had been charged with current.

Everyone filed out of the gym into a blizzard.

'Drill Sergeant, make the snow disappear,' said the Regimental Sergeant Major.

'Aye, sir,' said the Drill Sergeant, who turned right, stamped his foot smartly and marched off, his pace stick swinging through the snow. Twenty minutes later, the blizzard stopped. There was even a threat of sunshine. Further proof of the Divinity of a Guards Sergeant Major is not required.

The Regimental Colonel, HRH the Duke of Kent, had been grounded in London. Instead, the Major General of the Household Division had zoomed up on the first train from London and made the parade in time to hand out medals to the Guardsmen. With the Commanding Officer, he went from man to man as the Regimental Band in bearskins and greatcoats played along with the Pipes and Drums. The families stood shivering in tents. A languid roll of the snare drum announced 'Highland Cathedral' from the musicians as the Major General got to the platoon of wounded men at the end of the line. Lance Sergeant Jamieson again struggled from his wheelchair but overbalanced forward. The Major General put his arms out and caught him.

'That's right, Sergeant Jamieson, lean on me. That's what Generals are for,' he said, and then placed a medal in the man's one remaining hand.

After lunch, the men piled back into the gym for the Tug o' War. They'd painted faces blue and white and scrounged tartan from company lines. The 'Rabbits' of C Company went out first, followed by Right Flank. The bruisers from the Motor Transport Platoon then put Headquarter Company into the final ahead of B Company. Left Flank took their positions on the rope. At the front stood Major Rupert Kitching, and Guardsman Maciu Kabunicaucau was the anchor.

'Last time I saw that Guardsman, I was giving him first aid in Said Abdul and half his face was shot off,' said a startled Captain Rowe.

'Look at that,' said the Pipe Major. 'Someone's going to win as the clock strikes 16:42.'

'Aye, but shame the clock's an hour fast,' said the Sergeant Major.

Left Flank crowded round their team, chanting, 'Easy, easy, easy.' And it was.

The Commanding Officer called the men into a three-sided square around him and handed out cups to the best three teams.

'Well, I think it has been a fantastic day,' he said and then walked over to a wheelchair.

'Guardsman Watson, do you think it's been a fantastic day?'

'Oh aye, sir,' said Guardsman Watson. 'But I reckon we should have a ten o'clock start tomorrow morning.'

The whole Battalion cheered.

*

The next morning I drove out of the barracks for the last time, suitably hungover. I thought of the men left behind and the 10,000 British ambassadors still in Helmand Province and of those that would follow them, still looking for their war, and of the system that sends them. Coleridge's words played over in my head:

> The many men, so beautiful!
> And they all dead did lie;
> And a thousand thousand slimy things
> Lived on; and so did I.

'An Aspect of Realism'

> If one goes on arranging one's affairs, organising one's life in harmony with the lives of one's hosts, whose companionship one seeks and without which one would sink into disorientated craziness, one must eventually give way, or at any rate partially give way. If one must act as though one believed, one ends in believing, or half-believing as one acts.
>
> Sir E. E. Evans-Pritchard,
> *Witchcraft, Oracle, and Magic among the Azande*

It is now over two years since the events depicted in this book began. In that time, the campaign in Helmand, and across Afghanistan, has changed. So too have those who fought over that country in 2010. I have kept in touch with some of those I got to know that year, and have tried to keep myself briefed on events, though I am yet to return to Helmand.

*

'The children,' replies Piper Johnnie McIntyre instantly when I ask him about his strongest memory from Helmand. 'The looks on the children's faces. I remember I got my parents to send me colouring books and colouring pencils. And during the *shuras*, the kids, I'd be giving them these colouring books and pencils, and saying, "colour them in for us". And, you know, the fact that they felt they had to ask permission to use different colours – that was the big thing that done it for me.'

McIntyre, who by rights should choose being shot in the chest by a sharpshooter as his stand-out moment from Herrick 12, was speaking to me from Edinburgh in February 2012. He was coming to the end of his Class III Bagpiping Course. Learning the pipes had always 'been in the back of my mind' for the Glaswegian. The Pipe Major had told the young Guardsman McIntyre to go away and get some life experience before trying out for the Pipes and Drums. Months in Checkpoint Inzargul with Left Flank and his Casevac back to Birmingham have certainly given him that.

His pipes will be packed away come September 2012, when it seems he and most of 1st Battalion Scots Guards will redeploy to Helmand Province. 'It is a hard concept more for my family than for myself,' he says. 'I know what to expect, it's leaving the family guessing again. The wife had a bit of a bad time of it last week, but she's reassured now, she's happy again. I think it's being new parents: we had a baby boy last year.'

Captain Will Tulloch, promoted after the tour like so many Scots Guardsmen, has been busy since returning to Britain in October 2010. A stint of Ceremonial Duties in London, training Jordanian soldiers in the desert, and a succession of career progression courses have all been 'hugely enjoyable' for him. 'I do constantly think back on the prior tour – to be honest, with fondness more than anything else. I don't look back on it in a very gloomy way. It is genuinely very positive.'

If there are moments that stand out for Tulloch, it is those moments of doubt, when incidents called into question his presence in Helmand. Whenever a member of his platoon was injured, Captain Tulloch would retreat into himself and weigh up the cost of the campaign. 'There were times when I was very much looking on the side that maybe it's not worth people losing life and limb, but, overall and having had time to contemplate it as a whole, I would reject that. And, actually, I would come away thinking it may not be a very visible progression, but it is a progression nonetheless.'

In my opinion, it was this faith, constantly tested, that kept men like Captain Tulloch motivated in the most trying of circumstances. An irritating phrase, especially when used by senior officers pandering to the public perception of their profession, is the description of themselves as a 'simple' soldier/sailor/airman. While those in uniform may delight in doing certain simple tasks well – stripping a weapon, keeping a checkpoint clean – these are not simple folk. They spend more time thinking about the whys and wherefores of their job than most of us civilians. The reasons for this are quite obvious.

'Probably the incident with [Guardsman] Kabu[nicau-cau]. That plays on my mind quite a lot. Nothing bad, it's just experiences,' says Lance Corporal Ritchie Carr when I ask him what stands out from Herrick 12. Lance Corporal Carr, still only 20, picked up his first promotion in January 2012, and will be a trusted veteran on the next tour. He spends much of his time passing on what he learned in Checkpoint Said Abdul to a new generation of Guardsmen. Carr makes one of those remarks that would have stopped me a few years ago, but which I now understand better: 'To be honest, I think – apart from all the bad stuff that happened – I think it was the best time of my life, really. The bond you have with the lads, it's just really good. I'm looking forward to the next one – this one coming up.'

One man Lance Corporal Carr won't have to rely on in

2012–13 is Colour Sergeant Colin Kirkwood. Along with two other flying non-commissioned officers, Kirkwood was selected to represent the Scots Guards at the Royal Military Academy, Sandhurst. They completed the tough selection course, and began instructing the next generation of junior officers in September 2011.

'You see the potential in them here, and it's very good. Every cadet, no matter if they're Household Division or Royal Logistics Corps, wants to know about Afghanistan – it is the war of the moment.'

As well as grilling potential Scots Guards officers about his Regiment's history, Kirkwood tells them about the tour. 'Trust your non-commissioned officers – that's my biggest point. When Captain Murly-Gotto was shot, myself, Sergeant Walker and Sergeant McFarlane put him on the Pedro. And as it was taking off, and the downwash of the rotors was going, it hit me in that moment that I'm now the Platoon Commander. You've got that slight . . . I'm going to have to lead these guys into whatever is next. That's my strongest memory.'

Some have more negative recollections. Colour Sergeant Tony Gibson, also instructing at Sandhurst, 'can still see stuff. It depends on what I'm doing, how much I'm talking about it, what's on telly, what I've seen. If I want to go back to an incident, I can recall it. It's pretty much going to be there until the end of time, or my time. It's an experience that I'll never, ever be able to get rid of. But it's probably something I wouldn't want to get rid of, because it has made me who I am today.'

★

Others bear more visible scars.

Lance Sergeant Gary Jamieson knew he had lost his legs. Coming round in Birmingham, realising he had also lost an arm was 'a bit of a shock to the system. But every time I woke up, my wife was there, or a doctor was there, and they kept telling me everything. So when I came off the drugs I knew all my injuries. It took two or three days for it to really sink in.' His treatment plan was explained to him while he was still in Selly Oak Hospital. 'Ever since then,' he says 'I've never looked back on it – always tried to push myself to get that bit better.'

When he returned to his home village of Stonehouse, South Lanarkshire, a surprise welcome home party was held in his honour. 'The whole village was out, big banners up, stuff like that.' That welcome has continued. Jamieson will remain in the British Army until his treatment concludes, around three years after he received his wounds. Work placements are being arranged, and this man with three prosthetic limbs intends to 'walk straight into another job', perhaps as a major facilities manager with DHL. 'Everything is going forward. There's nothing I can sit back and go, "I'd change this or change that".'

I was unable to reach his fellow triple-amputee, Guardsman David Watson. This was because he was skiing in the Alps. Guardsman Watson had hoped to compete in the 2012 London Olympics, but a shoulder injury in 2011 has kept him out of the team for javelin and shot-put. He is clearly getting more use out of his one remaining limb than most able-bodied people do with four. Captain Gary Dunning is the Scots Guards Battalion Welfare Officer, and has been looking after their casualties since October 2010: 'It is just amazing, particularly the families, how positive and upbeat they are. It really has blown me away. It certainly has been a humbling experience from my point of view.'

Colour Sergeant Tam O'Donnell's career reading list has changed somewhat since a round shattered his knee in February 2010. Then, he was a Platoon Sergeant with

Right Flank. Now, he manages the Officers' Mess in Catterick. 'The Defence Napkin Folding Guide is part of my bookshelf now,' he laughs. Colour Sergeant O'Donnell has recovered well from his injuries. 'My focus over the last two years was getting fit to the stage where I can be fit to deploy back on operations,' he says. In February 2012 he was given the green light and will head back to Afghanistan with Battlegroup Headquarters.

I wonder why a wounded man would want to return. Unfinished business? 'No. Not at all,' he replies, 'and I've never felt that from the start. There's an enemy out there and they've got a job to do. You can't bear any grudges for somebody having a pot-shot at you – that's just bad luck, or some people would say [choosing a] poor fire position, but I beg to differ.'

Instead, it is the bond with his fellow soldiers that makes Colour Sergeant O'Donnell wish to head back to a war zone. In 2010, he watched his Battalion march back into Catterick without him at the end of a hard tour. It hurt. 'I don't want to be in that position again,' he thought to himself. Thanks to his hard work, it looks like he won't be. The next tour will be a family affair for Colour Sergeant O'Donnell. His son-in-law is now a Scots Guardsman, and his young boy has also joined. 'He wants to go to Afghanistan, and my hat goes off to him because obviously he seen what I went through, you know, seen me lying on my bed, tubes and . . . it was pretty horrific for a 15–16 year old at the time. And he still made the decision: "I want to join the Army." I'm so chuffed.'

The Battalion seems poised on the start line for another operational cycle. A rewarding and well-received Queen's Birthday Parade on Horseguards in June 2011 is a satisfying if fading memory. A summer in Canada and then the lengthy Mission Specific Training Cycle have ensured that laurels won in 2010 are less in their thoughts than what will face them when they return to Helmand. But, what awaits them?

★

While the Scots Guards will not, I believe, return to Lashkar Gah District, I wanted to find out what happened there after the narrative of this book ended. What was the wider picture beyond that six-month snapshot? Were successes built on? Were things that were left undone resolved?

'It wasn't what did we achieve on Herrick 14 in the summer of 2011,' says Colonel Alistair Aitken OBE, Late SCOTS, 'it was what did we achieve on Herrick 12, 13, 14 and 15 that was the important thing.' He had led The Highlanders, 4th Battalion the Royal Regiment of Scotland, to Lashkar Gah in the spring of 2011 as part of Operation Herrick 14. They had relieved 2 SCOTS, who had relieved the Scots Guards. A 'Scottish strand' had been responsible for securing Helmand's most populous district.

The buzzword for 2011 was 'transition', in the way that 'partnering' had been the rage in 2010. A timeline had been set for eventual withdrawal. Telling an enemy, among whose greatest strengths is strategic patience, that you'll vastly reduce your presence in Helmand in a few years regardless of conditions on the ground seems faintly dangerous. But politically, Western governments have had to strike a bargain with populations tired of a conflict that was never fully explained to them. (The bargain made with the Afghan people in 2001 is, presumably, easier to forget.)

On the ground, it seems that this deadline has had some positive outcomes. 'Once we told the Afghan forces that they were in charge,' says Colonel Aitken, 'and once we started to tell the population, and they started to tell the population that they were in charge – guess what: they were in charge.'

This is positive news. However, there must be some concern about whether partnering was given enough time to really bite into the ANSF's culture and operating ability. While many members of the myriad branches (ABP, ANA, ANCOP, ALP, ANP, AUP, NDS – keep up at the back) are brave individuals who seek solutions to their country's problems, there are significant operating issues – logistical support being one obvious one – where autonomy is a long way off. Weaning the Afghan forces off Isaf support is one answer in the long run. However, this comes with the risk that, as the British hand over, the good work of 2009–2010, when individual relationships between British and Afghan soldiers produced discernible progress, may be in jeopardy.

Take checkpoints. In 2010, these were partnered in Combined Force Lashkar Gah. For Colour Sergeant Gibson, this is a stand-out part of his tour: 'The partnering side of life: that was the biggest achievement for the Company. The Counter-Insurgency operations we were carrying out. I definitely think that the checkpoints we were manning made a difference in that area.' A year on, it appears that most checkpoints were Isaf-only or ANSF-only (quite apart from those, such as Checkpoint Tapa Paraang, that had been abandoned entirely). However, this separation between men who are supposed to be fighting as brothers against a common enemy is explicable. No type of incident in Afghanistan causes more comment in home nations than when a member of the ANSF turns his weapon on Isaf soldiers. The French suspended their training programme in January 2012 when a member of the ANA killed four of their troops. 'The French army is not in Afghanistan to be shot at by Afghan soldiers,' President Nicholas Sarkozy rightly said.

It could be argued that separating Afghans and foreign troops mitigates the risk of such tragedies. However, the positive results of leaning into this risk, the paradox of taking more risk in short term in order to protect yourself in the long term, were obvious to anyone who witnessed them. Others would argue that Afghan-only checkpoints demonstrate the ANSF's progression to independence. Clearly, doctrinal orthodoxies change, but the Prime Minister confirmed to the House of Commons on 25 April 2012 that in Afghanistan 'at all times, of course, paramount in our minds is the safety and security of our brave armed forces'.

Around the various company areas of Combined Force Lashkar Gah, real progress appears to have been made since October 2010. The great physical transformation has been the roads. Route Mars is now fully tarmacked – presumably the neo-cell netting wasn't as IED resistant as had been hoped – and this has led to a huge increase in economic activity. In Bolan South, where men from 45 Commando were based on Herrick 14, there were traffic jams as locals tried to get goods to market along a tarmacked Route Elephant. 'The amount of trade going on was quite impressive,' says Captain Matt Hills, Royal Marines, who led a small company through a tour where the Queen's Royal Lancers had spent the previous summer. According to Colonel Aitken, the Bolan market to the west of the city was an ever-expanding hub of 'free-market economy. Because they are mercantile people who love to make money, and love to trade. And the key element of trade was freedom of movement. Freedom of movement for trade was the key to security.'

This long-term investment in infrastructure is a good example of where the British got something right in Helmand: it was driven through by successive brigades and brought tangible benefits to the people. Amazingly, there was not a single IED incident on Route Mars throughout the 4 SCOTS tour. The reason for this appears to have been the very bold approach taken in Loy Adera.

'I think we – British Forces, Isaf – had perhaps struggled at times with our understanding of the back story of Babaji [of which Loy Adera is one part] over the previous twenty years,' says Colonel Aitken. His predecessors in 2 SCOTS had engaged with the local population. They came to understand that the insurgency and the population were, largely, the same. *Kalay* by *kalay*, the population had been fighting to defend their hyper-local interests against perceived threats. 'That is what they had been doing since 1979,' says Colonel Aitken, 'it is just that who they were fighting had changed according to what day of the week it was.'

Afghan and British forces had used the winter of 2010–11 to make an expansive offer to these people. Colonel Mazalum of the ANP had conducted *shuras* throughout the area and asked the elders to 'give me your young men.' The men, he promised, would go to Lashkar Gah, be trained as policemen, and then return in uniform to guard their own villages. These new policemen were the very men who had shot at and placed bombs at the feet of Left Flank in 2010. 'Hand on heart, some of our predecessors would have called them insurgents,' says Colonel Aitken, 'and we called them brothers in arms and partners, because they were the same people. And in the Pashtun mind, this just wasn't an issue, this just wasn't a problem. We'd fought bravely against each other, now we're fighting bravely with each other.'

For some Scots Guardsmen this must be unpalatable – a lot of blood was spilt on that road. But if this approach helps protect British and Afghan forces – and, of course, the local population – as well as defeating the hardline insurgency, then it must be a good thing. Many soldiers also have a professional respect for their opposite numbers. Piper McIntyre bears little ill-will towards the man who shot him: 'to be honest with you, if I ever met the guy who did it, I'd probably shake his hand and say well done: it was a pretty damn good shot.' Colour Sergeant Gibson is more hard-nosed, but still has regard for the men who caused him such grief. 'I'd probably not shake them by the hand, but definitely, the enemy we encountered were far better-trained than the picture that had been built up for those individuals. From what we could see of the rural farmer and all that sort of stuff, he definitely had years' of experience. Shake his hand? Maybe wring his neck . . . But, no, I have a new-found respect for them. They aren't stupid, they aren't just farmers, they aren't archaic. These people have got skills. Real skills.' I can only conclude that having some of them in a government uniform must be of use to the campaign in Helmand.

Could this have happened earlier, thereby saving Left Flank a lot of heartache in 2010? Probably not. The police-training programme in Lashkar Gah had not developed sufficiently to make this part of the 'offer' to the people of Loy Adera. Security had to be won, and in 2010, that often had to be done with the use of force. Left Flank had requested ANP for their area, but there was not capacity in the system until late in their tour. When the ANP did arrive, the ANA and the Scots Guards were suspicious of them – rightly, as it seems the membrane between insurgency and support for the Afghan Government is highly permeable in Loy Adera. It is to the credit of those who followed there that trust was established and the area calmed down significantly. Recent press reports suggest that Loy Adera is now denuded of all Isaf forces. This is the progression that needs to be attained across Helmand, and is an achievement that everyone who served in that area can be proud of.

There has also been a significant shift to the west, across the Stabilisation Bridge and into Bolan North. Isaf have drawn down to one checkpoint – Spina Kota – and left recently promoted Major Israel to his own devices in Yellow 14. Over the course of Herrick 14, British commanders had forcibly told the local ANP that they were closing their checkpoints in the area. When they followed through on this promise, commanders like Israel had to take responsibility for their areas. 'We were forcing the issue, forcing the pace,' says Colonel Aitken.

At the same time as disengaging with the ANSF, the British also stepped back from their relationship with the Afghan Government. 'There was a natural point,' says Colonel Aitken, 'where we began to understand, not the limitations of government, but an aspect of realism.' There seems to have been, from the start, a mismatch between the expectations the British had for the government in rural Lashkar Gah and the politicians' desire to get involved with this hinterland. The Afghans realised the limits of their ambitions, and thought their resources were best spent in Lashkar Gah itself. The British, understandably, wanted government involvement in areas their troops were securing at great cost. Into this fracture, the British initially poured cash and projects. By 2011, the policy changed. The Stabilisation Representative's 'Bank of Babaji' in Patrol Base Nahidullah was brought under control. The proposed Government Outreach Office was allowed to die a quiet death. Instead of holding *shuras* in Isaf checkpoints, the Afghans were told to set them up themselves, and if British officers attended at all, they would sit at the back and keep quiet. When this approach was challenged, the people were told, 'We are an army, that's not what we do. You should go to your government.' Rather than tracking disputes between rival factions, British commanders stepped back and took a slightly more modest approach. 'There were so many back-stories,' Colonel Aitken says of the rivalries in Bolan North. 'Did we ever really know what was going on? Not 100 per cent.' It seems the British Army in Helmand, rather like a weary academic, has learned enough about their subject to realise how little they know, perhaps ever can know, about it.

As the British, a powerful tribe with money and guns, revised their presence, some locals predicted chaos. This does not appear to have materialised. Instead, the population has engaged with Afghan Government and travels into Lashkar Gah for help resolving its problems. Whether the insurgents will re-infiltrate these areas is largely up to the Government: if they don't engage with the people, allow them to improve their lot, and resolve their disputes, the insurgents will make a powerful counter-offer, probably based on poppy and justice.

In the meantime, the security the Government provides allows farmers to get their products to market. 'The population', says Colonel Aitken, 'had suddenly realised that they could back the Government and get away with it. Because they could make money and get away with it.'

As Herrick 14 got under way, responsibility for Bolan South was finally handed to Nad-e-Ali. Just as with the Queen's Royal Lancers the previous summer, the men of 45 Commando had a tour that focused less on securing the area and more on convincing the Afghan Government to pay some attention to this poor, dry area. Eventually, District Governor Habibullah was persuaded to come and visit. The local commander, Captain Hills, was unsure of his motives: 'That was certainly a demonstration that, yes, you are a part of Nad-e-Ali and we are here to help you. Whether that was just for Isaf's benefit or our Political Adviser's benefit I'm not sure, but it certainly moved in the right direction.'

Just as in 2010, plans for infrastructure projects like

schools stalled. Captain Hills describes the three wells put
in during his time in Bolan South as 'baby steps, really'.
For Hills, the tour – casualty-free and reasonably calm in
his area – was 'completely different' to his previous two
tours of Helmand. 'The enemy are suppressed,' he says,
'they haven't got the power. Now we need to seize the
initiative and line up the political players and make sure
we take this relatively quiet period and capitalise on it.'
However, in words that echo the views of his predecessors
on Herrick 12, Hills concluded: 'My thoughts on the
Bolan area was that neither the Afghan Government or
the insurgents were that interested in it.'

Out to the east of Lashkar Gah, Highway 601 continues
to be an area where Isaf struggled with the question of what
they could really offer the people. Colonel Sitar and his
sons had been the victim of a political move and replaced.
The ANP continued to suffer from internal threats: 12 of
them were killed in what are widely known as 'insider jobs'
during the summer of 2011. Drug abuse, especially at the
fringes of the area, remained an issue in some parts of the
police. The priority remained keeping the road secure.
'The Afghan Government are very interested in bringing
security to the area,' said Colonel Aitken. 'Will they bring a
massive amount of governance? No, I don't think they will.
And we were very cautious about giving the impression to
the local population that either the Afghan Government or
we were coming. Because there's a finite resource, there's a
finite amount they can do.'

This lack of engagement along the 601 and in other
areas clearly risks opening a door to the insurgency's offer.
One area they can clearly best the Afghan Government is
over poppy. Lashkar Gah were encouraging self-eradica-
tion, where the farmers themselves destroy the poppy
crops, in Helmand – backed up with promoting other,
legal, crops. A full-scale eradication programme was also

tackling the more industrially cultivated areas. This will affect the relationship between the people and the government. The British, though, had stood back. 'This was an Afghan-led area and an ANP focus,' says Colonel Aitken. 'Poppy eradication in Helmand was conducted by the Afghans at the direction of the Provincial Governor. Physically we were not involved in it; we didn't provide any security to it.' This appears to me to be some distance from the lead-nation role for counter-narcotics that the British Government adopted in a fit of bravado in 2001.

One area where the Afghan Government was keen to make its mark was where the British had their lightest footprint: Lashkar Gah. The city transitioned to Afghan-led security in July 2011. Colonel Aitken had assumed this was a mere formal recognition of the *de facto* state of affairs in the provincial capital. 'I completely misjudged it,' he admits. 'I had completely not understood the subtlety of *Pashtunwalli* that made it fundamentally different: it made the ceremony massively important. Because what transitioned was their ability to conduct security operations on their own.'

Planning for the ceremony held on 20 July at the compound of Helmand Province's Governor, Gulab Mangal, was meticulous. Insurgents had promised to disrupt the day with violence. General Rahim Wardak, the Afghan Defence Minister, stood up to make a speech. His words stuck in Colonel Aitken's mind. 'He said: "This is the moment that all your sacrifices have worked towards. This is what all those British deaths and injuries have been about. This is why mothers have lost their sons. For this moment. For when we, the Afghans, say that we are truly capable of running our own security. This is a huge deal for our nation." I wish I could have recorded what he said and played it back to all those on Herrick 12 and 13 in 2010–11 as well.'

★

It seems the Scots Guards will return to a different Helmand than the one they left. I suspect their ability to operate freely will be severely restricted by various imperatives channelled through Brigade Headquarters in Lashkar Gah. If this results in a quieter tour, with fewer casualties than in 2010, then that is good. Men like Colour Sergeant Gibson who will remain in Britain will be watching carefully. 'I volunteered my services to the Regimental Sergeant Major to go there if anything goes wrong. To which I got the answer: "No, you're doing a job now, you need to stay there." That will stay firm: I'll always offer myself to them because I know how bad it is. I am British Army, they've given me everything that I've got in life today, and I will give them my career.' Piper McIntyre returns to Helmand with a souvenir of his last tour: two fragments of the copper jacket of the round that hit his chest. They are lodged just above his heart. 'It's not actually that long ago that we were out there,' he says. Guardsman Wannuwat, now a senior guardsman at 27, will redeploy as a Light Machine Gunner. He still thinks back on the bad memories from 2010, but is ready to go again. 'If they give me a Vallon,' he says, 'then I will be happy to take it. I'm kind of looking forward to it, and I'm not at the same time. I'm looking forward to working with the boys . . . and also, I'm not looking forward to getting blown up again.' It seems that the next tour will be his, and the Scots Guards', final tour of Helmand. 'Yeah,' he says, 'I hope so.'

*

'I hadn't realised how bad it was over there until I read your book,' a great friend said. It was the worst review. One of the aims of this book was to try to help bridge the gap between the civilian and military worlds. In my friend's case, one could argue, the book achieved this – this person now has a clearer picture of the level of sacrifice in Helmand. However, the point the book does not make clearly enough is the extent to which those in uniform accept these circumstances. To corrupt L. P. Hartley's quote, the Army is a foreign country: they do things differently there.

For a while, I learned to accept this alternative normality. It is a frequent reaction amongst those who investigate the society of others. In my own minor way, and rather like the anthropologist quoted at the top of this chapter, I yielded to my hosts' beliefs. They were what kept them together in those unusual months. It was a kind of faith, and one that I retain.

A NOTE ON SOURCES

The primary source material for this book was spending a great deal of time with the members of 1st Battalion Scots Guards and other members of Combined Force Lashkar Gah, who were all unstintingly patient with me. This time translated into days of interviews recorded on Dictaphone, hundreds of photos and videos, notebooks stuffed with snippets of conversation and an extensive personal diary. This was reinforced with a generous look at private papers, war diaries, after action reviews and other operational record-keeping notes. Current military doctrine stresses the importance of 'dwell patrols' – a typical piece of army effects lexicon. I dwelt with the Scots Guards for over a year and it was this time that forms the true basis of this book. There was never a wasted minute. I am very lucky indeed.

This access was secured through the agreement of one ground rule: the regiment got to read what I wrote before it was published. During the drafting stage, they were casually interested in my writing and pointed out factual errors but never made me change my conclusions or lent over my shoulder. Though they must disagree with some of what is written, they were polite enough not to let it show (too much).

A more formal contract was negotiated through the Directorate of Media and Communications in the MoD's

Whitehall Headquarters. This covered everything from my bed and board in Helmand ($50 per diem – paying to be in a war zone: amazing), to the requirement to have every word I wrote checked for factual accuracy, operational and personal security implications, and a number of other legal criteria. The wounded were consulted about the treatment of the incidents they were caught up in, and the next of kin of those who did not return alive were invited to give their blessing and comment on what had been written about their loved ones. Like the Scots Guards, the MoD had no editorial input – that remained with the publishers and me. In addition, I voluntarily signed the Official Secrets Act so that there was no question of betraying any privileged information encountered during this process. Once the MoD had finished reading the manuscript, a list of around 50 comments came back to the publisher. I immediately conceded about three quarters of the points, and over the course of a week negotiated the rest to a wording that the MoD, the publisher and I were happy with. The MoD then had a final sign-off on the manuscript before it went to print. Any remaining errors are entirely my own.

Copies of the interviews conducted before, during and after the tour are held in the Scots Guards Archive at Regimental Headquarters, Wellington Barracks, London along with many photos. I am sure Lance Sergeant Kevin Gorman, who was so helpful in checking my account of the Regiment's history, will look after them well.

APPENDIX I

Operational Honours and Awards

From the *London Gazette* of Thursday, 23 September 2010, Supplement No. 1
Queen's Commendation for Bravery
Lance Sergeant David WALKER, Scots Guards (killed in action)

From the *London Gazette* of Thursday, 24 March 2011, Supplement No. 1
Member of the Military Division of the Order of the British Empire [MBE]
Lance Corporal Isobel Ann HENDERSON, Royal Army Medical Corps [attached Scots Guards]

Military Cross
Lance Corporal Stephen Daniel MONKHOUSE, Scots Guards (killed in action)
Acting Corporal Matthew James STENTON, Royal Dragoon Guards (killed in action)

Mention in Dispatches
Lance Corporal Andrew Christopher ATHERTON, Scots Guards [attached Brigade Reconnaissance Force]
Sergeant Anthony Carl GIBSON, Scots Guards

Lance Sergeant Christopher LEYDEN, Scots Guards
Guardsman Glen McNALLY, Coldstream Guards [attached B Company, Scots Guards]
Lieutenant William John Lewis TULLOCH, Scots Guards

Queen's Commendation for Valuable Service
Lieutenant Colonel Lincoln Peter Munro JOPP MC, Scots Guards
Major Rupert Edward Charles KITCHING, Scots Guards
Lance Sergeant Cameron MACDOUGALL, Scots Guards
Lance Corporal Paul Edward RAMSAY, Scots Guards

Command Structure of Combined Force Lashkar Gah

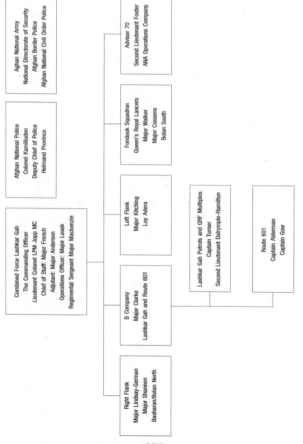

Combined Force Lashkar Gah
The Commanding Officer
Lieutenant Colonel LPM Jopp MC
Chief of Staff: Major French
Adjutant: Major Anderson
Operations Officer: Major Leask
Regimental Sergeant Major Mackenzie

Afghan National Police
Colonel Kamilluden
Deputy Chief of Police
Helmand Province

Afghan National Army
National Directorate of Security
Afghan Border Police
Afghan National Civil Order Police

Right Flank
Major Lindsay-German
Major Shannon
Basharan/Bolan North

B Company
Major Clarke
Lashkar Gah and Route 601

Left Flank
Major Kitching
Loy Adera

Fondouk Squadron
Queen's Royal Lancers
Major Walker
Major Cossens
Bolan South

Advisor 70
Second Lieutenant Foster
ANA Operations Company

Lashkar Gah Patrols and QRF Multiples
Captain Turner
Second Lieutenant Dalrymple-Hamilton

Route 601
Captain Alderman
Captain Gow

APPENDIX III

Command Structure of Left Flank

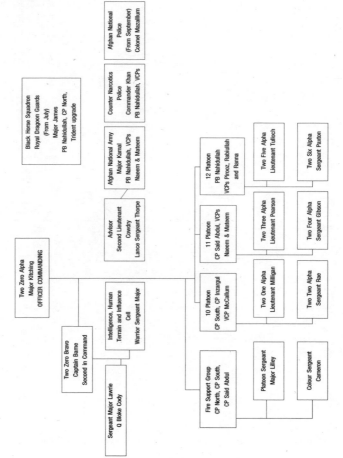